The Fernandes Guide to Apologetic Methodologies

By Phil Fernandes
IBD Press
Bremerton, WA

Dedication

This book is dedicated to the love of my life, my best friend next to Jesus, my wife Cathy. Without her encouragment, I would not be all God called me to be.

I also dedicate this book to my daughter Melissa and my grandson Nathan.

Ackowledgements

Thanks are due to numerous people who made this book possible:

First, I am eternally thankful for my wife Cathy, my encouragement and my best friend next to Jesus.

Also, thanks go out to Sam Whittaker and Rebecca Nessly for hours of work formatting this manuscript.

Further thanks go to Norman Geisler, Gary Habermas, Barry Leventhal, Wayne Detzler, and Richard Howe, my former apologetics professors.

I am also grateful to the leaders and members of Trinity Bible Fellowship, the Institute of Biblical Defense staff, and my students at Crosspoint Academy, Shepherds Bible College, and Columbia Evangelical Seminary. Through their questions and discussions, they have strengthened my apologetic thought.

Finally, let all the glory and praise be to the Triune God of the Bible, the God who has created us and provided salvation for us.

The Fernandes Guide to Apologetic Methodologies
By Phil Fernandes

IBD Press
Bremerton, WA

Published by IBD Press
A ministry of the Institute of Biblical Defense

P. O. Box 3264
Bremerton, WA 98310
(360) 698-7382
instituteofbiblicaldefense.com

ISBN-13: 978-1540715562
ISBN-10: 1540715566

Contents

Chapter 1

The Biblical Basis of Apologetics

For many Christians, apologetics is a forgotten art. Though Christian laymen and ministers usually know how to share their faith, they are often unable to defend it. Due to the anti-Christian climate currently prevalent in America and throughout the Western world, believers need to be informed about this discipline.

Before examining the many different ways to do apologetics, the term must be defined. Apologetics comes from the Greek word *apologia*, meaning "a verbal defense, a speech in defense."[1] Therefore, apologetics is dedicated to defending the beliefs of biblical Christianity.

Apologetics is a biblical concept. The word *apologia* is found in Peter's first epistle. Peter declares, "sanctify Christ as Lord in your hearts, always being ready to make a defense to everyone who asks you to give an account for the hope that

---

[1]W.E. Vine, *Expository Dictionary of New Testament Words* (Grand Rapids: Zondervan Publishing House, 1952), 61.

is in you, yet with gentleness and reverence" (3:15).[2] In this passage, the word *apologia* is translated "defense."

Apologetics is vital to the Christian church today. Those who share the gospel must also defend the gospel. People are seeking answers to their questions. Through apologetics we can find those answers. We can remove intellectual stumbling blocks that stand between lost souls and Christ. We can communicate the gospel in such a way that the "modern" man will understand it. We must, as the inspired writer instructs us, "contend earnestly for the faith" (Jude 3).

Some scholars believe that the gospel should not be defended. These scholars are called fideists.[3] They maintain that one's beliefs should not be rationally defended. Instead, according to this school of thought, one should accept his or her theological views by a leap of blind faith. One should not look for or provide evidence for religious beliefs. To do so, according to fideists, is to elevate human reason above divine revelation.

If fideism is true, then apologetics is an unbiblical exercise. However, if the practice of apologetics is found to be based in the scriptures, then fideism is unbiblical.

The Bible Commands Believers to Defend the Faith

The Bible clearly teaches that Christians are to defend the faith. In fact, believers are commanded to do apologetics. The apostle Peter instructs believers to always be "ready to make a defense" of the Christian hope (1 Pet. 3:15).

---

[2]*New American Standard Bible* (La Habra: The Lockman Foundation, 1973). All biblical quotations are taken from the NASB unless otherwise noted.

[3]*The Zondervan Parallel New Testament in Greek and English* (Grand Rapids: Zondervan Bible Publishers, 1975), 691.

Jude, the half-brother of Christ, also commands Christians to defend the faith. He tells believers to "contend earnestly for the faith which was once for all delivered to the saints" (Jude 3).

The apostle Paul states that those who are appointed as elders or overseers of local churches should be able to do more than just teach sound biblical doctrine. Paul states that those who hold this office must also be able "to refute those who contradict" the teachings of the Bible (Titus 1:9). In Paul's letter to the Colossian believers, he made the following statement: "Conduct yourselves with wisdom toward outsiders, making the most of the opportunity. Let your speech always be with grace, seasoned, as it were, with salt, so that you may know how you should respond to each person" (Col. 4:5-6).

These biblical passages show it is sufficiently clear that the Word of God commands believers to defend the faith. Therefore, the accusations of the fideists are false—apologetics is biblical.

Jesus Gave Evidence for Belief

The Lord Jesus Christ Himself did not expect people to believe in Him without evidence. Luke tells us in the Book of Acts that Jesus gave His followers "many convincing proofs" that He had indeed risen from the dead (Acts 1:3). When the Jewish religious leaders wanted to stone Jesus for blasphemy, He told them, "If I do not do the works of My Father, do not believe Me; but if I do them, though you do not believe Me, believe the works, that you may know and understand that the Father is in Me, and I in the Father" (John 10:37-38). Jesus was saying that if his listeners were thinking of rejecting His teachings, they should change their minds because of the evidence He presented for His claims—His miracles.

On another occasion, Jesus said, ". . . for the works which the Father has given Me to accomplish, the very works that I do, bear witness of Me, that the Father has sent Me" (John 5:36). Again, Jesus was saying that the miracles He did were evidence that His claims to be God, Savior, and Messiah were true.

When asked for a sign to prove He had authority over the temple, Jesus said the only sign He would give proving His authority would be His bodily resurrection from the dead (John 2:18-21). Therefore, anyone who rejects traditional apologetics is being inconsistent with the teachings of Jesus on this subject. Fideists (those who say Christians should never defend the Gospel) and presuppositionalists (those who teach that Christians should refute false religions but should not provide evidence for Christianity) are wrong to condemn giving evidence for Christian truth claims. Jesus gave evidence for faith; if we are able, we should do the same.

The Bible Speaks of Natural Revelation

The Bible not only commands Christians to defend the faith, but also speaks of God revealing Himself in nature.[4] This is called *natural revelation*. Natural revelation is also known as general revelation since it gives evidence of God's existence to all mankind.[5] When God made Himself known to man in the Bible, He miraculously had to guide human authors to record His Word without error. This is why the Bible is

---

[4]Henry Clarence Thiessen, *Lectures in Systematic Theology* (Grand Rapids: William B. Eerdmans Publishing Company, 1979), 7-8.

[5]Ibid.

called *supernatural revelation* (also known as special revelation). However, in natural revelation no supernatural work of God is needed. God has given evidence of His existence in the universe He created. The Bible declares the following regarding God's revelation of Himself in nature:

> The heavens are telling of the glory of God; and their expanse is declaring the work of His hands. Day to day pours forth speech, and night to night reveals knowledge (Ps. 19:1-2).

> For the wrath of God is revealed from heaven against all ungodliness and unrighteousness of men, who suppress the truth in unrighteousness, because that which is known about God is evident within them; for God made it evident to them. For since the creation of the world His invisible attributes, His eternal power and divine nature, have been clearly seen, being understood through what has been made, so that they are without excuse. For even though they knew God, they did not honor Him as God, or give thanks; but they became futile in their speculations, and their foolish heart was darkened. Professing to be wise, they became fools . . . (Rom. 1:18-22).

These passages teach that though no one has ever seen the invisible God, the visible work of His hands can be seen in His creation. If someone finds a watch, he knows a watchmaker must exist, though he has never seen him.[6] Therefore, when man sees the beauty and order of the universe, he knows that it must have been caused by an intelligent and powerful Being.

---

[6]John Hick, ed. *The Existence of God* (New York: The Macmillan Company, 1964). 99-103.

Since God has revealed Himself in nature, Christians can argue from the effect (the universe) to its cause (God). To gaze at the starry sky on a clear night and still believe that the universe is a product of chance is an insult to human reason.

Another aspect of natural revelation deals with the fact that God has revealed His law in the conscience of each person. The apostle Paul affirms this in the following words: "For when Gentiles who do not have the Law do instinctively the things of the Law, these, not having the Law, are a law to themselves, in that they show the work of the Law written in their hearts, their conscience bearing witness, and their thoughts alternately accusing or else defending them . . ." (Rom. 2:14-15).

Because God has given all men a glimpse of His moral law in their consciences, believers can argue from this moral law to the existence of the moral Lawgiver. Since the moral laws are above all men, the moral Lawgiver must also be above all men. Since evidence for God can be found in nature, philosophical apologetics (which argues for God's existence from the evidence of nature) is a biblical practice.

The Bible Speaks of Historical Evidences

As mentioned above, the Bible teaches that God has revealed Himself to man in nature. However, besides this evidence in nature, the Bible declares that evidence for the Christian faith can also be found in history.[7] While attempting to prove the resurrection of Christ from the dead, as well as the future resurrection of all believers, the apostle Paul lists the eyewitnesses of Christ's post-resurrection appearances:

---

[7]Ibid., 8-9.

For I deliver to you as of first importance what I also received, that Christ died for our sins according to the Scriptures, and that He was buried, and that He was raised on the third day according to the Scriptures, and that He appeared to Cephas, then to the twelve. After that He appeared to more than five hundred brethren at one time, most of whom remain until now, but some have fallen asleep; then He appeared to James, then to all the apostles; and last of all, as it were to one untimely born, He appeared to me also (1 Cor. 15:3-8).

From this passage it is clear that the apostle Paul was willing to refer to the evidence of eyewitness testimony in order to provide a defense for the truth of the gospel. Therefore, there is a biblical basis for historical apologetics. Historical apologetics utilizes historical evidences to argue for the truth of the Christian faith.

The Early Church Defended the Faith

The Bible commands believers to do apologetics. The scriptures speak of both natural revelation and historical evidences. And, finally, the early church did apologetics. The fact that Jesus was willing to give evidence for His claims has already been noted. The apostles followed the example of Christ; they were also willing to defend the gospel.

The apostle Peter defended the faith. On the day of Pentecost, Peter preached his famous sermon. Three thousand people were saved and added to the church. During that sermon Peter stated, "This Jesus God raised up again, to which we are all witnesses" (Acts 2:32). Peter often defended the faith during his sermons by appealing to eyewitness testimony (Acts 3:15; 5:30-32; 10:39-41).

7

The apostle John also defended the faith. In fact, he claimed that the main purpose for writing his Gospel was to provide eyewitness accounts of Christ's miraculous life in order to persuade others to believe (John 20:30-31). *Luke* willingly shared proof of Christ's claims. When Luke wrote the book of Acts, he stated that Christ "presented Himself alive, after His suffering, by many convincing proofs, appearing to them over a period of forty days" (Acts 1:1-3). Luke shared with Theophilus, the person to whom the book of Acts was addressed, eyewitness evidence of the post-resurrection appearances of Christ. Thus, Theophilus would not have to exercise blind faith in order to believe. Luke knew that biblical faith is based upon evidence, not an irrational leap.

The apostle Paul was also a defender of the faith. The scriptures say that he kept "confounding the Jews who lived at Damascus by proving that this Jesus is the Christ" (Acts 9:22). Paul's custom was to enter various synagogues and reason with the Jews from the scriptures (Acts 17:1-3; 18:4). If the Jews rejected the gospel message, he would then go and proclaim it to the Gentiles:

> And he entered the synagogue and continued speaking out boldly for three months, reasoning and persuading them about the kingdom of God. But when some were becoming hardened and disobedient, speaking evil of the Way before the multitude, he withdrew from them and took away the disciples, reasoning daily in the school of Tyrannus. And this took place for two years, so that all who lived in Asia heard the word of the Lord, both Jews and Greeks (Acts 19:8-10).

While in Athens, Paul stood on Mars Hill and preached one of his greatest sermons (Acts 17:16-34). There, he was confronted by Greek philosophers: the Epicureans and the Stoics. The Epicurean philosophers believed that God did not exist, while the Stoic philosophers equated God with the universe.

Paul noticed that the Athenians had devoted a statue to "an Unknown God." Paul then claimed to personally know this God of whom they were ignorant. Twice he quoted from the works of ancient Greek poets to establish his case as he began to share the gospel. Finally, when Paul spoke of God raising Jesus from the dead, many of the Greek philosophers sneered, while others asked Paul if he would be willing to speak to them again. Though the idea of a bodily resurrection had been repugnant to the Greeks since the days of Plato (427-347BC),[8] some Greeks were willing to give Paul a second hearing. This was probably due to the fact that he had proved himself to be well-read in Greek philosophy, even though he held the belief of Christ's bodily resurrection.

As demonstrated in Paul's case, apologetics enables a person to speak to the "intellectual elite." Paul chose to "become all things to all men" (1 Corinthians 9:19-22). He chose to use anti-Christian philosophies in order to refute the false beliefs of his listeners and to lead them to Christ. No defender of the faith can do less.

And, finally, Apollos used apologetics. He was a great defender of the faith. Luke records this about him: "Now a certain Jew named Apollos, an Alexandrian by birth, an eloquent man, came to Ephesus; and he was mighty in the scriptures . . . for he powerfully refuted the Jews in public, demonstrating by the scriptures that Jesus was the Christ" (Acts 18:24-28).

---

[8]William S. Sahakian. *History of Philosophy* (New York: Harper Perennial, 1968). 55-56.

Conclusion

Apologetics is taught in the Bible. The Bible commands us to defend the faith. The scriptures also speak of natural revelation and historical evidences for the Christian faith. And finally, the early church defended the faith. Apologetics is squarely based in the Bible.

Chapter 2

Great Apologists of Church History

In the last chapter, it was demonstrated that the apostolic church did apologetics—they defended the faith. In this chapter, it will be shown that, throughout the centuries, Christian thinkers have defended the faith. Eventually, a standard way to defend the faith called "classical apologetics" developed.

Apologists of the Early Church

Ignatius (died 107ad) was the Bishop of Antioch of Syria.[9] He wrote several letters while being transported to his martyrdom. In his letters, Ignatius refuted the ancient heresy called *Docetism*. Docetism denied the genuine humanity of Jesus; it taught that Jesus only pretended or appeared to be a man—He did not really become a man. He was only a spirit being without a real body. Docetists claim that only a phantom died on the cross—Jesus did not really physically die on the

---

[9]Eusebius, *The History of the Church.* Trans. By G. A. Williamson (London: Penguin Books, 1965), 97.

cross. Ignatius refuted Gnosticism by arguing that Jesus really was God incarnate, God in the flesh. He was physically born to the virgin Mary, was physically crucified, and bodily rose from the dead.[10] However, though Ignatius was defending the true and full humanity of Jesus, he also stated, numerous times, in his letters that Jesus was also "God and Savior."[11]

Justin Martyr (100-165ad) was converted to Christianity from paganism. In his writing entitled *Dialogue With Trypho*, he answered Trypho's accusations that Christians violate the Mosaic Law since they worship a human being.[12] Justin Martyr argued from Old Testament passages that Jesus is God and He fulfilled the Mosaic Law. Also in the second century, *Aristides*, *Tatian*, *Athenagoras*, and *Theophilus* all argued that Christianity is superior to the pagan religions.[13]

Irenaeus became the Bishop of Lyons in 177ad.[14] He wrote a work entitled *Against Heresies*. In this work, he refuted Gnosticism by teaching that: 1) evil is not co-eternal with God, 2) matter is not evil, and 3) Jesus rose bodily from the dead.[15] Irenaeus also wrote *Proof of the Apostolic*

---

[10]J. B. Lightfoot and J. R. Harmer, eds., *The Apostolic Fathers* (Grand rapids: baker Book House, 1984), 148, 156-157.

[11]Ibid., 137, 139, 142, 144, 149, 150, 156, 162.

[12]Earle E. Cairns, *Christianity Through the Centuries* (Grand Rapids: Zondervan Publishing House, 1981), 106-107.

[13]Ibid.

[14]Justo Gonzalez, *A History of Christian Thought*, vol. 1. (Nashville: Abingdon Press, 1987), 157.

[15]Ibid., 158-162.

Preaching. In this writing, he demonstrated that Jesus fulfilled Old Testament prophecies.[16]

Tertullian wrote between 196 and 212ad. In his work entitled *Apology*, he defended Christian beliefs against heresy and argued that Christians should be tolerated, not persecuted.[17] Tertullian also wrote five books called *Against Marcion.* In these works, he defended the use of the Old Testament by Christians and the oneness of God.[18] In another work, *Against Praxeas*, Tertullian defended the doctrine of the Trinity (God eternally exists as three equal Persons). Praxeas was a modalist—he believed that Jesus and the Father were the same person. Tertullian argued that the Father, Son, and Holy Spirit are three distinct Persons, yet one God.[19]

Many theologians have mistaken Tertullian for an irrationalist or a fideist (i.e., someone who rejects apologetics and believes Christianity is to be accepted by blind faith). However, Tertullian was only opposed to anti-Christian philosophy, not Christian philosophy and apologetics. Tertullian was opposed to the faulty wisdom of man, not the true wisdom that comes from God (whether through natural or supernatural revelation).[20]

Origen (185-254) wrote *Against Celsus*, in which he answered pagan objections to the Christian faith. Origen also spent a lot of his efforts refuting the Gnostic heresy.

---

[16]Ibid., 159.

[17]Tony Lane, *Exploring Christian Thought* (Nashville: Thomas Nelson Publishers, 1984), 18.

[18]Ibid., 18-19.

[19]Ibid., 19.

[20]Gonzalez, vol. 1, 175.

Unfortunately, Origen himself taught the heretical doctrines of the preexistence of souls and universal salvation and was later condemned by the church.[21]

Athanasius

Athanasius (296-373ad) was the greatest Bishop of Alexandria. In his work *Against the Heathen* he argued that God could be known in two ways: through the soul and through nature.[22] He believed that since the soul was created in God's image, it is capable of seeing God. Still, sin dims the light of God in the human soul.[23] But, Athanasius also believed that through the visible creation we can find the invisible God. We do not see the invisible God, but we do see the work of His hands—the creation.[24] Therefore, we know He exists. Athanasius added that the order and unity of the universe shows that God guides the universe through His reason or wisdom. Jesus is God's wisdom in that He is called the Logos (i.e., the Word). Hence, Jesus guides the universe.[25]

In another writing entitled *On the Incarnation*, Athanasius defended the Christian doctrine of the incarnation (i.e., God the Son became a man). He reasoned that since we must become new creations to be saved (and only God can create), then only God can save us. The Savior must therefore be God; anything less than God cannot save. Still, the Savior

---

[21]Lane, 21-24.

[22]Gonzalez, vol. 1, 293-294.

[23]Ibid.

[24]Ibid., 294.

[25]Ibid.

must be a man to die for our sins. Athanasius stated that God became a man so that man could become divine (i.e., the restoration of the image of God in man).[26]

Athanasius also refuted the Arian heresy—the false view that Jesus was a lesser god and is not one in Being with the Father. Arius (the originator of the Arian heresy) taught that Jesus was a lesser god and the first thing God the Father created. After being created, Jesus created everything else. Athanasius refuted this heresy by making two points. First, Arianism is a unique form of polytheism (i.e., the belief in more than one god) since it teaches there are two gods (i.e., God the Father and Jesus the lesser god). Second, Athanasius argued that a lesser god cannot save. The Savior must be fully God. Hence, Jesus is one is Being with the Father; He is not a lesser god.[27]

Augustine

Augustine (354-430) was the Bishop of Hippo in North Africa. Many people consider him to be the greatest church leader between the apostle Paul and Martin Luther. Early in his life, Augustine had accepted a dualistic religion called Manicheanism. This religion taught that God (light) and matter (darkness) are both eternal. The Manicheans believed that both good and evil existed throughout all eternity. This, they reasoned, removed any responsibility from God for the evil that exists in the universe.[28]

---

[26]Ibid., 296-297.

[27]Ibid., 297-298.

[28]Vernon J. Bourke, *Augustine's Quest of Wisdom* (Albany: Magi Books, 1993), 17-18.

Under the preaching of Ambrose, Augustine became a Christian. He began to see that evil was not coexistent with God. Rather, God alone is eternal, and all that He created is good. Yet, by giving angels and men free will, God permitted evil to come into existence. Therefore, evil is a privation (a lack of the good that should be there). Evil does not exist on its own, but must exist in something good (just as rust cannot come into existence without the metal it corrupts). Therefore, Augustine concluded, evil exists as a corruption or perversion of God's perfect creation. God created the universe perfect, but angels and men brought evil into the universe through their free choices.[29]

As one of the greatest theologians in the history of the church, Augustine wrote many works defending Christianity. He provided evidence for God's existence, attempted to reconcile faith and reason, and correctly saw and defended the fact that mankind has inherited a corrupted nature from Adam.

Augustine offered a two-fold refutation of the skeptics of his day. The skeptic claims to suspend judgment on all things; he claims man cannot know truth. Augustine argued that skepticism is both rationally inconsistent and practically inconsistent. Skepticism is rationally inconsistent because skeptics are not skeptical about their skepticism. In fact, the claim that man cannot know truth is a claim to know the truth that man cannot know truth. Hence, skepticism is self-refuting. But, it is also practically inconsistent because skeptics cannot live consistently with their skepticism—they do not suspend judgment when they eat, communicate, or protect themselves.[30] Having refuted skepticism, Augustine concluded that truth is attainable.

---

[29]Norman L. Geisler, ed., *What Augustine Says* (Grand Rapids: Baker Book House, 1982), 181-200.

Augustine was greatly influenced by the thought of the Greek philosopher Plato. He accepted Plato's view of the invisible world of unchanging, eternal ideas or truths. But, Augustine placed these ideas in the eternal, unchanging mind of God. Since our time-bound, changing minds are not capable of causing the existence of these ideas, Augustine viewed these eternal, unchanging truths (i.e., mathematical truths, the laws of logic, etc.) as evidence for the existence of God (i.e., the eternal, unchanging Mind). Only an eternal, unchanging Mind is the adequate source of the eternal, unchanging ideas.[31]

Augustine utilized several other arguments for God. He used a cosmological argument for God's existence—he reasoned from the existence of the changing, time-bound world to the existence of an eternal, unchanging Creator. He also argued from the design in the world (i.e., the human eye) to the existence of the Designer of the world. This is called the teleological argument. And, he argued from the concept of perfection to the most Perfect Being or Form.[32]

Augustine had a very balanced view of the relationship between faith and reason. He rejected extreme rationalism (which leaves no room for faith) and extreme fideism (which leaves no room for reason). Augustine understood that even when we reason, faith is involved. For, whether we are using our reason when dealing with natural revelation (what God has revealed to man in nature) or supernatural revelation (what God has revealed to man through miracles and the Bible), it is revelation from God in either case. And, a healthy faith is a

---

[30]Frederick Copleston, *A History of Philosophy*, vol. 2 (New York: Image Books, 1950), 52-53.

[31]Bourke, 136. See also Geisler, *What Augustine Says*, 22.

[32]Geisler, *What Augustine Says*, 20-21.

rational faith (though faith does at times go beyond the limits of human reason); it is a faith based on the evidence.[33]

Augustine's most famous debate was with a monk named Pelagius. Pelagius believed that each person is born in the same state in which Adam was created. Thus, each person is *not* contaminated by Adam's sin. In Pelagius' view, Adam merely set a bad example for his offspring—it is possible for man to live without sin. Augustine refuted Pelagius by pointing out that the scriptures teach that each person inherits Adam's sin nature. Therefore, no one can please God through human effort. Man must rely solely on God's grace to be saved.[34]

Though Augustine rightly defended both divine sovereignty and human free will, his later writings exhibited an extreme view of predestination that seemed to cancel out any real human freedom in the area of salvation. Man, in Augustine's view, believes in Christ only because God predestined him to do so.[35] A millennium later, the great reformer John Calvin would systematize and popularize Augustine's view of predestination and free will.

Augustine also argued for the historical truths of Christianity. He considered miracles, Jesus' resurrection, and the Bible's fulfilled prophecies as evidence that Christianity is true.[36]

In his writings Augustine defended the doctrine of the Trinity, the deity of Christ, and salvation by God's grace.

---

[33]Ibid., 13-20, 24-31.

[34]Justo Gonzalez, *A History of Christian Thought*, vol. 2 (Nashville: Abingdon Press, 1971), 29-34.

[35]Ibid., 46-49.

[36]Geisler, *What Augustine Says*, 24-28.

Augustine's two greatest works were *Confessions* and *The City of God*. *Confessions* is an autobiographical work detailing Augustine's conversion. This work is very philosophical in that it deals with his intellectual and spiritual journey to God. Augustine found that there was no rest or satisfaction for man until he found genuine, lasting rest in his Creator.[37]

The City of God was Augustine's view of history.[38] It represented his greatest philosophical and apologetic work. For Augustine, the city of God consists of all angels and men who love and serve God, while the city of the Devil is comprised of those angels and men who oppose the God of the Bible. These two cities are in constant battle. Eventually, the city of God will triumph over the city of man. Augustine's *City of God* is an early example of cultural apologetics—he argued that the pagan attack on Rome was not due to Christendom's rejection of the pagan gods. Instead, argued Augustine, the Roman Empire was comprised of two cities: the City of God (made up of true Christians) and the City of Man (comprised of pagans). The sack of Rome was a great loss to the City of Man. But, the City of God does not seek material wealth; it is an eternal city. Hence, Augustine defended Christianity against the charge that it's rejection of the pagan gods had led to Rome's demise.

---

[37]Saint Augustine, *Confessions*, trans. by R. S. Pine-Coffin (London, Penguin Books, 1961), 21.

[38]Saint Augustine, *City of God*, trans. by Gerald G. Walsh, Demetrius B. Zema, Grace Monahan, and Daniel Honan (New York: Image Books, 1958).

Anselm

Anselm (1033-1109) was the archbishop of Canterbury. His three main writings are: *Proslogium*, *Monologium*, and *Why the God-Man?* Anselm is famous for his ontological argument for God's existence. He believed that God's existence could be proven by reason alone. He concluded that God must exist since His nonexistence is inconceivable. For God is, by definition, the greatest conceivable being. The greatest conceivable being must exist. If He did not exist, then one could conceive of a being greater than Him—a being with all His attributes *and* who did exist. But then this being would be the greatest conceivable Being. Hence, according to Anselm's reasoning, God must exist.[39]

Anselm had another way of stating his ontological argument. He declared that since God is by definition the most perfect being, He must lack no perfection. Since Anselm believed that existence was a perfection, he reasoned that it is impossible for God to lack existence. Therefore, God must exist. Many philosophers today reject the ontological argument for God's existence.[40] Still, it has provoked much thought and debate even in this modern era.

It should also be noted that Anselm did not limit his apologetics to the ontological argument for God's existence. Anselm also used the cosmological argument when attempting to prove God's existence. He argued from the

---

[39]Saint Anselm: *Basic Writings*, trans. by S. N. Deane (Lasalle, IL: Open Court Publishing, 1962), 7-22.

[40]Norman L. Geisler and Winfried Corduan, *Philosophy of Religion* (Grand Rapids: Baker Book House, 1988), 148-149.

existence of good things in the world to the existence of the supreme Good.[41]

Anselm also wrote a work entitled *Why the God Man?* In this work, Anselm defended the Christian doctrine of the incarnation (i.e., God the Son becoming a man). Anselm reasoned that in order for God's wrath against man's sin to be satisfied, only an infinitely worthy sacrifice would suffice. In other words, the sacrifice for man's sins had to be God in order to satisfy God's wrath. But, the sacrifice also had to be man in order to represent man and to be able to die for man, for God as God cannot die.[42]

Thomas Aquinas

Thomas Aquinas (1225-1274) was the greatest scholastic thinker of the middle ages. Scholasticism was an attempt by medieval Christian scholars to use reason to reconcile traditional Christian theology with the philosophy of Aristotle. Aquinas was born in Aquino, Italy. He studied under Albert the Great in Paris and Cologne. Aquinas, like Albert, utilized Aristotle's philosophy in structuring his theological thought; but, unlike Albert, Aquinas developed a complete system.[43]

Although Aquinas held a high view of human reason, he was not a rationalist. He believed that being precedes knowing. Hence, he did not attempt to prove his beliefs with logical necessity. Instead, he used the principle of existential necessity or actual undeniability. He argued for God's

---

[41]Lane, 88.

[42]Ibid., 89.

[43]Copleston, vol. 2, 308-311.

existence and other truths based upon actually undeniable premises.[44]

Aquinas rejected the ontological argument for God's existence.[45] Like Aristotle, he believed that all human knowledge begins in the senses and that the human mind begins life as a "blank slate" upon which nothing is written. He taught that everything in the mind was first in the senses except the mind itself.[46] In other words, man starts life with no data in his mind, though his mind does have the innate ability to draw information from sense experience. The mind has the capacity to draw more out of sense data than sense data itself. The mind does this by reasoning and making judgments on the information gained through sense experiences. Still, knowledge must begin with sense experience. Therefore, according to Aquinas, one cannot argue from the idea of God to His existence (the ontological argument). Instead, one must argue from the data of the physical world to its ultimate Cause.[47] This is why Aquinas used the cosmological and teleological arguments for God's existence. The cosmological argument reasons that finite things such as the universe need an infinite Cause. The teleological argument concludes that design and order in the universe is evidence for the existence of an intelligent Designer of the universe.

Aquinas is famous for his five ways to prove God's existence.[48] The first four ways are cosmological arguments,

---

[44]Norman L. Geisler, *Thomas Aquinas, An Evangelical Appraisal* (Grand rapids: baker Book House, 1991), 71, 73.

[45]Copleston, vol. 2, 337-338.

[46]Ibid., 339. See also Geisler, *Thomas Aquinas*, 86.

[47]Copleston, vol. 2, 340.

while the fifth way is a teleological argument. In his first way to prove God's existence, Aquinas argued from the movement or change in the universe to an unmoved Mover. Second, Aquinas argued from effects in the universe (which cannot account for their own present existence) to their uncaused Cause. Third, Aquinas argued that the existence of beings that have the possibility of nonexistence must have their continuing existence grounded by a Being which has no possibility of nonexistence. Fourth, Aquinas reasoned that since there are different degrees of perfections among beings, there must be a most perfect Being. And, in Aquinas' fifth way, he concluded that since the non-intelligent things in nature progress towards definite goals, they must be directed towards these goals by an intelligent Being.[49]

Aquinas also attempted to solve the problem of evil. He agreed with Augustine that God did not create evil, but that evil is merely a corruption of God's good creation. God did however, according to Aquinas, create the possibility for evil by giving man and angels free will. Fallen men and angels brought evil into the universe by choosing to rebel against God. Aquinas reasoned that God allows evil for the purpose of a greater good. Evil is necessary in order for man to have free will. Since God is all-good and all-powerful, He will one day defeat evil. He accomplishes this through the atoning work of Christ.[50]

Aquinas attempted to solve the problem of religious language. Aquinas rejected univocal knowledge of God.

---

[48]Saint Thomas Aquinas, *Summa Theologiae: A Concise Translation*, edited by Timothy McDermott (Westminster: Christian Classics, 1989), 12-14.

[49]Ibid.

[50]Geisler, *Thomas Aquinas*, 151-162.

Words used of the infinite God cannot have exactly the same (univocal) meaning when used and applied to finite man, for God's existence far transcends man's existence. (Man is not good in exactly the same way God is good.) On the other hand, if words used of man have totally different (i.e., equivocal) meanings when applied to God, then man can have no knowledge of God whatsoever. (When we say "God is good" it would have no meaning.) This rules out equivocal knowledge of God. Aquinas settled this dilemma by his doctrine of analogical predication. A term used both of God and man will be defined the same (univocal). Still, the term will be not be attributed to man and God in exactly the same way. The terms will be infinitely applied to God, but finitely applied to man (i.e., analogical predication). Man must remove all limitations from terms before attributing them to God.[51]

Aquinas believed that God has revealed Himself in both nature and the scriptures. Some truths can be proven by reason (i.e., God's existence, that there is only one God, etc.), but other truths (i.e., the doctrine of the Trinity) are above reason and must be accepted by faith alone.[52] Still, according to Aquinas, there is much evidence for accepting the Bible as God's Word. In fact, miracles (especially Jesus' resurrection), fulfilled prophecies, and the beneficial impact of Christianity upon mankind add to the philosophical arguments to further confirm the truth of Christianity.[53]

---

[51]Ibid., 137-149.

[52]Copleston, vol. 2, 312-313. See also Geisler, *Thomas Aquinas*, 67-69.

[53]Bernard Ramm, *Varieties of Christian Apologetics* (Grand rapids: Baker Book House, 1976), 101.

Aquinas spent much time philosophically defending the orthodox attributes of God. In Aquinas' thought, since God is infinite, He cannot be limited. Hence, He must be immutable, eternal, simple (not composed of parts), one (two or more infinite beings cannot exist—they would limit each other and not be infinite), all-knowing, all-good, everywhere present, and all-powerful.[54]

Aquinas also argued for the existence of natural law—that God's moral laws are written within the hearts of men. Through reason, man can discover God's moral laws (even apart from Scripture).[55]

Thomas Aquinas was one of the greatest defenders of the Christian faith of all time. To this day, many scholars rely heavily upon his thought. Whether Catholic or Protestant, scholars who utilize his system of apologetics are called Thomists.

Bonaventure

Bonaventure (1221-1274) was a contemporary of Thomas Aquinas. Bonaventure used many different arguments for God's existence. He reasoned that our idea of imperfections assumes the existence of the Perfect (by which the imperfections are compared). Bonaventure argued that since beings that are produced exist, there must exist a first Cause of their existence. The existence of changeable beings declares the existence of an unchangeable Being. Bonaventure stated that since from nothing, nothing can come, there must be a self-existent Being as the ground of all other existence.

---

[54]Copleston, vol. 2, 347-362.

[55]Geisler, *Thomas Aquinas*, 164-169.

Beings which have the possibility of nonexistence necessitate the existence of a Being which cannot not exist.[56]

Bonaventure believed that God's existence is self-evident to all men. God's existence is a truth that is naturally implanted in the human mind. Still, he viewed this knowledge to be dim and implicit, rather than obvious and explicit. He considered the atheist to be one who has chosen not to reflect upon this truth. Thus, God's existence can be doubted by men.[57]

Bonaventure also utilized Anselm's ontological argument for God's existence. Since God is the greatest conceivable being, He must exist. For if He did not, one could conceive of a being greater than Him, a being that shared all God's attributes but did exist. Therefore, God must exist.[58] Bonaventure borrowed from Augustine as well. He reasoned from the existence of eternal truths to the existence of an eternal Mind.[59]

Bonaventure, however, had a major disagreement with Thomas Aquinas. Aquinas believed that it was philosophically possible for the universe to be eternal, while Bonaventure believed it could be philosophically proven that the universe had a beginning. Both men agreed that the universe was created and was not eternal. This was clear from the scriptures (Genesis 1:1; John 1:1; Colossians 1:15-17). However, Aquinas agreed with Aristotle that there is nothing logically contradictory with an eternal universe. To refute this view, Bonaventure showed that it is impossible to both add to

---

[56]Copleston, vol. 2, 251-252.

[57]Ibid., 252-253.

[58]Ibid., 255-256.

[59]Ibid., 256-257.

an infinite number and to pass through an infinite series. For, if the universe is eternal, then present events would be adding to the infinite number of past events. But the infinite cannot be added to since it is already infinite. Also, if the universe is infinite, then one could never reach the present moment since one would have to pass through an infinite series of past events to arrive at the present. But, this is impossible due to the fact that no matter how many past events are traversed, there will always be an infinite number more to pass through before the present moment can be reached. Therefore, Bonaventure showed in convincing fashion that it is philosophically contradictory to hold to the possibility of an eternal universe.[60]

John Calvin

John Calvin (1509-1564) was the famous Geneva reformer. Like Luther, he broke from the Roman Catholic Church. He defended the scriptural doctrine of salvation only by God's grace through faith in Christ.[61] At a time when the Roman Catholic Church was elevating human effort in the attaining of salvation, Calvin, like Luther before him, stressed God's grace in salvation.

When one looks at Calvin's *Institutes*, one can detect Calvin's apologetic methodology. Although presuppositionalists, verificationalists, and reformed

---

[60]Ibid., 262-265.

[61]John Calvin, *On the Christian Faith: Selections from the Institutes, Commentaries, and Tracts.* Edited by John T. McNeill (Indianapolis: The Bobbs-Merrill Company, 1957), 82-88.

apologists claim Calvin as their own, it appears that Calvin utilized a mild form of classical apologetics.[62]

Calvin acknowledged that God has revealed Himself to man through His revelation in nature. First, man was created with a natural sense of divinity—man has this knowledge of God by natural endowment. This is not, according to Calvin, an innate idea of God. Rather, it is the witness of God within each person. This sense of divinity produces man's religious attitude and nature. Man's creativity, giftedness, intelligence, and moral sense all point to God.[63]

Second, God reveals Himself to man through creation. Calvin believed that God has given man innumerable evidences of Himself in His creation. The skillful ordering of the universe and God's continual providence over nature display His existence to mankind. Calvin points to both the design in nature and God's care for nature as evidence for God. The seasons make agriculture possible. The abundance of animals for food and their ability to do much of man's work point to God. It is no coincidence that what man needs is provided.[64] Calvin even sees God's control over human history as a clue to God's existence.[65]

In short, Calvin argued for both the immediate knowledge of God and the mediate knowledge of God. The immediate knowledge of God is the inner witness of God within the heart of man. This is man's sense of God. The mediate knowledge of God is the external witness of creation

---

[62]Ramm, *Varieties of Christian Apologetics*, 163-178.

[63]Ibid., 165-166.

[64]Ibid., 167.

[65]Ibid., 167-168.

to God's existence. Because of the immediate and mediate knowledge of God, man has no excuse for rejecting God.[66]

Besides natural revelation of God, Calvin also argued for supernatural revelation from God, when God reveals Himself to man through miracles and the Bible. Calvin believed that man has no excuse for rejecting God's obvious revelation of Himself in nature. Still, due to man's depravity and fallen state, God's general revelation of Himself in nature (i.e., creation) cannot produce in man either true knowledge of God or true worship of God. Calvin argued that the brilliant thought of great philosophers cannot overcome human depravity. Hence, natural revelation (without the acceptance of supernatural revelation) inevitably leads to false religion. Only through God's supernatural revelation can man's depravity be overcome and a true knowledge of the true God be attained. Therefore, God's supernatural revelation in Scripture is needed.[67]

Calvin also reasoned that the witness of the Holy Spirit is necessary to persuade and illuminate man so that all doubt is overcome. Only the Holy Spirit can establish God's truth in the heart of each person. The Holy Spirit empowers the believer to know that God exists with certainty. Only God's special and supernatural revelation in Scripture can produce saving knowledge of God through Jesus Christ.[68]

It seems that Calvin can be classified as a mild classical apologist or evidentialist. Still, he did not believe certainty came from human reason or arguments for God.

---

[66]John Calvin, *Institutes of the Christian Religion*. Trans. by Henry Beveridge (Grand rapids: Eerdmans, 1989), 51-63.

[67]Ibid., 64-73.

[68]Ibid., 68-73.

Certainty only comes from the Holy Spirit. But, on this point, many classical apologists and evidentialists would agree. They would also agree with Calvin that salvation cannot be attained through natural revelation (i.e., God revealing Himself in nature). God's supernatural revelation in Scripture is essential for a person to have a saving knowledge of the gospel.

Rene Descartes

Rene Descartes (1596-1650) was a Roman Catholic philosopher. He decided that something was not worth believing unless one could be certain about it.[69] He decided to reject any beliefs that could be doubted. In this way, he would attempt to find a belief that could not be doubted. This belief would be his point of certainty. From this belief, he would attempt to build an entire system of thought.[70] As Descartes searched for this starting point, he began to doubt more and more beliefs. He became skeptical about all things. Finally, he found what he believed to be this point of certainty. For, the more he doubted, the more he became certain of the existence of the doubter (himself). Descartes coined his famous phrase "*Cogito ergo sum*" (I think, therefore I am). From the starting point of his own existence, he attempted to build his system of thought. Descartes utilized Anselm's ontological argument for God's existence, as well as cosmological type arguments.[71]

---

[69]Rene Descartes, *Discourse on Method and the Meditations*, trans. by F. E. Sutcliffe (London: Penguin Books, 1968), 53.

[70]Ibid., 53-55.

[71]Ibid., 56-61.

Blaise Pascal

Blaise Pascal (1623-1662) was a great French thinker like Descartes. Pascal died while working on a defense of Christianity. It was later published in its incomplete form as *Pensees* (Thoughts). Pascal was opposed to the ultra-rationalism of Rene Descartes. He realized that man is more than merely a rational being. Often man's heart overwhelms his mind. Pascal understood that many of man's most important decisions are not made by man's reason. Since man is both fallen and finite, his reason is not an infallible arbiter of the truth. Man's intuition, will, desires, emotions, and biases often outweigh the influence of his reason. Pascal believed that, due to the Fall, man is incapable of using his reason in an unbiased manner. Hence, Pascal used pragmatic and psychological argumentation to show that man should be biased towards God (rather than against God) before looking at the evidence. There is no such thing as a human being who examines the evidence for or against God in an unbiased manner.[72]

Unlike Descartes and Aquinas, Pascal was opposed to using any of the traditional arguments for God.[73] Instead, he focused on a psychological examination of the nature of man, and then argued that man should hope that God exists before looking at the evidence for Christianity. Pascal pointed to the paradox of man—that man is both wretched and great. He argued that Christianity provides the best explanation for this.

---

[72]Blaise Pascal, *Pensees*, trans. by A. J. Krailsheimer (London: Penguin Books, 1966), no. 44, 110, 183, 188. (The numbers listed for *Pensees* are the numbers of the Pensees, not the page numbers.)

[73]Ibid., no. 84, 190, 449.

Man is great because he was created in God's image. Man is wretched because he has fallen into sin and perverted his nature.[74]

Pascal considered the sad state of the human condition—man is on a one way street to death. All humans are mortal; all humans will someday die.[75] Man can face this inevitable fate and wallow in despair. Or, he can ignore the human condition and divert his attention by amusing and entertaining himself, rather than face the misery of his coming death.[76] But the wise man, according to Pascal, will seek deliverance from death. He will wager his life on God. In other words, he will seek God with all his heart. Pascal said that only two types of men could be considered wise: those who serve God with all their hearts because they know Him and those who seek God with all their hearts because they do not know Him. To wager one's life on God's non-existence is the ultimate act of foolishness. For, one is risking eternity for the few decades of life on this planet.

Pascal is famous for his "wager" argument for God's existence. However, it is not actually an argument for God. Instead, it is an argument that the wise man will wager his life on God (i.e., live as if God exists). This is because the possibility of the infinite gain to be attained by embracing God's existence and eternal life and reward for those who serve Him far outweighs the gain to be attained if God does not exist. In fact, there is nothing to be gained (and the possibility of infinite loss) be wager against God's existence.[77]

---

[74]Ibid., no. 114, 116, 149, 200.

[75]Ibid., no. 165, 434.

[76]Ibid., no. 133, 137.

[77]Ibid., no. 418.

Pascal reasoned that since man uses his reason in a biased manner, we cannot reason to God. Instead, we must use our will. We must either choose to be open to God's existence, or we must reject Him. Pascal concluded that if we wager that God exists and we find that He does in fact exist, we gain eternal happiness. But if God exists and we reject Him, we have lost everything (infinite loss). On the other hand, if God does not exist, we would still lose nothing by wagering that He does. Pascal stated that when a person wagers on God, he will either win or lose. If the person loses, he loses nothing. But if the person wins, he wins everything. Therefore, the wise man will wager that God exists.[78]

As noted above, this is not an argument for God's existence. It is merely an argument that the wise man will be biased in favor of God's existence (i.e., he will wager his life on God) due to the possibility of infinite gain and no possibility of any loss. Only the foolish man will wager his life against God since there is nothing to gain by wagering against God, and there is the possibility of infinite loss. Hence, the wise man will be biased towards God before he uses his reason to examine the evidence for Christianity. According to Pascal, no man uses his reason in an unbiased way. Man must be either biased for God or against God at the outset. And, for pragmatic reasons, the wise man will be biased for God.

Once Pascal has convinced his readers that they should be biased for God (i.e., they should seek God and hope that He exists) before examining the evidence for Christianity, Pascal then makes his case for Christianity. Pascal then turns to the fulfilled prophecies of the Bible, the history and survival of the Jewish people (the chosen nation), and the miracles and

---

[78]Ibid.

resurrection for Jesus to prove Christianity is true.[79] Pascal knows that his case for Christianity will not persuade the hardened skeptic. Still, if the person is open to God's existence due to pragmatic reasons, he will see that the case for Christianity is rather strong.

Pascal is obviously not a classical apologist or an evidentialist. He is not a classical apologist because he rejects the traditional arguments for God's existence. He is also not a typical evidentialist (even though he does utilize historical evidences for Christianity). For, Pascal is adamant that the apologist must first convince the non-believer to be open to God's existence before presenting historical evidence for Christianity. Hence, Pascal is a psychological apologist who deals with man's will, desires, and emotions before making his case for Christianity. According to Pascal, only after moving the person's will towards God can an effective case for Christianity be made.

William Paley

William Paley (1743-1805) was the Archdeacon of Carlisle. Despite the widespread skepticism of his day, he was an aggressive defender of the Christian faith. He wrote several apologetic works: *A View of the Evidences of Christianity* and *Natural Theology*. His most famous contribution to Christian thought was his teleological argument for God's existence.

Paley's teleological argument is called the "watchmaker." In this argument, Paley reasoned that if one found a watch in the wilderness, he would have to conclude that there must have been a watchmaker who designed it.

---

[79]Ibid., 310, 322, 332, 451, 734.

Even if he had never seen a watch before, one would recognize the obvious design, order, and complexity of the watch and conclude that it was designed. Paley then asks his readers to consider the design in the universe and the human eye, and conclude with him that they also need an intelligent Designer.[80]

Paley defended the possibility of miracles against the objections of Scottish philosopher David Hume. Paley argued that if God exists, then miracles are possible. For, it is reasonable to believe that the God who created the universe might want to reveal Himself to mankind. Miracles would be a likely way to reveal Himself. When Hume argued that miracles are contrary to universal experience, this begs the question. When someone (like the Apostles) makes a miracle claim, it would simply be wrong to reject the miracle claim merely because we never experienced a miracle. Miracles claims should be judged by historical investigation; miracles should not be rejected because of a priori philosophical views. Paley argues that Hume is arguing in a circle—he is assuming what he is supposed to prove. Hume is assuming miracles never happen in order to prove that miracles never happen. Hence, miracles are possible, and the historical evidence for or against miracles needs to be examined before one can rule out a miracles.[81]

Next, Paley argued that the Gospels and the epistles are historically reliable. Paley argued that the eyewitnesses of the miracles of Jesus and the Apostles were willing to suffer for what they preached. Hence, their testimony should be

---

[80]William Paley, *Natural Theology: Selections*. edited by Frederick Ferre. (Indianapolis: Bobbs-Merrill, 1963), 3-4, 13.

[81]William Lane Craig, *Reasonable Faith* (Wheaton: Crossway books, 1994), 137-138.

considered reliable. Paley also argued that the widespread agreement among the early church fathers concerning the traditional authorship of the Gospels supports the church's long held belief that the Gospels were actually written by Matthew, Mark, Luke, and John. Paley also turned to the fulfilled prophecies found in the Bible as further confirmation of the truth of Christianity.[82]

Finally, Paley gave evidence for Jesus' bodily resurrection from the dead. He argued that the apostles were not trying to deceive others since they were sincere enough to suffer and die for their beliefs. But what if the apostles were themselves deceived? Paley argues against the hallucination theory—the idea that the apostles did not actually see the risen Christ; they merely had hallucinations. But, this cannot be the case. For, Jesus appeared to groups, not individuals. Many witnesses saw Him several times, not just once. These witnesses did not merely see Him—they ate with Him, touched Him, and talked with Him. And, His tomb was found empty. This would not have been the case if the apostles had merely hallucinated. Since Jesus was buried in a tomb near Jerusalem, it would have been very easy for the Jewish religious leaders to locate the corpse of Christ had the tomb not been empty. Hence, Jesus' bodily resurrection is the best explanation of the available data.[83]

---

[82]William Lane Craig, *The Son Rises: The Historical Evidence for the Resurrection of Jesus* (Eugene, OR: Wipf and Stock Publishing, 1981), 28-36.

[83]Ibid., 35-36.

Conclusion

In this brief survey of the history of Christian apologetics, certain points need to be emphasized. First, the vast majority of Christian apologists saw no inconsistency in providing evidence for the Christian faith. Even Jesus and the Apostles were willing to provide evidence for Christianity. Second, most apologists provided evidence for God from the creation. (Blaise Pascal is a notable exception to this.) Third, most apologists were willing to argue from history for the truths of the gospel. This is why arguing first for God's existence and then for the historicity of the Christian faith is called "Classical Apologetics."

In the pages that follow, the apologetic methodologies of more recent apologists will be discussed. It will be shown that there is no easy way to classify the many different ways to defend the faith that have been developed. As Christians are called to "contend earnestly for the faith," they will find a great arsenal of evidences from which to choose, as well as a great variety of approaches for defending the faith.

Chapter 3
Why Apologetics is Needed

Having discussed the definition, biblical basis, and history of apologetics, the issue of why apologetics is needed must now be examined. In this chapter, seven reasons why Christians need to defend the faith will be given. Though more reasons could be listed, these seven will suffice to demonstrate that Christian apologetics is a necessary discipline in the church.

GOD CREATED MAN TO THINK

Man was created by God to think. Man was created a rational being.[84] God wants man to use all that He has given him for His glory (1 Corinthians 10:31). God has given each man a mind; God wants him to use his mind.

God calls out to the unsaved and invites them to reason with Him that they might be saved (Isaiah 1:18). But God also commands the believer to love Him with all his mind (Mark 12:30). Whether saved or unsaved, God wants man to think

---

[84]John R. W. Stott, *Your Mind Matters* (Downers Grove: InterVarsity Press, 1972), 14-15.

and use his mind. For this reason, believers are to reason with others concerning the gospel (Colossians 4:5-6). God never meant for His gospel message to be considered "anti-intellectual." Therefore, the first reason why apologetics is needed is that God created man to think; He wants people to use the minds He gave them.

TO CONFIRM THE FAITH OF BELIEVERS

A second reason why apologetics is needed is to strengthen or confirm the faith of believers.[85] It is necessary to answer the many intellectual doubts that believers often have.

Our society enthusiastically promotes such ideologies as atheistic evolution and moral relativism. Because of this, Christians are often ridiculed. Born-again believers are often called old-fashioned or dull. It is often said that Christians believe outdated myths or fairy tales. This type of verbal persecution and peer pressure often lead believers to doubt their faith. For this reason, apologetics is needed. It helps answer the doubts a believer may develop in an anti-Christian society.

TO PERSUADE NONBELIEVERS

A third reason why apologetics is needed is that it can and has been used to persuade nonbelievers to accept Christ.[86]

---

[85]Gary R. Habermas, *The Resurrection of Jesus* (Lanham: University Press of America, 1984), 16.

[86]Ibid., 17.

This is done by removing intellectual stumbling blocks that often keep a person from Christ.[87]

Some believers disagree with this particular point. They are quick to point out that arguments cannot lead people to Christ. For only the Holy Spirit can lead a person to Christ. Several things must be mentioned here. First, it is true that only the Holy Spirit regenerates (John 3:3-6). Second, Jesus commands believers to share their faith (Matthew 28:19-20). Third, the Bible commands believers to defend the gospel (1 Peter 3:15). And, fourth, the people who make this objection still share their faith. This shows that they believe that though only the Holy Spirit regenerates, He has chosen to use believers as His instruments. And they are correct at this point. But their position is mistaken in that they fail to realize that the same God who told Christians to share their faith also commanded them to defend it. In other words, just as the Holy Spirit uses believers' sharing of the gospel, He can also use believers' defending of the gospel. Very few Christians, if any, actually believe that the Holy Spirit will lead people to Christ without using believers. Though He has the power to do so, He has chosen to use Christians in both the sharing and the defending of the faith.

It should also be noted that many people were led to Christ through apologetics. Josh McDowell, C. S. Lewis, Walter Martin, and John Warwick Montgomery are just a few outstanding Christian leaders who came to Christ through apologetics.

Those who don't do apologetics must stop witnessing when objections to the gospel are raised, for they do not believe in providing evidence for the gospel. But Christians

---

[87]J. P. Moreland, *Scaling the Secular City* (Grand Rapids: Baker Book House, 1987), 12.

who do apologetics can continue to witness. Defenders of the faith can attempt to answer those objections. And, if Christians really love their fellow man, they should be willing to answer his objections if possible.

TO REFUTE SYSTEMS OF FALSE BELIEF

A fourth reason why apologetics is necessary is that heretical movements must be refuted. If the truth is to be protected, then errors must be exposed and countered. The apostle Paul made it clear that pastors of local churches must be able to "refute those who contradict" the truths of the Bible (Titus 1:9).

If Christians refuse to do battle with belief systems that oppose Christianity, then non-Christian cults and religions will proclaim their false teachings without opposition. Many people who thirst for God will be led astray. Though most Christians shy away from confrontation, they must be willing to boldly combat the false teachings that they encounter. As the Lord confronted the legalistic and hypocritical Pharisees (Matthew 23), His followers must be willing to refute those who promulgate error.

If the Christian church does not oppose false religions and cults, then the essential differences between truth and error will be blurred. Therefore, apologetics is needed to refute non-Christian belief systems.

TO IMPROVE THE MORAL HEALTH OF AMERICA

Fifth, apologetics is needed to help improve the moral well-being of America.[88] The increase in crime, sexual promiscuity, and abortion have plagued this nation.

---

[88]Ibid.

Apologetics can be used to reverse these trends. This can be done in two ways. First, believers may lead others to Christ through apologetics. This will affect the behavior of these new converts. They will begin to live by biblical morality as opposed to the morality which the world promotes (James 2:26). Second, through the use of apologetics, Christians can defend biblical morality even when dealing with nonbelievers.

America needs moral direction. The Christian can encourage a return to traditional values through the use of apologetics. Christian thinkers should engage in public debates and dialogues with non-Christian thinkers concerning ethical issues. In this way defenders of the faith can argue for the superiority of Christian morality.

TO SHOW THE WORLD CHRISTIANITY IS NOT IRRATIONAL

A sixth reason why apologetics is needed is to declare to the world that the Christian faith is not a contradictory system of thought. The world must be shown that one does not have to throw away his or her mind to become a Christian. Many intelligent and educated people have been Christians in the past. Intelligent and educated people can still be Christians today.

Defenders of the faith need to engage in public debate with non-Christian thinkers. Even if no one is persuaded through apologetics (which is usually not the case), at least it will be shown that the Christian faith can be intelligently defended in the world of ideas. The Church must not allow others to call the gospel an outdated myth without responding to this accusation. Therefore, apologetics is needed to show the world that Christianity is not irrational.

TO STAND UP FOR WHAT IS RIGHT EVEN IF NO ONE IS LISTENING

Seventh, apologetics is needed to stand up for what is right even if no one is listening. God demands that Christians stand up for His truth even if it is rejected by all others. The apostle Paul preached the same gospel regardless of whether his listeners applauded him or stoned him (1 Corinthians 9:16; 2 Corinthians 11:23-33; Philippians 4:11-13; Galatians 1:10). The prophet Jeremiah's message was extremely unpopular to the people of Judah. Still, he proclaimed it (Jeremiah 37:15-17). Just because others may harden their hearts to the message, this does not relieve the Church from defending the faith.

In the midst of an immoral culture, someone must stand up for what is right. In the midst of an idolatrous society, someone must contend for the one true God. Anything less is to ignore the responsibilities entrusted to the Church. Paul stated, "I am appointed for the defense of the gospel" (Philippians 1:16) and "woe is me if I do not preach the gospel" (1 Corinthians 9:16). All Christians must proclaim and defend the gospel even if no one is listening.

CONCLUSION

In conclusion, apologetics is needed for several reasons. First, God created man to think. Therefore, the Church should be able to give reasons for why she believes what she believes. Second, apologetics helps to strengthen the faith of believers. Third, it is instrumental in persuading nonbelievers to accept Christ. Fourth, it is necessary since false belief systems must be refuted. Fifth, apologetics can help improve the moral health of society. Sixth, apologetics is needed to show the world that Christianity is not irrational.

And, seventh, apologetics is needed since God calls His followers to stand up for what is right even if no one else is listening.

WHY APOLOGETICS IS NEEDED

1) Because God created man to think

2) To confirm the faith of believers

3) To persuade nonbelievers

4) To refute systems of false belief

5) To improve the moral health of America

6) To show the world Christianity is not irrational

7) To stand up for what is right even if no one else is listening

Chapter Four

A Critique of Contemporary Classifications of Apologetic Methodologies

Currently, there are several exceptional books dealing with apologetic methodologies. Therefore, the question can be asked, "Why this book?" Why write a new book on apologetic methodologies? It is the contention of this author that there has been an oversimplification of the classification of the many different ways to defend the faith. There exists a variety of different ways to defend the faith, and several of these different methodologies are completely ignored. A brief survey of the leading books on apologetic methodologies will confirm this inadequate portrait of apologetic methodologies in books dealing with the subject.

Steven Cowan

Steven Cowan edited one of the most important works on apologetic methodologies in recent times. Cowan's work is called *Five Views on Apologetics*.[89] Five different apologists were asked to contribute to this book. William Lane Craig represented the classical method (i.e., arguing for God first, followed by historical evidences for Christianity).[90] Gary R. Habermas was selected to discuss the evidential method (starts with historical evidence for Christianity).[91] Paul Feinberg defended the cumulative case method (i.e., a method that uses numerous different arguments for the truth of Christianity).[92] John Frame was chosen to represent the presuppositional method.[93] Finally, Kelly James Clark contributed a chapter on the reformed epistemological method (usually associated with Christian philosopher Alvin Plantinga).[94] Each of the authors critiques the methodologies of their colleagues while defending their own method. Over all, this book is an excellent read.

However, several criticisms of this book can be made. First, only five methods are discussed in this book. This leaves the reader with the impression that there are only five ways to defend the faith. But, this is not really the case—there are many other ways to defend the faith (i.e., comparative religious apologetics, psychological apologetics, scientific apologetics, cultural apologetics, verificational, etc.).[95]

---

[89]Steven B. Cowan, ed., *Five Views on Apologetics* (Grand Rapids: Zondervan Publishing House, 2000).

[90]Ibid., 26-55.

[91]Ibid., 92-121.

[92]Ibid., 148-172.

[93]Ibid., 208-231.

[94]Ibid., 266-284.

[95]This current work will identify and discuss seventeen different apologetic methodologies. Most scholars try to sum up

Second, presuppositionalism is presented in such a way that it is implied that there is only one presupposiitonal method (i.e., that of Cornelius Van Til). Gordon Clark's presupposiitonal approach is completely ignored. In fact, Clark's earlier presuppositional approach (i.e., dogmatic pre-suppositionalism) differed from his later presuppositional approach (scripturalism). Hence, there are at least three distinct presuppositional apologetic methods, not one. In fact, Van Til and Clark were totally opposed to each other's apologetic methodology. Third, John Frame, the apologist tasked with defending the presuppositional approach, is not really a presuppositionalist at all. He is more accurately characterized as a verificationalist (i.e.., he allows his presupposition to be tested; his presuppositional is more accurately a hypothesis). Instead of being a strict Van Tillian presuppositionalist, he has one of the best critiques in print of Van Til's main argument—the transcendental argument.[96]

Phil Fernandes—*Contend Earnestly for the Faith*

My book *Contend Earnestly for the Faith: A Survey of Christian Apologetics* was published in 2008.[97] However, it was primarily based on research that I conducted in the mid to late 1990's. In *Contend Earnestly for the Faith*, I listed and described eight different apologetic methodologies:

---

all the different ways to defend the faith by listing four or five methods. But, this is far too simplistic.

[96]John Frame, *Apologetics for the Glory of God* (Phillipsburg, NJ: Presbyterian & Reformed Publishers, 1994), 67-74.

[97]Phil Fernandes, *Contend Earnestly for the Faith: A Survey of Christian Apologetics* (Baltimore: Publish America, 2008).

testimonial, presuppositional, psychological, philosophical, historical, scientific, comparative religious, and cultural.[98]

Testimonial apologists share their testimony (i.e., how Jesus has changed His life) with the non-believer. The testimonial apologist uses the evidence of a transformed life.[99] Presuppositional apologists do not argue to God; they argue from God—God is the starting point.[100] Psychological apologetics consists of defending the faith by appealing to the non-believer's will and psychological make-up, rather than attempting to appeal to his reason.[101] Philosophical apologetics utilizes the traditional philosophical arguments for God. It also attempts to provide a solution for the problem of evil and explain why miracles are possible.[102] Historical apologetics argues from historical evidences to the truth of Christianity; whereas scientific apologetics turns to scientific evidence to argue for the existence of a personal God. Comparative religious apologetics refutes non-Christian religions and cults. Finally, cultural apologetics argues for the positive effects of Christianity on culture, while noting the negative consequences of a culture which abandons God.[103]

In the years since the book was published, I realized that these eight different classifications of apologetic methodologies were inadequate in assessing the great variety

---

[98]Ibid.

[99]Ibid., 87-97.

[100]Ibid., 101-136.

[101]Ibid., 139-160.

[102]Ibid., 163-238.

[103]Ibid., 241-419.

that exists within the field of apologetics today. There are several ways to defend the faith that I had ignored. A few examples will suffice. First, I did not discuss Alvin Plantinga's reformed epistemology (i.e., God as a basic belief). Second, I did not mention verification apologetics or cumulative case apologetics. Third, I did not include David Clark's dialogical apologetics. Fourth, I made no mention of narrative apologetics or paranormal apologetics. Hence, there was a need to update my work and attempt to address those apologetic methodologies overlooked in my earlier work.

Also, I needed to utilize the terminology already present in the common ways apologetic methodologies are classified. For instance, I needed to use the currently accepted classifications "classical apologetics" and "evidentialism," and be able to differentiate between the two. What I referred to as philosophical apologetics is usually called classical apologetics. Whereas, what I titled historical apologetics is normally called evidentialism.

Kenneth Boa and Robert Bowman

Kenneth Boa and Robert Bowman wrote an excellent book on apologetic methodologies called *Faith Has Its Reasons* in 2005.[104] It is a very thorough book. Still, problems with classifying apologetic methodologies remain. The authors only list five different methods in this work: classical, evidential, reformed, fideist, and integrative. In the reformed apologetics section, the authors do have separate subsections dealing with the methodologies of Gordon Clark, Cornelius

---

[104]Kenneth D. Boa and Robert M. Bowman Jr., *Faith Has Its Reasons: An Integrative Approach to Defending Christianity* (Waynesboro, GA: Paternoster Books, 2005).

Van Til, and Alvin Plantinga.[105] But, giving the same classification for these three apologists does not do justice to their differences. Clark was opposed to Van Til's approach to defending the faith. Van Til was opposed to Clark's methodology. And, Plantinga would never claim that he uses the same apologetic approach as either Clark or Van Til. Too often, experts on apologetic methodologies try to simplify things by arbitrarily forcing apologists into classifications in which they do not really fit. If one wants to list all the different ways to defend the faith, the number of methods would far exceed five.

Still, Boa and Bowman are right to draw a distinction between classical apologetics and evidentialism.[106] They are also right to add a section on integrative apologetics (what is called combinationalism in this work).[107] All in all, Boa and Bowman's book is a must read if anyone wants a thorough introduction into the thought of leading Christian apologists.

Scott Burson and Jerry Walls

In 1998, Scott Burson and Jerry Walls co-authored a book detailing the apologetic methodologies of C. S. Lewis and Francis Schaeffer.[108] Though the book did not deal with apologetic methodologies in general, it did focus on

---

[105]Ibid., 221-334.

[106]Ibid., 49-218.

[107]Ibid., 425-523.

[108]Scott R. Burson and Jerry L. Walls, *C. S. Lewis and francis Schaeffer: Lessons for a New Century from the Most Influential Apologists of Our Time* (Downers Grove, IL: Intervarsity Press, 1998).

classifying the apologetic methodologies of Lewis and Schaeffer. The authors note that Schaeffer was not a Van Tillian presuppositionalist, even though Van Til was one of Schaeffer's seminary professors. Van Til often harshly critiqued, both verbally and in writing, Schaeffer's apologetic methodology.[109] Van Til clearly disagreed with the way Schaeffer defended the faith. Hence, Burson and Walls are correct in their assessment that Francis Schaeffer was not a true presuppositionalist—he was a verificationalist. He used the Christian presupposition, not in a dogmatic way, but as a hypothesis that he was willing to submit to testing and verification. In fact, Burson and Walls also classify C. S. Lewis as a verificationalist.[110]

Burson and Wills deserve credit for recognizing the difference between presuppositionalism and very-ficationalism. Presuppositionalism dogmatically presupposes the Christian world view as its starting point and then argues *from* that starting point rather than *to* it. Verificationalism, on the other hand, uses the Christian world view, not as a presupposition, but as a hypothesis to explain reality. The verificationalist then allows the Christian hypothesis to be tested (i.e., verified). Too many apologists classify verificational apologists like Schaeffer, John Frame, and Edward J. Carnell as presuppositionalists when that was not actually the case.

---

[109]Ibid., 148.

[110]Ibid., 161-163.

Bernard Ram

In 1962, Bernard Ramm wrote *Varieties of Christian Apologetics*.[111] This was a revised edition of an earlier work.[112] Ramm, in *Varieties of Christian Apologetics*, classifies apologetic methodologies into three categories based on what they stress: 1) subjective immediacy, 2) natural theology, and 3) revelation. Ramm discusses three apologists in each of the three categories.

Ramm lists Blaise Pascal, Soren Kierkegaard, and Emil Brunner as apologists who stress subjective immediacy.[113] This view focuses on religious experience being self-authenticating. Most apologists would probably classify this type as fideism. Some would question whether fideism is even a way to defend the faith or a rejection of apologetics.

Ramm's second category deals with apologists who start with natural theology. These apologists start with God's revelation in nature and argue to God's existence, or they use historical evidences to argue for Christianity. Ramm discusses Thomas Aquinas, Joseph Butler, and F. R. Tennant in this section.[114]

The third category Ramm discusses is apologetic systems that stress God's revelation. In this category, Ramm writes about the apologetic methodologies of Augustine, John

---

[111]Bernard Ramm, *Varieties of Christian Apologetics* (Grand Rapids: Baker Book House, 1962).

[112]Bernard Ramm, *Types of Apologetic Systems* (Wheaton: Van Kampen Press, 1953).

[113]Ramm, *Varieties*, 31-85.

[114]Ibid., 89-144.

Calvin, Abraham Kuyper.[115] These apologists start with God's revelation in Scripture and then argue to the truth of Christianity. This methodology is now often called presuppositionalism, though it is debatable whether Augustine and John Calvin were truly presuppositional in their apologetic approaches.

Though Ramm over-generalizes apologetic methodologies by listing only three distinct classifications, he should be commended for dividing each classification into three sub categories. So, in essence, Ramm describes nine different approaches rather than just three. Still, if one is to truly list all the different ways an apologist can defend the faith, one will have to list more than nine methodologies. This present work will try to show that the discipline of Christian apologetics is much more multi-faceted than previous works on apologetic methodologies have shown.

Gordon Lewis

Gordon Lewis wrote his latest edition of *Testing Christianity's Truth Claims* in 1990.[116] In this important work, he discussed the thought of several different apologists. The classifications he gave for each apologist were based upon examining each apologist's arguments. Lewis should be commended for this. Too often, researchers of apologetic methodologies start with preconceived notions of the different apologetic methods, and then attempt to artificially force different apologists into these preconceived categories. When this is

---

[115]Ibid., 147-195.

[116]Gordon R. Lewis, *Testing Christianity's Truth Claims: Approaches to Christian Apologetics* (Lanham, MD: University Press of America, 1990).

done, the thought of several apologists is commonly misrepresented. Unless one is willing to concede that the number of apologetic methods is much higher than is often portrayed (as this present work will show), Lewis' example should be followed. He allows the thought and nuances of each individual apologist to dictate how to classify that particular apologist.

Lewis discusses the "pure empiricism" of J. Oliver Buswell, Jr. and the "rational empiricism" of Stuart Hackett.[117] Lewis, unlike many other students of apologetic methodologies, clearly differentiates the approaches of the leading presuppositionalists Gordon Clark and Cornelius Van Til. Too often all presuppositionalists are placed under one methodology. Not so with Gordon Lewis. He appreciates the differences between Clark and Van Til. Lewis classifies Gordon Clark's method as "rationalism," whereas he refers to Cornelius Van Til's approach as "biblical authoritarianism."[118] Lewis also discusses what he calls the "mysticism" of Earl E. Barrett.[119] This approach argues for Christianity based on one's personal experience of God. Most apologists would call this methodology "fideism." Many apologists (including this author) do not even consider fideism an apologetic method. Instead, fideism is the rejection of defending the faith; it is "anti-apologetics."

Gordon Lewis closes his book with four chapters on the different aspects of Edward J. Carnell's verificational approach.[120] By doing this, Lewis rightly shows that Carnell

---

[117]Ibid., 45-98.

[118]Ibid., 100-149.

[119]Ibid., 151-173.

was not a strict presuppositionalist. Instead, Carnell treated Christianity as a hypothesis or explanation that could be verified by testing. Lewis also shows that Carnell was also somewhat of a combinationalist in that he was willing to combine several different approaches when defending the faith.

Lewis should be commended for allowing the work of each apologist to define his own method, for drawing a distinction between the presuppositionalists Van Til and Clark, and for distinguishing between presuppositionalism and verificationalism. *Testing Christianity's Truth Claims* is a must read for those who desire to learn about apologetic methodologies.

Norman L. Geisler

In his extensive work entitled *Baker Encyclopedia of Christian Apologetics*, Norman Geisler includes an article dealing with apologetic methodologies.[121] He lists five different ways to defend the faith. First, there is the classical approach. This approach first argues for God's existence and then provides historical evidence for the truths of Christianity. Second, evidentialism uses historical evidences as well as other evidences for Christianity. Geisler calls the third method "historical apologetics." He, unlike most apologists, distinguishes between evidentialism and historical apologetics. He sees evidentialism as more eclectic than historical apologetics; whereas historical apologetics limits itself to historical evidences. Fourth, Geisler discusses what he calls "experiential apologetics." Experiential apologetics

---

[120]Ibid., 176-283.

[121]Norman L. Geisler, *Baker Encyclopedia of Christian Apologetics* (Grand Rapids: Baker Book House, 1999), 41-44.

focuses on the self-authenticating power of religious experience. (Many apologists would not consider this a way to defend the faith.) Finally, Geisler lists presuppositionalism as the fifth approach to defending the faith. However, unlike many apologists, Geisler does not lump together all so-called presupposiitonalists. He differentiates between four sub-categories of presuppositionalism. This is to his credit because far too many apologists act as if all presuppositionalists use the same approach. This ignores the many differences that exist between different types of presuppositionalists (i.e., Cornelius Van Til, Gordon Clark, Carl Henry, etc.).

Problems with the Current Classifications of Apologetics Methodologies

There are several problems with the way apologetic methods have been classified. First, too often the important differences between distinct presuppositional approaches are ignored by non-presuppositionalists. However, true presuppositionalists are very passionate about these distinctions. Hence, these distinctions should not be ignored. There are different ways to do presuppositional apologetics. This is why Gordon Clark and Cornelius Van Til (though both were presuppositionalists) often passionately disagreed with each other's approach to defending the faith.

Second, too often verificationalists (those who treat Christianity like a hypothesis to be tested) are classified as presuppositionalists when they are not really presuppositionalists. Verficiationalism should be recognized as an apologetic methodology distinct from presuppositionalism.

Third, many ways to defend the faith are often ignored. Some apologists only use scientific evidences to defend the faith. Hence, scientific apologetics should be accepted as its own way to defend the faith. Comparative religious apologetics is often ignored. The same could be said for many other ways to defend Christianity (i.e., testimonial, psychological, cultural, narrative, dialogical, paranormal, basic belief, etc.).

Hence, this work will try to give a more exhaustive classification of the many different ways to defend the faith. This work will also show that since there is so much diversity in classifying apologetic methodologies, it is probably best to discuss each apologist as an individual and then detail the different approaches or evidences he uses. Still, the many different ways to defend the faith can be used as a way to chart the many different apologists and their different approaches.

Chapter 5
The Apologetic Methodology of Norman Geisler

INTRODUCTION

Norman Geisler may be the leading Christian apologist of the latter half of the twentieth-century. Geisler founded the Evangelical Philosophical Society and the International Society of Christian Apologetics, and is also a former president of the Evangelical Theological Society. He has successfully debated, in defense of Christianity, some of the world's leading non-Christian thinkers.

Geisler earned his Ph.D. in philosophy at Loyola University. Over the decades, he has established himself as the leading evangelical Thomist (someone who utilizes the philosophical thought of Saint Thomas Aquinas). He has taught theology, philosophy, and apologetics at some of America's leading evangelical schools such as Dallas Theological Seminary, Trinity Evangelical Divinity School, and Liberty University. Geisler helped found Southern Evangelical Seminary (one of today's leading training grounds for Christian apologists) in North Carolina and taught apologetics and theology there. It is hard to find an evangelical apologist who has had a greater impact on the evangelical thought of his day.

Geisler is a prolific author. Some of his most notable works that deal with apologetics and his apologetic methodology are: *Christian Apologetics,*[122] *Philosophy of Religion*[123] (co-authored with Winfried Corduan), *I Don't Have Enough Faith to Be an Atheist*[124] (co-authored with Frank Turek), *When Skeptics Ask*[125] (co-authored with Ronald Brooks), and *The Baker Encyclopedia of Christian Apologetics.*[126] In this chapter, we will examine his apologetic methodology. First, we will look at his seminal work *Christian Apologetics.*

METHODOLOGY—HOW DO WE FIND TRUTH?

Geisler is one of the most thorough apologists—he begins his apologetic system asking the question: How do we find truth?[127] In an attempt to answer this question, he examines several options before identifying what he believes to be the correct method of finding truth. Once he identifies

[122]Norman L. Geisler, *Christian Apologetics* (Grand Rapids: Baker Book House, 1976).

[123]Norman L. Geisler and Winfried Corduan, *Philosophy of Religion*, 2nd ed. (Grand Rapids: Baker Book House, 1988).

[124]Norman L. Geisler and Frank Turek, *I Don't Have Enough Faith to be an Atheist* (Wheaton: Crossway Books, 2004).

[125]Norman L. Geisler and Ron Brooks, *When Skeptics Ask: A Handbook on Christian Evidences* (Wheaton: Victor Books, 1990).

[126]Norman L. Geisler, *Baker Encyclopedia of Christian Apologetics* (Grand Rapids: Baker Book House, 1999).

[127]Geisler, *Christian Apologetics*, 11-147.

this method, he applies it to worldviews (i.e., different ways to explain reality), testing them to determine the true world view. Once he finds the true world view, he then turns to historical evidences to defend Christianity.

Geisler examines and critiques several proposed methods for finding truth. First, he looks at *agnosticism*.[128] Hard agnosticism is the view that man cannot know truth. Geisler shows that hard agnosticism is self-refuting, for it is a claim to know something—that man cannot know anything. But, if man can know that man cannot know, then, at least, man can know this. Hence, agnosticism fails—man can know truth. Geisler critiques the agnostic Immanuel Kant. Kant argued that we can only know reality as it appears to us, not reality as it is. However, Geisler points out that if Kant is correct, then man can know the reality that we cannot know reality—but, this is knowledge of reality. Hence, Kant's agnosticism is self-refuting. Since agnosticism fails, it is possible for man to know truth.

Second, Geisler focuses on *rationalism* as a test for truth.[129] Pure rationalism fails as a test for truth for several reasons. Rationalism can prove that which is false (i.e., contradictions cannot be true) and it can show what is possible; but, by itself, it is unable to prove that which is true. Also, if man can prove everything through reason alone, then we would be able to prove our first principles (i.e., our starting points) through reason alone. But, then these would not be our first principles since there would be premises that precede them. And these premises would need proof as well. Hence, pure rationalism leads to an infinite regress of premises and

---

[128]Ibid., 13-27.

[129]Ibid., 29-46.

knowledge can never get started. Therefore, pure rationalism fails as a method to find truth.

Third, Geisler shows *fideism* to be an inadequate test for truth.[130] Fideism is the view that we must merely believe things without evidence for them. Applied to religion, fideists contend that we must blindly believe religious tenets without evidence. Geisler points out that fideism fails because it refuses to test truth claims—it asks us to merely believe. The fideist says we should not use reason to defend our religious beliefs, yet the fideist himself, by claiming to be a fideist, uses the law of non-contradiction (a rational principle). In essence, the fideist is using reason in an attempt to argue against reason.

Fourth, Geisler identifies the problems with using *experientialism* as the test for truth.[131] Geisler points out that no experience is self-interpreting—we interpret our experiences through the lenses of our world view (i.e., our view of reality). Also, there is no way to adjudicate between conflicting truth claims if experientialism is the sole test for truth. Each person would hold to their own experience, but there would be no way to prove one experience true and the other experience false.

Fifth, Geisler declares *evidentialism* to be an inadequate test for truth.[132] Facts do not come with their own built-in interpretations—again, they must be interpreted by the world view of the person. We interpret facts by our worldview and not the other way around. A mere appeal to

---

[130]Ibid., 47-64.

[131]Ibid., 65-81.

[132]Ibid., 83-99.

facts will not settle disputes between different world views; our test for truth must be more foundational than facts.

Sixth, *pragmatism* also fails as a test for truth.[133] Pragmatism is the belief that whatever works is true. Geisler points out that even though all truth must ultimately work, not everything that works is true. Often, lies work—when a doctor tells a patient he is recovering when he is not may help him rehabilitate more rapidly, but it is still a lie. Just because something works does not mean it is true. Also, Geisler points out that, as finite humans, we cannot always see the long range results of a view. Sometimes what works in the short term will fail in the end. Whatever the case, pragmatism fails as a test for truth.

Seventh, Geisler rejects *combinationalism* as a test for truth.[134] Merely adding together inadequate ways to find truth will not produce an adequate way to find truth. Geisler illustrates this point by stating that adding leaky buckets will continue to fail to hold water. Hence, merely combining inadequate tests for truth is equivalent to a new inadequate test for truth.

After showing the limitations of these seven failed tests for truth, Geisler proposes his own tests for truth. These tests are as follows: 1) *actual unaffirmability* as a test for the falsity of world views, 2) *actual undeniability* as a test for the truth of world views, and 3) *systematic consistency* (a combinational test for truth statements *within* a particular world view).[135]

Actual unaffirmability deals with things that are impossible to affirm without contradiction. For instance, if

---

[133]Ibid., 101-116.

[134]Ibid., 117-132.

[135]Ibid., 133-147.

someone says he does not exist, he must first exist in order to make the denial. Hence, my nonexistence is actually unaffirmable. Any world view that is actually unaffirmable must be false.[136]

Actual undeniability deals with truths that can only be denied with contradiction. An example of this is that it is actually undeniable that I exist; for, if I did not exist I would not be able to deny my existence. I must exist to be able to deny my existence. Hence, my existence is actually undeniable. Any world view that is actually undeniable must be true.[137]

Systematic consistency uses combinationalism, not to test the truth of a world view, but as a test for the truth of statements within a world view.[138] The three main components of Geisler's systematic consistency test are consistency, empirical adequacy, and experiential relevance. *Consistency* determines whether the beliefs within a world view are non-contradictory. *Empirical adequacy* says that a world view must explain all the relevant facts in question. If a world view is unable to explain relevant data, it is a weak world view. *Experiential relevance* declares that a world view must be livable. If it is not possible to live consistently with a world view, then that world view should be abandoned.[139]

Geisler uses the first two tests (actual unaffirmability, and actual undeniability) to test the main world views to determine which one is true. The world views he tests are: deism, pantheism, panentheism, atheism, and theism. Geisler

---

[136]Ibid., 141-143.

[137]Ibid., 143-145.

[138]Ibid., 145-147.

[139]Ibid., 147.

argues that theism is the true world view. Once this is settled, Geisler then uses the test of systematic consistency to determine which theistic religion is true.

THEISTIC APOLOGETICS—WHICH WORLD VIEW IS TRUE?

Deism is the world view that teaches that God created the universe but does not intervene—He does not perform miracles. Deism is based on a faulty view of science in which the laws of nature cannot be violated. In reality, the laws of nature do not prescribe what must occur; they describe what generally occurs. Natural laws do not rule out the possibility of miracles. If God cared enough to create the universe (a point agreed to by Deists), then it makes sense that He would care enough to communicate with His creatures through miracles. If God is powerful enough to create the universe (also accepted by Deists), then He is powerful enough to perform miracles. Hence, if Deism is true, then God is both willing and able to perform miracles. But, then Deism would be false.[140]

Pantheism is the world view that believes that God is everything—God is the universe. God is a non-personal force. In this world view, since all reality is one being (monism), man is God. Geisler exposes the weaknesses of pantheism by showing that it fails to adequately explain the existence of the finite self and the existence of evil. Also, pantheism teaches that God is beyond reason; hence, God is unknowable. But, this creates a problem for pantheism. For, how could the pantheist know that pantheism is true if God is unknowable? If God is completely unknowable, how could we know that

---

[140]Ibid., 151-171.

God is the universe and is non-personal. For these reasons, pantheism fails as a world view.[141]

Panentheism is the world view that professes belief in the existence of a God who has both a finite aspect and an infinite aspect to His basic nature. But, this is incoherent. For God cannot be both finite and infinite in His basic nature. If God has limitations in His basic nature, he would, by definition, be a finite, limited god. A changing, finite god would need to have his existence grounded by an infinite, non-changing God (i.e., the God of theism). Therefore, the panentheistic world view fails.[142]

Atheism is the world view that teaches there is no God. This world view fails for several reasons. First, Geisler shows that arguments for atheism are invalid and self-refuting. Second, atheism offers no adequate explanation for the existence of the universe, personality, intelligence, and morality. The existence of the universe, personality, intelligence, and morality provide good evidence for theism (i.e., the belief in a personal God who is both transcendent and immanent).[143]

After showing the weaknesses of the above world views, Geisler argues that the theistic world view is actually undeniable.[144] First, Geisler argues that "some things undeniably exist." For example, I must exist in order to deny my existence—I cannot consistently deny my own existence. Therefore, I undeniably exist. Second, "my nonexistence is possible." There was a time I did not exist. I depend on the existence of other things for my continued existence. Third,

---

[141]Ibid., 173-192.

[142]Ibid., 193-213.

[143]Ibid., 215-235.

[144]Ibid., 237-259.

"Whatever has the possibility not to exist is currently caused to exist by another." Fourth, "There cannot be an infinite regress of current causes of existence," for then each cause would also be an effect. There would be no cause for the continuing existence of the entire series. Fifth, "Therefore, a first uncaused cause of my current existence exists." If this were not the case, then no finite things would now exist. Sixth, Geisler shows that "this uncaused cause must be infinite, unchanging, all-powerful, all-knowing, and all-perfect." If this were not the case, then the infinite cause of all finite existence would not really be infinite. However, an infinite uncaused cause must exist in order to ground the continuing existence of all finite things. Geisler argues that "this infinitely perfect being is appropriately called 'God,'" for there cannot be two infinite beings. Hence, God exists. This God is identical to the God of the Bible. Therefore, the God of the Bible exists.[145]

Dr. Geisler, through his argumentation, has shown that the existence of the God of theism is actually undeniable. Since all other world views contradict theism, they must be false. Only theism is the true world view.

CHRISTIAN APOLOGETICS—WHICH THEISTIC RELIGION IS TRUE?

Once Geisler proves theism to be true, he then moves on to argue that Christian theism is true, whereas Islamic theism and Jewish theism are false. Christianity, Islam, and Judaism are the three great theistic religions. Geisler turns to history to argue for the truth of Christian theism. He shows that, through the study of ancient history and by using the

---

[145]Ibid., 238-250.

principle of systematic consistency, the truth of the Christian world view can be established.

First, Geisler argues that miracles are possible. If the theistic God (a personal, all-powerful God who created the world but sustains its existence) exists, then miracles are possible. Miracles cannot be ruled out a priori (before examining the evidence for particular miracle claims).[146]

Second, Geisler argues that history is objective—there is a real history independent of any particular historian's speculation about history. History is as objective as modern science since both deal with probabilities (not certainties). Hence, miracle claims must be tested.[147]

Third, Geisler argues that the truth of Christian theism can be verified through an examination of history. First, he argues for the historical reliability of the New Testament manuscripts. Second, he argues for the deity and authority of Jesus Christ. Third, he argues for the inspiration and authority of the Bible.

Geisler points to several pieces of evidence for the historical reliability of the New Testament manuscripts. He shows that the New Testament has greater manuscript evidence for its reliability than any other ancient writing. It has more copies, a smaller gap between the earliest extant copies and the original, and a higher percentage of agreement between existing ancient copies. No ancient writing comes close to the New Testament in reference to manuscript evidence.[148] By referring to archaeological confirmation, ancient secular writings, and the writings of the early church fathers, Geisler presents strong arguments for the early dates

---

[146]Ibid., 263-283.

[147]Ibid., 285-304.

[148]Ibid., 305-308.

of the New Testament books, thus showing that they were written by eyewitnesses who knew Jesus (or people who knew eyewitnesses).[149]

Next, Geisler argues that Jesus did in fact claim to be God on numerous occasions. Jesus claimed to be Jehovah and equal with God. He accepted worship, taught others to pray in His name, and placed His words on the same level as the words of God.[150] Geisler argues that Jesus proved His claims to be true by rising from the dead, fulfilling numerous Old Testament messianic prophecies, and performing miracles.[151] Therefore, Jesus is God.

As God, Jesus verified that the Bible is God's Word. He taught that the Old Testament is God's Word and promised that the Holy Spirit would guide His followers into all the truth, thus producing the New Testament.[152] Since the Bible is God's Word, it is without errors—it it totally true in the original manuscripts. Hence, other religions that disagree with the Bible are false.[153]

GEISLER'S TWELVE STEP APOLOGETIC ARGUMENT

In more recent times, Norman Geisler has spelled out his apologetic case for Christianity, in a more simplified fashion, in a twelve-step argument. This argument can be

---

[149]Ibid., 308-327.

[150]Ibid., 330-334.

[151]Ibid., 339-351.

[152]Ibid., 353-376.

[153]Ibid., 376-377.

found in his work, co-authored with Frank Turek, *I Don't Have Enough Faith to be an Atheist*:

1. Truth about reality is knowable.

2. The opposite of true is false.

3. It is true that the theistic God exists.

4. If God exists, then miracles are possible.

5. Miracles confirm a message from God.

6. The New Testament is historically reliable.

7. The New Testament says that Jesus claimed to be God.

8. Jesus' claim to be God was miraculously confirmed by:

    a. His fulfillment of Old Testament prophecies.

    b. His sinless and miraculous life.

    c. His prediction and accomplishment of His resurrection.

9. Therefore, Jesus is God.

10. Whatever Jesus (who is God) teaches is true.

11. Jesus taught that the Bible is the Word of God.

12. Therefore, the Bible is God's Word and anything opposed to it is false.[154]

First, truth about reality is knowable. If someone says "there is no truth," he contradicts himself. For the statement "there is no truth" would be true. Hence, truth exists. If someone says "man cannot know truth," then this would be a truth known by man. Hence, it is also self-refuting. Therefore, truth exists and man can know it.

Second, the opposite of true is false. That which contradicts the truth must be false. If the statement "God exists" is true, then the statement "God does not exist" must be false. Contradictory statements cannot both be true.[155]

Third, it is true that the theistic God exists. Geisler now uses several arguments for God's existence. He uses two types of cosmological arguments: the argument from the beginning of the universe and the argument from the continuing existence of the universe. Geisler argues that whatever has a beginning needs a cause, and that the universe has a beginning—this is confirmed by the big bang model, the expansion of the universe, and the second law of thermodynamics. Therefore, if the universe had a beginning, it needs a cause. Geisler also argues that it is impossible for only contingent beings to exist—beings whose continued existence is dependent on the existence of other things. Eventually, we must arrive at a being that is necessary, a being that cannot not exist. This being grounds the continuing existence of everything else that exists.[156]

---

[154]Geisler and Turek, *I Don't Have Enough Faith to be an Atheist*, 33.

[155]Ibid., 35-69.

[156]Ibid., 73-94.

Geisler also uses two forms of the teleological argument for God—the argument from design.[157] The first type of design argument argues from the Anthropic Principle that universe was fine-tuned to support human life on the planet earth. This cannot be a coincidence—an intelligent Designer must have pre-planned the universe for the purpose of supporting human life on the planet earth. The second type of design argument deals with the specified and irreducible complexity of life. Even a single cell animal contains enough genetic information to fill 1,000 complete sets of Encyclopedia Britannica. That amount of highly complex information could not have come about by chance. Life—even the most basic forms of life—had to be intelligently designed.

Geisler also uses the moral argument for God's existence. Everyone appeals to an absolute standard of morality when we condemn the actions of others. But, if there exists an absolute moral law, there must exist an absolute moral Lawgiver. If there exists no universal moral law, then there is no real difference between living a life like Mother Theresa or living a life like Adolph Hitler.[158]

Fourth, if God exists, then miracles are possible. Since Geisler has already shown that the evidence indicates that the theistic God does exist, then miracles cannot be ruled out beforehand. Miracles are possible, for the theistic God is both willing and able to perform miracles. Hence, we must examine the historical evidence to determine if certain miracles have occurred.[159]

---

[157]Ibid., 95-167.

[158]Ibid., 169-193.

[159]Ibid., 197-217.

Fifth, God uses miracles to confirm a message from Him. God does not perform miracles to entertain; He performs miracles to place His stamp of approval on the message that is being proclaimed.[160]

Sixth, Geisler argues that the New Testament is historically reliable. Geisler builds a strong case that the New Testament presents early eyewitness testimony to the life, teachings, miracles, death, and resurrection of Jesus. Ancient non-Christian authors confirm what the early church believed. The New Testament has more extant copies than any other ancient writing. These copies have a far greater percentage of agreement than any other ancient writing. The gap between when the New Testament was originally written and the oldest copies we currently have is a smaller gap than that of any other ancient writing. The writings of the early church fathers show the New Testament books to be first century ad documents. This shows that the New Testament was written while the apostles (who personally knew Jesus) were still alive. Hence, the New Testament accounts were not legends that developed decades or centuries after Jesus lived; they were reliable historical accounts that accurately depicted the life and ministry of Jesus.[161]

Seventh, the New Testament (which we have shown to be authored by the generation that knew Jesus) portrays Jesus as a man who claimed to be God on numerous occasions. Hence, the earliest evidence indicates that Jesus thought of Himself as equal to God.[162]

---

[160]Ibid., 216-217.

[161]Ibid., 221-297.

[162]Ibid., 327-354.

Eighth, Jesus' claim to be God was confirmed by His fulfilling Old Testament prophecies of the coming Messiah,[163] His miraculous works, and His bodily resurrection from the dead. Geisler and Turek present numerous evidences for Jesus' bodily resurrection and refute alternative, naturalistic theories used to explain away the resurrection.[164] Therefore, Jesus is God and whatever He teaches is true (i.e., points 9 and 10 above).

Jesus taught the Old Testament is the inerrant Word of God and promised to complete God's revelation through the teachings of His apostles (i.e., the New Testament). The Holy Spirit would guide the apostles into the truth and bring to their remembrance all that Jesus taught them. Hence, Jesus (who is God) taught that the Bible is God's Word (point 11).[165]

Finally, since the Bible is God's Word, whatever it teaches is true. Whatever contradicts the Word of God must therefore be false.[166] This concludes Norman Geisler and Frank Turek's case for Christianity.

Geisler's Scientific Case for Creation

Norman Geisler has also established himself as a leading scientific apologist. This section will draw heavily upon the information found in the book *Origin Science* by Norman L. Geisler and J. Kirby Anderson.[167]

---

[163]Ibid., 329-336.

[164]Ibid., 299-320.

[165]Ibid., 355-376.

[166]Ibid., 375.

[167]Norman L. Geisler and J. Kirby Anderson, *Origin Science* (Grand Rapids: Baker Book House, 1987), entire book.

HISTORY OF THE CREATION-EVOLUTION DEBATE

The creation model is the view that God created the universe without using evolution. The creation model dominated modern science before 1860.[168] Modern science was started by men who believed in the existence of the God of the Bible. Galileo, Isaac Newton, Francis Bacon, Johannes Kepler, and Blaise Pascal are just a few who fit into this category.[169] Their belief in God's existence formed the foundation for modern science. They believed that a reasonable God created the universe in a reasonable way, so that through reason man could find out about the universe in which he lives.[170] In other words, the universe makes sense only because God designed it to make sense. Today, however, atheistic evolutionists have rejected this base for modern science.[171] They have rejected the existence of a reasonable God. But the question that they must face is this: "Without a reasonable God, can a person really expect the universe to make sense?"

The evolution model is the view that life spontaneously evolved from non-life without intelligent intervention.[172] The evolution model dominated modern science after 1860.[173] Charles Darwin published his book *The*

---

[168]Ibid., 37-52.

[169]Ibid.

[170]Ibid., 37-40, 51.

[171]Ibid., 52.

[172]Ibid., 82-86.

[173]Ibid.

Origin of Species around that time.[174] Darwin proposed a naturalistic explanation for the origin of the universe, first life, and new life forms.[175] He taught that nature can be explained without appealing to a supernatural origin. Darwin's proposal quickly became the predominant "scientific" view.

THE SCIENTIFIC METHOD

Evolution is not a scientific fact. The scientific method consists of six steps: 1) observation, 2) proposal of a question or problem, 3) hypothesis (an educated guess), 4) experimentation, 5) theory (a hypothesis with a high degree of probability), and 6) natural law (a theory thought to be valid on a universal scale).[176] Evolution is not a scientific law or theory, let alone a scientific fact. The supposed evolutionary changes from one species to another cannot be observed.[177] They supposedly occurred in the past. Therefore, since observation is the initial step in the scientific method, evolution cannot be proven through the scientific method.

The creation view is in the same category as evolution. Creation, scientifically speaking, is not a fact, law, or theory. Like evolution, the supposed creation is a singular event in the past. It cannot be observed. Therefore, both creation and evolution are only *scientific models*; they represent different ways to interpret the same evidence.[178]

---

[174]Ibid.

[175]Ibid.

[176]Tom M. Graham, *Biology, the Essential Principles* (Philadelphia: Saunders College Publishing, 1982), 6.

[177]Geisler and Anderson, 15.

[178]Ibid.

This does not mean that creation and evolution cannot claim to be scientific. Contrary to popular belief, the scientific method is not the only way to search for truth in the field of science. Forensic science (crime scene investigation) does not use the scientific method, for the crime can no longer be observed. Still, forensic science is a legitimate science.[179] Science can be separated into two main divisions: operation science and origin science. Operation science deals with the repeatable; it is science of the observable present. It uses the scientific method. Forensic science, creation, and evolution do not fall into this category.[180] Origin science, on the other hand, deals with the non-repeatable; it deals with the singular events of the past. Origin science does not utilize the scientific method since singular events of the past can no longer be observed.[181] Forensic science, creation science, and evolutionary science fall into this category.

ORIGIN SCIENCE

Since the non-repeatable events of the past cannot be observed, origin science does not make use of the scientific method. Instead, origin science uses the principles of analogy (also called uniformity) and causality to determine whether or not a model is plausible.[182] The principle of analogy states that when a scientist observes a cause bringing about a certain effect in the present, he should posit the same kind of cause

---

[179]Ibid., 25.

[180]Ibid., 36.

[181]Ibid., 127-132.

[182]Ibid.

for a similar effect in the past.[183] In other words, similar effects usually have similar causes. The principle of causality states that every event must have an adequate cause.[184] A scientist should use these two principles to determine the plausibility (or lack of plausibility) of a particular model.

Since the creation model and the evolution model fall under the heading of origin science, the principles of analogy and uniformity must be applied to them to determine which model is more plausible. It must be understood that the creation model and the evolution model both deal with the same evidence. An example of this is common anatomy. Common anatomy deals with the similarities in the body parts of different species. Examples of common anatomy are the similarities that exist concerning the arm of a man, the arm of an ape, the wing of a bird, and the fin of a shark. Both creationists and evolutionists agree to the common anatomy between different species of animal life. However, the two models interpret the evidence differently. The evolution model teaches that common anatomy proves common ancestry.[185] Common ancestry is the view that all species are related since one species has evolved into another. The creation model teaches that the same data (common anatomy) proves the existence of a common Designer. Animals often share common anatomy due to their being created and designed by the same God.[186]

---

[183]Ibid., 131-132.

[184]Ibid., 130-131.

[185]Morris, *Many Infallible Proofs* (El Cajon, California: Master Books, 1974), 252-255.

[186]Ibid.

Which model is more plausible? In order to answer this question, the principles of analogy and causality must be applied to the origin of the universe, the origin of first life, and the origin of new life forms. Both the creation model and the evolution model must be tested in these three areas to ascertain which model is more plausible.

THE ORIGIN OF THE UNIVERSE

Did the universe have a beginning, or did it always exist? This is a very important question. For if the universe had a beginning, it would need a cause. It could not have evolved into existence from nothing. If the universe is eternal then it may not need a cause. Fortunately, science is not silent on this question. The second law of thermodynamics is called energy deterioration. This law says that the amount of usable energy in the universe is running down.[187] Eventually, all the energy in the universe will be used up. This means that the universe is winding down. If it is winding down, it had to have been "wound up." If the universe is going to have an end, it had to have a beginning. There had to be a time when all the energy in the universe was usable; this marks the beginning of the universe.

The expansion of the universe and the big bang model also confirm the beginning of the universe.[188] In 1929, astronomer Edwin Hubble discovered that the universe is expanding at the same rate in all directions.[189] As time moves forward the universe is growing apart. This means that if one

---

[187]Graham, 75.

[188]William Lane Craig, *Apologetics: An Introduction* (Chicago: Moody Press, 1984), 81-83.

[189]Ibid., 82.

went back in time the universe would get denser. If one goes back in time far enough, the entire universe would be contained in what scientists have called "a point of infinite density."[190] But, a point can only be finitely dense. For a point to be infinitely dense it would have to be non-existent. Therefore, the universe came into existence from nothing a finite time ago.

There have been two main attempts to refute the proposition that the universe had a beginning. The first is the steady-state model. This view holds that the universe had no beginning. Instead, it always existed in the same state. However, because of the mounting evidence for the big bang model, this view has been abandoned by most of its adherents.[191]

The second attempt to evade the beginning of the universe is called the oscillating model. This model teaches that, at some point during the universe's expansion, gravity will halt the expansion and pull everything back together again. From that point there will be another big bang. This process will be repeated over and over again throughout all eternity. However, the oscillating model fails for three reasons. First, there is no known principle of physics that would reverse the expansion of the universe into another big bang. Second, current scientific research has shown that the universe is not dense enough for gravity to pull it back together again. Third, even if one could prove that several big bangs have occurred, the second law of thermodynamics would still require that there was a first big bang.[192]

---

[190] Ibid.

[191] Ibid., 83.

[192] Ibid., 83-88.

Therefore, science has shown that the universe had a beginning, but, since from nothing, nothing comes, something must have caused the universe to come into existence. Everything that has a beginning needs a cause. Since the universe needs a cause, the creation model is more plausible than the evolution model. If the universe were eternal, then the evolution model could claim some type of plausibility. But, for the above reasons, this is not the case. The universe is not eternal; it had a beginning. Something separate from the universe had to cause it to come into existence.

THE ORIGIN OF FIRST LIFE

Evolution teaches spontaneous generation—that life came from non-life without intelligent intervention.[193] However, spontaneous generation violates the law of biogenesis and the cell theory. The law of biogenesis states that "all living things arise only from other living things."[194] The cell theory defines the cell as the most basic unit of life, and declares that "new cells arise only from pre-existing cells."[195] Both the law of biogenesis and the cell theory are accepted by evolutionists; the evolutionists merely assume that first life is the exception to these principles. But, a model that violates scientific theories and laws should be abandoned. This is especially true when there is a rival model that does not violate scientific theories and laws.

The creation model posits the existence of an intelligent Being in order to bridge the gap from non-life to life. The creation model recognizes that the specified complexity (highly

---

[193]Morris, *Many Infallible Proofs*, 260.

[194]Graham, 18.

[195]Ibid., 12.

complex information) found in a single-celled animal could not be produced by chance. A single-celled animal has enough genetic information to fill one volume of an encyclopedia.[196] Just as an explosion in a print shop cannot randomly produce one volume of an encyclopedia, there is no way that a single-celled animal could have been produced by mere chance. Intelligent intervention was needed.[197]

Natural laws by themselves do not produce specified complexity. Geisler illustrates this point by stating that though natural laws can explain the Grand Canyon, they cannot explain the faces on Mount Rushmore.[198] The faces on Mount Rushmore reveal evidence of intelligent design.

Evolutionists often offer the Miller and Urey experiments as evidence that life has been produced from non-life in the laboratory. In response, several things should be noted. First, Chandra Wickramasinghe, one of Britain's most eminent scientists, calls these experiments "cheating." Miller and Urey start with amino acids, break them down, and then recover them. They do not produce something that wasn't there to begin with.[199] Second, Geisler states that the Miller and Urey experiments do not produce life. They only produce amino acids, which are the building blocks of life. Amino acids are to life what a single sentence is to one volume of encyclopedia.[200] Third, Geisler points out that even if these experiments did produce life from non-life in the laboratory

---

[196]Geisler and Anderson, 162.

[197]Ibid., 162-163.

[198]Ibid., 141.

[199]Varghese, Roy Abraham, *The Intellectuals Speak Out About God* (Dallas: Lewis and Stanley, 1984), 34.

[200]Geisler and Corduan, 105-106.

(which they don't), it would support the creation model, not the evolution model. The reason for this is clear. The experiments would merely prove that to get life from non-life intelligent intervention (i.e., the scientists) is needed. The experiments would not prove that life spontaneously arose from non-life.[201]

Therefore, the creation model is more plausible than the evolution model when explaining the origin of first life. Intelligent intervention is necessary to produce life from non-life. It could not have happened by accident.

THE ORIGIN OF NEW LIFE FORMS

Many people believe that the fossil record proves evolution, but, this is not the case. In the fossil record, new life forms appear suddenly and fully developed.[202] There is no evidence of transitional forms (missing links). There are no fins or wings becoming arms. There are no intermediate forms. The gaps between forms in the fossil record are evidence against evolution, not for evolution.

Evolution teaches that single-celled animals eventually evolved into human beings. Of course, evolutionists claim this took long periods of time to be accomplished. A single-celled animal contains enough information to fill one volume of encyclopedia,[203] but the human brain contains enough information to fill twenty million volumes of encyclopedia.[204] Natural law, no matter

---

[201]Geisler and Anderson, 138-139.

[202]Ibid., 150-152.

[203]Ibid., 162.

[204]Ibid.

85

how much time is involved, can never produce twenty million volumes of encyclopedia from one volume. Intelligent intervention is needed to produce more complex information.[205]

Evolutionists often point to mutations as the process by which evolution takes place.[206] However, mutations do not add more complex information to the genetic code. Instead, they merely garble the already existing genetic code.[207] For evolution to take place, new genetic information is needed. For example, single-celled animals would need new genes for the development of teeth, yet mutations produce no new genetic information.[208]

Simple life forms do not go to complex life forms through natural law alone.[209] Time plus chance plus natural laws can never produce more complex information.[210] Something must impart more information. Therefore, the creation model is more plausible than the evolution model concerning the origin of new life forms.

---

[205]Ibid., 163.

[206]Morris, *Many Infallible Proofs*, 256.

[207]Ibid.

[208]Charles Caldwell Ryrie, *You Mean the Bible Teaches That . . .* (Chicago: Moody Press, 1974), 111.

[209]Geisler and Anderson, 150.

[210]Scott M. Huse, *The Collapse of Evolution* (Grand Rapids: Baker Book House, 1983), 94.

CONCLUSION OF GEISLER'S SCIENTIFIC CASE
FOR GOD

The scientific case for creation is very strong. Though it is true that creationists have never seen the invisible Creator, evolutionists also have never seen the supposed evolutionary changes of the past. The principles of analogy and causality support creationism as a superior model to evolution. Blind chance and natural laws are inadequate causes for the origin of the universe, first life, and new life forms. An intelligent Cause is needed in each case. The cause of the beginning of nature cannot be nature itself. No being can preexist its own existence in order to cause its own existence. Therefore, nature needs a supernatural Cause. This supernatural Cause must be an intelligent Being to bring life from non-life and complex life forms from simple life forms. Hence, the creation model is more plausible than the evolution model.

CONCLUSION

Dr. Geisler's apologetic methodology is a thorough, consistent type of classical apologetics. Geisler is indebted to the philosophy of Thomas Aquinas—his apologetic system is Thomistic.

There are three main steps in his defense of Christianity. First, he identifies the appropriate tests for truth—a step ignored by most apologists. Second, he proves the existence of the theistic God with actual undeniability. And third, he shows Christianity to be true with a high degree of probability. (Historical events of the past can only be proven with probability.)

Geisler uses other evidences for the Christian faith besides philosophical and historical evidences. He is willing to utilize scientific apologetics in his defense of the faith. Refusing to put God's truth in a pre-determined "box," he is willing to use evidence for God wherever that evidence is found.

Norman Geisler's apologetic methodology should serve as a model for other apologists. He deals with important issues often ignored by most apologists (i.e., the concept of truth, finding proper tests for truth, the objectivity of history, the possibility of miracles, etc.). Though Geisler's apologetic methodology is somewhat complex, he was willing to simplify it and break it down for Christian lay people in order to assist them in their defense of the faith. Geisler's apologetic methodology has established him as one of the foremost Christian apologists of the twentieth and early twenty-first centuries. One cannot consider oneself knowledgeable in contemporary apologetics without reading the apologetic works of Norman Geisler. Even if a Christian apologist chooses to use a different methodology to defend the Christian faith, he does a disservice to himself if he chooses to ignore the contribution Norman Geisler has made to the history of Christian thought and the evidences and arguments he has developed. Geisler laments that contemporary evangelicals have ignored the work of Thomas Aquinas.[211] It would also be unfortunate if evangelicals choose to neglect the thought of Dr. Geisler.

---

[211]See Norman L. Geisler, *Thomas Aquinas: An Evangelical Appraisal* (Grand Rapids: Baker Book House, 1991).

Chapter 6

The Apologetic Methodology of William Lane Craig

William Lane Craig may be the world's leading Christian debater alive today. Craig is a research professor for Talbot School of Theology. He has debated some of the world's leading non-Christian thinkers. Craig is a classical apologist who utilizes several arguments for God's existence. He also defends the deity and bodily resurrection of Jesus.

The Kalam Cosmological Argument

Craig utilizes the kalaam cosmological argument for God's existence. This argument is as follows: 1) whatever began to exist must have a cause, 2) the universe began to exist, 3) therefore, the universe had a cause.[212]

Premise #1 uses the law of causality—non-being cannot cause being. In other words, from nothing, nothing comes. Since nothing is nothing, it can do nothing. Therefore,

---

[212]William Lane Craig, *Reasonable Faith: Christian Truth and Apologetics* (Wheaton: Crossway Books, 1994), 92.

it can cause nothing. Hence, whatever began to exist needs a cause for its existence.[213]

Premise #2 contends that the universe had a beginning. Scientific evidence for the beginning of the universe includes the second law of thermodynamics (energy deterioration) and the Big Bang Model. The second law of thermodynamics is one of the most firmly established laws of modern science. It states that the amount of usable energy in a closed system is running down. This means that someday in the finite future all the energy in the universe will be useless (unless there is intervention from "outside" the universe). In other words, if left to itself, the universe will have an end. But if the universe is going to have an end, it had to have a beginning.[214] At one time, in the finite past, all the energy in the universe was usable. Since the universe is winding down, it must have been wound up. The universe is not eternal; it had a beginning. Since it had a beginning, it needs a cause, for from nothing, nothing comes.

It should also be noted that, due to energy deterioration, if the universe is eternal it would have reached a state of equilibrium in which no change is possible an infinite amount of time ago. All of the universe's energy would already have been used up. Obviously, this is not the case. Therefore, the universe had a beginning.[215]

The Big Bang Model also indicates that the universe had a beginning.[216] In 1929, astronomer Edwin Hubble discovered that the universe is expanding at the same rate in all directions. As time moves forward the universe is growing

---

[213]Ibid., 92-94.

[214]Ibid., 113-116.

[215]Ibid.

[216]Ibid., 100-113.

apart. But this means that if we go back in time the physical universe would get smaller and smaller. Eventually, if we go back far enough in the past, the entire universe would be what scientists call "a point of infinite density" or "a point of dimensionless space." However, if something is infinitely dense, it is non-existent, for existent things can only be finitely small. The same can be said for points of dimensionless space. If a point has no dimensions, it is non-existent for it takes up no space. Therefore, if the Big Bang Model is correct, it shows that the universe began out of nothing a finite time ago.

Craig points out that there have been two main attempts to refute the beginning of the universe. The first is called the steady-state model.[217] This view holds that the universe never had a beginning. Instead, it always existed in the same state. Because of the mounting evidence for the Big Bang Model, this view has been abandoned my most of its adherents.

The second attempt to evade the beginning of the universe is called the oscillating model.[218] This model teaches that, at some point during the universe's expansion, gravity will halt the expansion and pull everything back together again. From that point there will be another big bang. This process will be repeated over and over again throughout all eternity. However, the oscillating model fails. First, there is no known principle of physics that would reverse the collapse of the universe and cause another big bang. Second, current scientific research has shown that the universe is not dense enough for gravity to pull it back together again. And third, even if it could be proven that several big bangs have

---

[217]Ibid., 102-103.

[218]Ibid, 103-107.

occurred, the second law of thermodynamics would still require that there was a first big bang.[219]

Many scientists accept the beginning of the universe, but believe that it does not need a cause. The evidence proposed by these scientists consists of speculation dealing with quantum physics (the study of subatomic particles). Appeal is made to Heisenberg's Principle of Indeterminacy in order to claim that quantum particles pop into existence out of nothing, entirely without a cause. However, Heisenberg's Principle does not necessitate such an absurd interpretation.[220] Simply because scientists cannot presently find the causes does not mean that the causes do not exist. All that Heisenberg's Principle states is that scientists are presently unable to accurately predict where a specific subatomic particle will be at a given time. If this principle proved that events can occur without causes then this would destroy one of the pillars of modern science—the principle of causality (every event must have an adequate cause). It is obvious that the principle of causality is on firmer epistemological ground than the belief that things can pop into existence without a cause. Non-being cannot cause being. If the universe had a beginning, then it needs a cause.

Besides this scientific evidence there is also philosophical evidence for the beginning of the universe. If the universe is eternal, then there would be an actual infinite number of events in time. However, as Zeno's paradoxes have shown, it is impossible to traverse an actual infinite set of points.[221] If we assume the existence of an infinite amount of

---

[219]Ibid.

[220]William Lane Craig and Quentin Smith, *Theism, Atheism, and Big Bang Cosmology* (Oxford: Oxford University Press, 1993), 142-146.

[221]*Reasonable Faith*, 94-100.

actual points between two locations, then we can never get from location A to location B, since no matter how many points we have traversed, there will still be an infinite number of points left. If the universe is eternal, then there must exist an actual infinite set of events in the past, but then it would be impossible to reach the present moment. Since the present moment has been reached, there cannot be an actual infinite set of events in the past. There could only be a finite number. Therefore, there had to be a first event. Hence, the universe had a beginning.

It should also be noted that if it is possible for an actual infinite set to exist outside of a mind, contradictions and absurdities would be generated. To illustrate this point, let us look at two infinite sets. Set A consists of all numbers, both odd and even. Set B contains only all the odd numbers. Set A and Set B are equal since they both have an infinite number of members. Still, Set A has twice the number of members as Set B since Set A contains both odd and even numbers, while Set B contains only odd numbers. It is a clear contradiction to say that Set A and Set B have an equal amount of members, while Set A has twice as many members as Set B. Therefore, actual infinite sets cannot exist outside the mind. Actual sets existing outside the mind can only be potentially infinite, not actually infinite. These sets can be added to indefinitely; still, we will never reach an actual infinite by successive addition.[222] Therefore, the universe cannot have an infinite number of events in the past. The universe had a beginning.

Since the universe had to have a beginning, it had to have a cause. For from nothing nothing comes. But if the universe needs a cause, what if the cause of the universe also needs a cause? Could we not have an infinite chain of causes and effects stretching backwards in time throughout all

---

[222]Ibid., 98-100.

eternity? Obviously, the answer is no, for we have already shown that an actual infinite set existing outside of a mind is impossible. Therefore, an infinite chain of causes and effects is also impossible. There had to be a first uncaused Cause of the universe. This uncaused Cause would be eternal, without beginning or end. Only eternal and uncaused existence can ground the existence of the universe.[223]

Craig completes his kalam cosmological argument for God's existence by stating that an eternal cause can only cause a temporal effect if the eternal cause is a personal Being. For the only adequate reason for an eternal cause to produce a temporal effect would be if the eternal cause is a personal agent who chose to create the universe in time. Otherwise, if the cause is non-personal, the effect would also have to be eternal. Only a personal choice can account for a temporal effect caused by an eternal cause. Hence, the uncaused cause of the universe must be a personal Being.[224]

The Design Argument for God

Craig argues that, during the last generation, scientists have discovered that the initial conditions of the big bang appear to have been fine-tuned to permit life. This is often called the anthropic principle. This principle states that there are approximately fifty quantities and constants present in the big bang which must be fine-tuned this way if the universe is to permit life. If any of these quantities or constants were

---

[223]Ibid., 116-117.

[224]Ibid., 117.

slightly different, there would now exist no intelligent life in the universe.[225]

Craig states that life-prohibiting universes are much more probable than life-permitting universes. Craig argues that the best way to explain the incomprehensible precision of the fine-tuning of the universe for the existence of intelligent life is to aknowledge that the universe was designed. Natural laws and chance both fail as adequate explanations of the fine-tuning of the universe. Hence, the universe was designed.[226]

The Moral Argument for God

Craig reasons that if God does not exist, then objective moral values do not exist. Craig points out that several leading atheists have agreed with him on this point (i.e., Bertrand Russell, Frederick Nietzsche, Michael Ruse, etc.). If atheism is true and no God exists, then though rape and child abuse may be socially unacceptable behavior, these actions are not really objectively wrong. Craig appeals to man's sense of right and wrong. He argues that, deep down inside of us, we know that rape and child abuse really are objectively wrong. We really know that objective moral values do exist. But, if God does not exist, there can be no objective moral values. Since objective moral values exist, God also exists as the ultimate Cause of these objective moral values.[227]

---

[225]Ibid., 118-122.

[226]Ibid., 122.

[227]Ibid., 66-68.

Evidence for Christ's Deity and Bodily Resurrection

Craig also provides historical evidence for the deity of Christ and Christ's bodily resurrection. In these areas, Craig argues in a similar fashion to his colleague and friend, Gary Habermas of Liberty University. The chapter on Habermas will give the reader a more thorough presentation of the historical evidence for Christ's deity and resurrection. Still, a few highlights of Craig's historical case for Jesus should be mentioned.

Craig turns to the almost unanimous consensus of current New Testament scholarship to build his historical case for Jesus. He points out that New Testament scholars acknolwedge that the early church, within twenty years of the crucifixion, worshiped Jesus as God incarnate. The earliest prayers, creeds, and sermons of the church refer to Jesus as Lord and God.[228]

Craig argues that Jesus referred to Himself as the "Son of Man." Most New Testament scholars today acknolwedge the Son of Man sayings as authentic. When the Son of Man sayings of Jesus are examined, it becomes evident that Jesus thought of Himself as having the authority of God and being the Savior of the world.[229]

But, Jesus also thought of Himself as the "Son of God." Jesus called God His "Abba," indicating He believed He had a unique Father-Son relationship with God the Father that no one else had. In a passage consider authentic even by liberal New Testament scholars, Jesus referred to Himself as the Son of God when He acknowledged that He did not know the day or hour of His return (Mark 13:32).[230]

---

[228]Ibid., 233-254.

[229]Ibid., 243-244.

Craig points out that Jesus spoke and acted as if He believed Himself to have the authority of God.[231] He did not refer to the oral traditions of the rabbis when interpreting God's Word. Instead, he equated His own authority with the divine authority of the Old Testament; He considered His interpretation of God's Law to be on the same level as God's Law itself. This is why His hearers were schocked that he spoke with such authority. His interpretation of the Torah (the Law of Moses) held as much authority as the Torah itself.

Using the accepted principles of current New Testament scholarship, Craig shows that Jesus believed He was able to forgive sins and perform miracles, and that a person's eternal destiny would be determined by how they responded to Him.[232] In short, using contemporary New Testament critical scholarship, a strong case can be made that Jesus believed Himself to be God incarnate.

Craig then argues that Jesus proved His claims to be God by bodily rising from the dead. Craig argues for the bodily resurrection of Jesus from the fact of the empty tomb and the fact of the post-crucifxion appearances of Jesus.[233] Craig builds a powerful case for the tomb being found empty just days after Jesus' death. He also shows that the reports of Jesus appearances after His death are on solid evidential ground. Craig also shows that the bodily resurrection (i.e., the empty tomb and post-resurrection appearances) is the only adequate explanation of the origin and growth of the early church. If there had been no resurrection, the Christian church

---

[230]Ibid., 244-245.

[231]Ibid., 246-247.

[232]Ibid., 247-251.

[233]Ibid., 272-298.

would have never come into existence.[234] Craig once again builds his case for Christianity on the findings of contemporary New Testament scholarship. From these findings, he argues that Jesus did in fact bodily rise from the dead and appear to His disciples on several occassions.

Assessment of Craig's Apologetic Methodology

Like Norman Geisler, William Lane Craig is a classical apologist. He begins his case for Christianity with philosophical and scientific evidence for God's existence. After establishing the existence of God, Craig then turns to historical evidences for Christ's deity and bodily resurrection. Craig has had much success defending Christianity in debates with some of the world's leading non-Christian thinkers—his apologetic methodology should not be overlooked.

---

[234]Ibid., 288-289.

Chapter 7

The Apologetic Methodology of J. P. Moreland

J. P. Moreland earned his Ph.D. in philosophy from the University of Southern California. He is the professor of philosophy at Biola University's Talbot School of Theology. He is one of today's top defenders of the faith and he has debated several leading atheists. Moreland's primary apologetics work is entitled *Scaling the Secular City: A Defense of Christianity*.

Moreland's Cosmological Argument

J. P. Moreland begins his case for Christianity with the cosmological argument—the argument for God from the existence of the universe. Though Moreland likes the Thomistic cosmological argument (i.e., that the continuing existence of contingent beings prove the existence of a totally necessary Being) and the Leibnizian cosmological argument (i.e., that everything that exists must have a sufficient reason for its existence; eventually, we must arrive at the existence of a Being who explains its own existence—a self-explained

Being), he chooses to spend the most time discussing the kalam cosmological argument. In fact, he and William Lane Craig are currently the two leading proponents of the kalam cosmological argument. The kalam cosmological argument argues from the beginning of the universe to God as its cause.[235]

The kalam cosmological argument has three major premises: 1) the universe had a beginning, 2) the beginning of the universe was caused, and 3) the cause for the beginning of the universe was personal.[236] Moreland uses set theory to show the impossibility of an actual infinite set of finite things existing outside of a mind. This shows that the universe could not be eternal, for that would entail an actual infinite set of finite moments existing in the past. Since this is impossible there must be a first moment; the universe had a beginning.[237]

Moreland also uses Zeno's paradoxes to show the impossibility of traversing an actual infinite set of points.[238] This means that if the universe was eternal, one would never reach the present moment for one would have to traverse (or pass through) an actual infinite number of moments to reach the present moment. But, no matter how many moments one has traversed, there will still be an infinite number more to traverse. Hence, since man has reached the present moment, there is only a finite number of moments in the past. Once again, the universe had a beginning; it had a first moment.

---

[235]J. P. Moreland, *Scaling the Secular City: A Defense of Christianity.* (Grand Rapids: Baker Book House, 1987), 15-42.

[236]Ibid., 19.

[237]Ibid., 19-22.

[238]Ibid., 30-33.

Moreland finds scientific confirmation that the universe had a beginning in big bang cosmology and the second law of thermodynamics (entropy or energy deterioration).[239] Basically, the big bang model (which is presently accepted by most scientists) shows that the universe is expanding as one moves forward in time. But, this means that if one were able to move backward in time the universe would eventually be infinitely dense—it would not be there. Hence, the big bang model strongly indicates that the universe had a beginning; it is not eternal.

The second law of thermodynamics shows that the amount of usable energy in the universe is running down. Therefore, given enough time, the universe will die—it will run out of usable energy. If the universe is winding down, it had to be wound up. If it will have an end (if left to itself), it had to have a beginning.

But, argues Moreland, if the universe had a beginning, it must need a cause. Nonbeing cannot cause being. Nonbeing is nothing, and nothing has no ability whatsoever, let alone the ability to create. Hence, since the universe had a beginning, something else had to cause it to come into existence. The universe needs a cause.[240]

Either the cause of the universe must be personal or non-personal. Moreland argues that the cause of the universe must be personal for the following reason: the only adequate explanantion for the first event (creation) to spontaneously arise from a timeless, spaceless, changeless cause would be if the cause was a personal agent who spontaneously chose to create. A non-personal cause can act out of necessity; but, it cannot act volitionally. Only a personal agent can choose to

---

[239]Ibid., 33-38.

[240]Ibid., 38-41.

create. But, for an eternal cause to create a temporal effect, the eternal cause must be a personal (i.e., volitional) Being. Hence, the eternal, uncaused Cause of the universe must be a personal Being.[241]

Moreland's Design Argument

Moreland points out that there are different kinds of design found in the universe. There are: order, purpose, simplicity, complexity, beauty, sense and cognition (man's thinking ability), information, and the cosmic constants necessary for life on earth.[242] Moreland argues that our universe is not a universe of chaos, but of order. Things in the world operate according to the laws of nature (i.e., in an orderly fashion). This order in the universe points to intelligent design behind the universe.[243]

The evidence for purpose in the universe is due to the fact that even the mindless things of nature work together for some goal or end. This is evident in the fact that mindless acorns become mature oak trees and not something else. The mindless things of nature, moving towards the same goals time and time again, implies the existence of a Mind behind the mindless things of nature.[244]

The simplicity and unity in the world seems to imply the existence of one, rational, efficient Mind. Yet, the vast

---

[241]Ibid., 41-42.

[242]Ibid., 43-54.

[243]Ibid., 62.

[244]Ibid., 45-47.

complexity of the universe reveals evidence of tremendous intelligence behind the organizing of the universe.[245]

The beauty found in the world, whether it be the beauty of a sunset or the beauty of the mathematical theories which accurately describe its workings, point to the existence of a cosmic Artist. This cosmic Artist is able to produce a universe which far surpasses the beauty of anything produced by human artists.[246]

Moreland agrees with those philosophers who believe that man's ability to accurately perceive the world and think about it is evidence that these abilities were designed by an intelligent Designer for these purposes. The validity of man's thinking ability (i.e., human reason) can only adequately be explained by the existence of cosmic Reason.[247]

Moreland notes that the genetic information of living things contain both information and order. Scientists call this specified complexity. The information is ordered and arranged in such a way that it is as complex and as orderly as volumes of encyclopedia. This amount of specified complexity is not a product of natural laws, time, plus chance. This amount of specified complexity is clearly the product of intelligent Design.[248]

Finally, Moreland discusses the cosmic constants that permit life on the planet earth. Moreland mentions just a few of the constants necessary for life to be possible. If these constants (and many others) were just slightly different, there would be no possibility of life on the planet earth. Some of the

---

[245]Ibid., 47-48.

[246]Ibid., 48-49.

[247]Ibid., 49-51.

[248]Ibid., 51-52.

103

cosmic constants noted by Moreland include: 1) the rate of the expansion of the big bang, 2) the even distribution of the observable universe, 3) the values of the gravitational constant and the electromagnetic force, 4) the balance of matter to antimatter, 5) the factors on earth necessary for life, 6) the earth being the right size and shape, 7) the earth being the right distance from the sun, 8) the earth having the right rotational speed, 8) the sun being precisely the right size and shape, and 9) the perfect combination of a vast number of factors to bring about life from nonlife. Again, Moreland notes that a tiny messing with any of these constants would eliminate any possibility of life on earth. It is as if the entire universe was "fine-tuned" for the purpose of supporting life on the planet earth. It is extremely doubtful if not impossible) that these factors all came together accidentally in order to produce and sustain life on earth. It is far more likely that the universe was designed for the purpose of producing and sustaining life on planet earth.[249]

Moreland, after refuitng several objections to design arguments, concludes that the apparent design found in the universe makes it extremely unlikely that the universe was produced by accidental and random events. Just as machines were intelligently designed, it appears that the universe is also a product of intelligent design. It is far more reasonable that God exists and that He designed the universe, than it is to believe that the design in the universe is the outcome of accidental and random processes. At the very least, the design argument shows that theism (i.e., the belief in a personal God) is far more reasonable than atheism (i.e., the rejection of belief in God).[250]

---

[249]Ibid., 52-54.

[250]Ibid., 74-75.

The Argument from Mind

Next, Moreland argues for the existence of non-material mind. He concludes that if man has a non-material mind, it is more likely that a non-material Mind exists as its cause than it is to believe that mind evolved from matter. Though Moreland has a chapter dealing with his argument for mind and God as its cause, he also dealt with this topic when interviewed by Lee Strobel in Strobel's book *The Case for a Creator*.[251]

In that interview, Moreland refutes physicalism (the view that only material things exist; there is no non-material mind). Moreland argues that if physicalism is true then there would be no first-person point of view. If everything is material, then everything would be explained from a third-person perspective.[252] Second, if physicalism is true, then there would be no free will and human responsibility; all our choices would be biologically determined.[253] Third, if physicalism is true then there would be no disembodied intermediate state. Moreland provides evidence, from near death experiences, that persons can still perceive things even while their brains have ceased to function.[254]

Next, Moreland turns to positive evidence for the existence of the non-material soul or mind. First, Moreland turns to the research of neurosurgeon Wilder Penfield.[255]

---

[251]Lee Strobel, *The Case for a Creator* (Grand Rapids: Zondervan Publishing House, 2004), 247-272.

[252]Ibid., 255.

[253]Ibid., 255-256.

[254]Ibid., 256-257.

Penfield was able to use electrical stimulation of some of his patients' brains to get them to move their limbs. However, to Penfield's surprise, they stated, "I didn't do that. You did." Apparently, his patients thought of themselves have existence apart from their bodies. Penfield's research concluded that, no matter where he prodded the human brain, there is no location in the brain that will cause a person to decide. Decisions are made in the conscious, not in the brain.[256] Second, Moreland argues that ideas can be classified as true or false, but not so with brain states. Hence, ideas and brain states are not the same thing.[257] Third, consciousness is inner and private, whereas brain states are not. Moreland stated, "A scientist could know more about what's happening in my brain than I do, but he couldn't know more about what's happening in my mind than I do. He has to ask me."[258]

Moreland believes the case for the non-material mind presents great problems for atheistic evolutionists. It is impossible to get consciousness from material things. No matter how much time one has, matter will never produce mind. The only adequate way to explain the existence of finite minds is to acknolwedge the existence of infinite Mind as its cause.[259]

---

[255]Ibid., 258.

[256]Ibid.

[257]Ibid.

[258]Ibid., 259.

[259]Ibid., 264.

God and the Meaning of Life

Moreland argues that genuine meaning in life is a good indicator that God exists. He surveys different views concerning the meaning of life. He identifies serious problems with nihilism (i.e., there is no real meaning), temporal purpose or optimistic humanism (.e., we invent or create our own meaning and values), and immanent purpose and transcendentalsim (i.e., meaning and values genuinely exist as brute givens; they are just there). Then Moreland argues that the best explanation is that human existence has purpose, meaning, and real values because God created man and the universe that way. Life is meaningful if the God of the Bible exists. Meaning in life is a given if Christianity is true.[260]

Those who deny genuine meaning in life cannot live consistently with that denial. They live like life has meaning. Atheists who believe life has genuine, lasting meaning can provide no plausible explanation as to why this is so. Only theism (belief in a personal God) adequately explains why life has genuine, lasting meaning.[261]

The Historicity of the New Testament

Moreland argues that the evidence for the reliability of the New Testament manuscripts is very strong.[262] We have more extant copies of the New Testament than that of any other ancient writing. And, these copies are much closer in date to the originals than that of any other ancient writing. For

---

[260]Moreland, *Scaling the Secular* City, 105-132.

[261]Ibid., 128-129.

[262]Ibid., 133-157.

most ancient writings we possess, only a handful of copies still exist. These copies usually date to about one-thousand years after the originals were written. With the New Testament, there exist thousands of written copies. Also, there are thousands of quotations of the New Testament found in the writings of the early church fathers. Moreland states that most historians accept the reliability and textual accuracy of other ancient works based on far less manuscript evidence than is available for the New Testament.[263]

Moreland points out that the authors of the New Testament were either eyewitnesses or writers who knew the eyewitnesses. Their writings were compiled while the eyewitnesses who knew Jesus were still alive. These eyewitnesses would have been willing and able to refute any inaccuracies in the texts if needed. And, these authors were sincere enough to suffer and die for their beliefs. Hence, the New Testament is based on early, eyewitness, and reliable sources.[264]

Moreland argues that the disciples of Jesus, like disciples of other rabbis of the first-century, would have memorized some of Jesus' teachings. In fact, they may have also taken notes when He preached. There is every reason to believe that Jesus' disciples would have been able to accurately passed on His teachings to others.[265]

Moreland adds that the presence of unique material in Jesus' sayings (i.e., words or expressions used by Jesus and not by the early church), the presence of material that would have been considered irrelevant by the early church, and the absence of material that would be considered relevant by the

---

[263]Ibid., 134-137.

[264]Ibid., 137-142.

[265]Ibid., 143.

early church all show that the early church did not put the words into Jesus' mouth. He actually said and taught these things.[266] Also, the early church would surely not make up the embarassing or counterproductive features one finds in the New Testament. There was no motive for the early church to fabricate stories about Jesus the Messiah being baptized by John, mocked by His brothers, displaying anger, not knowing the precise time of His return, and being executed in the most shameful way known to man (i.e., crucifixion). The only reason for the early church recording these events would be if they really occurred.[267]

Moreland points to other factors to prove the historicity of the New Testament. Even the most critical of New Testament scholars accept at least seven of Paul's letters as being authentic. Yet, from the moment Paul began writing (around 50 ad), he already taught the full deity of Christ, His resurrection from the dead, and salvation through Jesus alone. This takes us to within twenty years of Christ's death, and He was already acknolwedged as God, Savior, and risen.[268] But, Moreland does not stop there. Ancient creeds and the ancient sermons of the first twelve chapters of Acts date back to the early thirties ad, for the theology is very primitive and undeveloped. Yet, these ancient creeds and sermons already proclaim Jesus as God, Savior, and risen.[269]

Moreland makes a strong case that Luke and Acts had to be written very early. This is because Acts is the sequel to Luke, so Acts had to be written after Luke's Gospel. Moreland

---

[266]Ibid., 145-146.

[267]Ibid., 146-147.

[268]Ibid., 147-148.

[269]Ibid., 148-151.

lists six reasons why Acts was written early. This would mean that Luke was written earlier still. First, though Jerusalem plays a very important role in Acts, there is no mention of the destruction of the temple which occurred in 70 ad. Second, no mention is made of Nero's persecution of Christians in the mid 60's ad. Third, the martyr's deaths of James, Paul, and Peter are not mentioned in Acts. They were all executed between 61 and 65 ad. Fourth, Acts deals with issues that were inportant prior to the 70 ad destruction of the temple. Fifth, several expressions found in Acts are early and primitive. And seventh, there is no mention of the Jewish war with Rome (which began in 66 ad). These six points taken together show that the Book od Acts was most likely written in the early 60's ad. And, of course, the Gospel of Luke would have to have been written even earlier. This means that at least one of the four Gospels was written within thirty years of Jesus' death.[270]

The ancient creeds and sermons going back to the early 30's ad, the writings of the Apostle Paul going back to the early 50's ad, and the Gospel of Luke and the Book of Acts going back to the early 60's ad show that the New Testament portrait of Jesus is very early. Moreland points out that A. N. Sherwin-White, an Oxford scholar who specializes in ancient Greek and Roman history, argues that two generations is not enough time for legend to wipe out core historical facts.[271] The New Testament portrait of Jesus was well established long before that time. Hence, there is no reason to doubt the historicity of the New Testament documents and their depiction of Jesus.

---

[270]Ibid., 152-154.

[271]Ibid., 156.

Defense of Jesus' Resurrection

Having built his case for the historicity of the New Testament, Moreland then provides his readers with a historical defense of Jesus' bodily resurrection.[272] Moreland argues for the historicity of the empty tomb and the post-resurrection appearances of Jesus. He then discusses four additional features that confirm the truth of the resurrection. Finally, Moreland shows that the resurrection accounts were not borrowed from pagan mythology. Instead, Jesus' resurrection from the dead did in fact happen in history.

Moreland lists numerous evidences for the empty tomb.[273] First, even critical scholars admit that the resurrection is proclaimed (or at least implied) in multiple, fairly early sources (the source material that sholars believe went into the Gospels, the ancient sermons, the ancient creeds, etc.). Second, the first preaching of the resurrection occurred in Jerusalem (near where the tomb was). Third, there was no early veneration of Jesus' tomb. This implies His remains were no longer there. Fourth, the response of the Jewish authorities (i.e., that the disciples stole the body) presupposed that the tomb was empty. Fifth, the pre-Markan passion account includes the empty tomb. Sixth, the ancient Jewish concept of resurrection was always a bodily resurrection. If the tomb was not empty, the apostles would not have procalimed Jesus as risen. Seventh, the apostles would not have fabricated the testimony that women were the first witnesses of the empty tomb. In first-century Judaism, a women's testimony was rarely permitted in a court of law. There was no evidential value to making this story up. Eighth,

---

[272]Ibid., 159-183.

[273]Ibid., 160-172.

the ancient creed found in 1 Corinthians 15 implies that the tomb was empty (i.e., He was buried. . . He was raised).[274]

Moreland points out that attempts to explain away the empty tomb are unconvincing. The wrong tomb theory and the stolen body theory fail. These two alternative, naturalistic explanations are so unlikely that virtually no scholars promote them today.[275]

Next, Moreland discusses the evidence for the post-resurrection appearances of Jesus. In 1 Corinthians 15:3-8 Paul quotes an ancient creed which lists some of the people Jesus appeared to after His death. Then Paul adds to the list Jesus' appearance to him. Scholars date this creed to the early 30's ad, just a few years after Christ's death. This creed is early eyewitness testimony that Jesus appeared to several indiviuals and groups (one group was comprised of over 500 people) shortly after His death by crucifixion.[276] Second, the apostles were not predisposed to believe in the resurrection of an individual. As first-century Jews, they believed in a general resurrection of all God's faithful followers at the end of the age. The apostles were not expecting a resurrection of one person before the final days judgment. Since they were not in the right frame of mind, it is highly unlikely they hallucinated. And, since Jesus appeared to groups, the hallucination theory is ruled out. Hallucinations cannot happen to groups of people; they are events that occur in a person's head. No two people have the same hallucination.[277] Hence, the most plausible

---

[274]Ibid., 160-171.

[275]Ibid., 171-172.

[276]Ibid., 174-175.

[277]Ibid., 175-178.

explanation of the historical data is that Jesus of Nazareth bodily rose from the dead and appeared to numerous people on different occassions.

Moreland adds four other features that confirm Jesus' resurrection. First, the transformed lives of James, Paul, and the apostles. If Jesus did not rise and appear to them there is no explanation for their changed lives.[278] Second, the early church was Jewish. Yet, it left the sacrificial system, changed the primary worship day from the Sabbath to Sunday, and began to worship and pray to Jesus long side the Father. This is hard to explain if Jesus had not actually risen from the dead.[279] Third, the two church ordinance only make sense if Jesus rose from the dead. Why celebrate Jesus' death duirng the Lord's Supper unless Jesus rose? And, water baptism was closely linked to Jesus' death and resurrection.[280] Fourth, the origin and existence of the church itself is impossible to explain had Jesus not been raised from the dead.[281] These four factors confirm that Jesus did in fact rise from the dead.

After providing his readers with a strong case for Jesus' resurrection, Moreland addresses the objection that the early church fabricated the resurrection accounts by borrowing data from ancient pagan myths.[282] Skeptics argue that the early church borrowed from pagan myths about dying and rising gods. Moreland's response is fivefold. First, the early church was rooted in Old Testament Judaism, not paganism. In fact, the early church, as were the jews before

---

[278]Ibid., 178-179.

[279]Ibid., 179-180.

[280]Ibid., 180.

[281]Ibid., 180-181.

[282]Ibid., 181.

her, was very exclusivistic. The early church refused to borrow from other religions. Second, the pagan myths of dying and rising gods centered on the seasonal cycles of the year; these stories were not based in any real history. Third, the parallels between these myths and the resurrection accounts are apparent and not real. They only sound like real parallels if Christian terminology is smuggled into the pagan myths. Fourth, the differences outweigh the supposed similarities. The pagans were polytheistic, while the early church was montheistic. The pagans were very syncretistic, while the early church was very exclusivistic. And fifth, the vast majority of real parallels date after Christianity. Hence, if borrowing occurred, it was the pagan myths that borrowed from Christianity; it was not the other way around. For these reasons, contemporary scholars reject the idea that the early church borrowed its ideas from the ancient pagan myths.[283]

Science and Christianity

J. P. Moreland is one of the most well-informed contemporary apologists when it comes to scientific issues. His grasp of the philosophy of science is to be commended. In his book *Scaling the Secular City*, in the chapter entitled "Science and Christianity," Moreland discusses the debate between scientific realists (scienctists who believe science can give us real knowledge about the real world) and scientific anti-realists (scientists who believe we attain no real knowledge about the real world through science; at best, we find formulas that work). Though the discussion is rather techical, Moreland makes it clear that the relationship between Christianity and science is much deeper than merely the

---

[283]Ibid., 181-183.

creation-evolution debate. Before moving on, Moreland makes a case for a humble scientific realism.[284]

Moreland points out that science has its limitations. The view that truth can only be found through science is itself self-refuting since there is no way to scientifically (i.e., empirically) prove the statement to be true. Hence, there are more ways to find truth than merely through science. Moreland also states that there are several necessary presuppositions that must be held before science can get started. These include: the reliability of sense perception, the validity of human reason, the uniformity of nature, the knowability of the universe, the reality of the laws of logic, the reality of truth, the existence of numbers, the meaningfulness of language, the results of scientfic experiements should be reported honestly, and that the moral value called honesty is real. Scientists must assume the truth of all these things; yet, none of them are provable by science (i.e., by the five senses). Hence, certain philosophical assumptions must be made before scientific studies can even start. Therefore, science does not have a monopoly on truth.[285]

After discussing different models of integrating science and theology, Moreland points out that sometimes the subject matter studied by the theologian overlaps the subject matter being studied by the scientist. Science and theology do not always operate in two entirely different domains.[286]

At this point, Moreland begins to discuss creation science. Moreland answers several popular objections raised against creation science being a legitimate way to do science. Moreland argues that to limit science to finding only natural

---

[284]Ibid., 185-197.

[285]Ibid., 197-200.

[286]Ibid., 200-208.

causes and to a priori rule out the possibility of finding any supernatural causes, is to stack the deck against creationism. The scientist should go wherever the evidence leads. If the scientific evidence points to a supernatural cause, then the scientist has no right to reject that supernatural cause. Hence, creation science is a legitimate type of science.[287]

Moreland informs his readers that creationists accept microevolution (gradual changes within lower levels of classifications), but reject macroevolution (that life evolved from non-life and all complex life forms evolved from simple life forms). Often the evolutionists will present evidence for microevolution, but then act as if he has made a case for macroevolution.[288]

Moreland demonstrates that the second law of thermodynamics rules out the possibility of life evolving from non-life. Moreland states:

> . . . raw energy cannot bring order or information out of chaos any more than one can form a Boeing 747 by dropping a bomb on a machine shop. Raw energy needs a blueprint (such as DNA) to direct it and an energy-converting mechanism (such as the digestive system in animals) to convert the form of energy so it will be usable. But blueprints and energy-converting mechanisms are themselves produced only by life, so the process is a catch-22.[289]

---

[287]Ibid., 208-213.

[288]Ibid., 220.

[289]Ibid., 221.

Moreland also presents problems in the fossil record. According to Darwinism and neo-Darwinism, the fossil record should display millions of transitional forms that are intermediate between the different forms of life they ancestrally link together. But this is not the case. In the fossil record, new life forms appear suddenly and fully developed. This is clearly seen in the Cambrian explosion. Moreland writes that "The Cambrian period of the geological column (dated at around 570 million years ago) reveals a sudden explosion of all marine invertebrates which appear fully formed, unchanged to the present, and without a fossil record of ancestors before them or transitions among them." This lack of transitional forms in the fossil record shows that the creation model has not been ruled out.[290]

In fact, many neo-Darwinists are now abandoning their views for a view called puncuated equilibrium.[291] This view tries to defend evolution by arguing that the major evolutionary changes occurred so rarely and were so sporadic that scientists should not be surprised by the absence of transitional forms in the fossil record. However, this view seems to be using the absence of evidence for evolution as if it were evidence for evolution. Moreland acknolwedges that creation scientists are justified in viewing the absence of transitional forms in the fossil record as evidence for the creation model, and as evidence against any form of the evolution model. Whatever the case, Moreland concludes that "it is safe to say that science has not shown Christianity to be false or irrational."[292]

---

[290]Ibid., 221-222.

[291]Ibid., 222.

[292]Ibid., 223.

Four Final Issues

The four final issues Moral deals with in his apologetic work are: 1) the visibility of God, 2) God as a psychological projection, 3) religious experience, and 4) moral relativism. The visibility of God objection basically says, "I can't believe in God because I cannot see Him." But, this objection is weak. For, there are many things that exist that man cannot see: thoughts, propositions, values, numbers, other minds, the laws of logic, etc. Just because we cannot see God does not mean He does not exist. One is justified in believing in the existence of God by seeing His effects in the world.[293]

Moreland points out that many atheists (i.e., Sigmund Freud, Bertrand Russell, etc.) have accused theists of pyschologically projecting God. In other words, because humans sense a need for a father image to calm their fears and care for them, they project a concept of God outside themselves and give this concept "existence." Since this concept is irrational, the wise man will reject this belief in God.[294]

Moreland responds by refering to the work of psychologist Paul Vitz. Vitz argues that Christians do not fit into any one psychological control group. Yet, first-generation, militant atheists almost always come from families where the father was absent or passive. The relationship with the father was often one of hate. Vitz argues that atheism can be explained as the desire to kill the father image because one desires to be autonmous. Rejection of the paternal authority often leads to rejection of God.[295]

---

[293]Ibid., 226-228.

[294]Ibid., 228-229.

Second, it is the genetic fallacy to attempt to refute a view because the person who holds the view got it from an inadequate source. Even if belief in God was due to some type of psychological issue, that does not mean God does not exist. God might still exist even if those who believe in Him do so for less than adequate reasons.[296]

Third, Moreland credits theologian R. C. Sproul for pointing out that the demanding God of Christian theism is not the type of God humans would invent. If humans invented gods, these would be more like the idols condemned in the Bible, not the God of the Bible Himself. If humans invented a god it would be a more manageable god than the all-powerful God of the Bible.[297]

Next, Moreland discusses religious experience. When it comes to religious experience, Moreland tries to avoid two extremes. First, he advises his readers not to rest their entire case for Christianity on religious experience (i.e., a person's testimony). Second, he discourages his readers from making too little of religious experience by claiming it is merely subjective.

Religious experience can take many different forms. It can entail feelings of guilt, being in awe of a beautiful sunset, the feeling of being watched when alone, or the peace that overcomes a person when praying. The God hypothesis may be the best explanation of a person's trnasformed life (i.e., Paul, James, the apostles, etc.). The atheist may argue that the experience is merely psychological, or maybe it is the result of peer pressure. But, this is hard to maintain when the transformed person persistently exhibits a life of self-sacrifice

---

[295]Ibid., 229.

[296]Ibid., 229-230.

[297]Ibid., 230.

and a new zeal for holiness. When it can be shown that these transformational experiences have occurred to a great diversity of people from different cultures, places, and times, it is hard to explain these experiences away as mere emotional experiences. If the religious experiences is associated with an objective event (like the resurrection) and an objective interpretive grid (like the Bible), then the probability of it being a genuine experience of God increases.[298]

The Christian could maintain that God can be perceived by a "nonsensory form of seeing." It is possible that God is directly perceived (i.e., not perceived by the five senses). It is also possible that the person must be seeking God in order to directly perceive Him. If the atheist does not look for God, he will not find Him.[299] Moreland lists seven tests to distinguish true from false perceptions of God. First, the experienced object must not be an internally contradictory object. Second, is the experience similar to the experience of godly people of the past? Third, does the experience help the person live a morally better life? Fourth, the consequences of the experience should be good in the long run for the person having the experience. Fifth, the consequences of the experience should be good for tohers as well. Sixth, the depth and profoundness of the experience is a point in its favor. Seventh, does the experience conform to Holy Scripture, which is itself verified by objective evidence (i.e., fulfilled prophecies, historical evidence, etc.)? With these tests, one can ascertain the plausibility (or lack thereof) of an experience of the transcendent being authentic.[300]

---

[298]Ibid., 231-232.

[299]Ibid., 237.

[300]Ibid., 239-240.

Finally, Moreland deals with moral relativism. Some moral relativists believe that moral laws come from the society or culture in which a person finds himself. The society or culture is the final arbiter of what is right or wrong. However, if one accepts that Martin Luther King, Jr., Mahatma Gandhi, Moses, and Jesus were true moral reformers, then one must admit that these moral reformers appealed to a moral standard above their culture or society. Also, when one society condemns the actions of another society (i.e., Nazi Germany), then the society making the judgment is appealing to a moral law or standard above both societies. This makes no sense if moral relativism or cultural relativism is true.[301]

Moreland argues that one can know that torturing innocent babies is wrong even if one does not know how to prove it is wrong.[302] Man intuitively knows that certain things are wrong or right. Also, many moral relativists argue that people should be tolerant. But this belief is itself an absolute—we should all tolerate those who disagree with us. Hence, even moral relativists act like moral absolutists.[303] Hence, Moreland concludes that moral absolutes are real; there is a moral law above all individuals and societies.

Classifying Moreland's Apologetic Methodology

J. P. Moreland is clearly a classical apologist. He argues first for God's existence, using primarily philosophical arguments. Next, he turns to historical evidences for the

---

[301]Ibid., 241-243.

[302]Ibid., 245.

[303]Ibid., 247-248.

historicity of the New Testament and Christ's resurrection. This two step approach unambiguously identifies Moreland as a classical apologist. However, he has also established himself as a leading scientific apologist. In addition to classical apologetics and scientific apologetics, he argues from religious experience to God; hence, he is also willing to engage in testimonial apologetics. Therefore, Moreland is a classical apologist who also chooses to utilize scientific and testimonial evidences for God.

Chapter 8
The Apologetics of C. S. Lewis

British author and scholar C. S. Lewis (1898-1963) was one of the greatest Christian apologists of the twentieth-century. His writings have sold in the tens of millions of copies and have led many skeptics to find Christ, while confirming the faith of believers. His four main apologetic works were *The Problem of Pain*, *Miracles*, *Mere Christianity*, and *The Abolition of Man*. His fictional works also have apologetic value.

The Possibility of Miracles

Lewis argued against the atheistic world view called naturalism. Naturalism is the belief that all causes are natural causes; hence, miracles are impossible. But, the naturalist's arguments against miracles fail.

The naturalist often claims that the laws of nature rule out any possibility of miracles. But, the naturalist is reading too much into natural laws on this point. For natural laws are *descriptive*; they are not *prescriptive*. In other words, natural laws do not prescribe what can or cannot happen. Instead, natural laws describe the way nature generally operates.

Natural laws themselves cannot rule out miracles. If a God exists and He set the laws of nature in motion, then He can interrupt or suspend these laws any time He chooses to do so.[304]

Lewis' Argument from Reason

In his book Miracles, Lewis presented an argument for God from man's confidence in his reason (his thinking ability). Lewis argued that when we trust in the validty of human reason, we are acting as if we believe that human reason has a rational cause. Reason with a small "r" presupposes the existence of reason with a capital "R." Christians are right to have confidence in the validity of human reason since they believe we are creations of a rational God who created us in His image.[305]

But, the atheist believes his reason evolved from non-rational causes. Hence, the atheist has no reason to trust in his reasoning processes.[306] Yet, the atheist does place confidence in his reasoning processes when he does science or argues against God's existence. However, this is very inconsistent. For, if the atheist believes his reasoning ability evolved from non-rational causes, he should have no trust in what his reason is telling him.[307]

Only in a theistic universe should man have confidence in the validity of human reason. In a world without

---

[304]C. S. Lewis, *Miracles: How God Intervenes in Nature and Human Affairs* (New York: Collier Books, 1960), 55-62.

[305]Ibid., 14-15, 18-19, 21-24.

[306]Ibid., 18.

[307]Ibid., 18, 22.

God, if man's reason works, there is no way for man to know this. Only infinite Reason can ground our confidence in finite reason.[308]

Lewis Moral Argument for God

In Lewis' work *Mere Christianity*, Lewis articulated his moral argument for God's existence. Lewis argued that a universal moral law must exist; for, if this is not the case then we could not condemn the actions of others (such as the Nazis). Without a universal moral law, fulfilling promises and honoring treaties would hold no value. The fact that humans make excuses for breaking the moral law implies they acknolwedge its existence. Also, even those who deny the existence of the universal moral law act like it exists at least when they are victims of wrongdoing.[309]

Lewis argued that the moral law is not the product of herd instinct, for the stronger instinct or desire does not always win. Humans often feel morally obligated to stand up for the weak.[310] The moral law cannot be the mere creation of society, for people often criticize and try to reform their own society.[311] Lewis reasoned that the moral law cannot be identified as a law of nature. For, the laws of nature are descriptive; but, moral laws are precriptive—they prescribe

---

[308]Ibid., 22.

[309]C. S. Lewis, *Mere Christianity* (New York: Collier Books, 1952), 17-21.

[310]Ibid., 22-23.

[311]Ibid., 24-26.

the way humans ought to act.[312] Hence, the universal moral law is real.

Lewis argued that moral laws come from a mind and not from mere matter. Hence, there must exist a Mind above mankind that has given man the universal moral law. The moral law-giver must be all-good since He is the source of all else that is good.[313]

The Problem of Pain

In *The Problem of Pain*, Lewis dealt with the problem of evil and human suffering. He believed that God allows evil and human suffering for several reasons. First, if God did not permit any evil man would have no free will. Lewis believed that it would be morally unworthy for God to force His will upon mankind.[314] Second, God allows evil for purposes of a greater good. There are some good things that could not be attained in our world without God allowing evil.[315] Third, God often draws people to Himself through their suffering and pain. Lewis stated that "God whispers to us in our pleasures, speaks in our conscience, but shouts in our pain: it is His megaphone to rouse a deaf world."[316]

---

[312]Ibid., 27-28.

[313]Ibid., 34-35.

[314]C. S. Lewis, *The Problem of Pain* (New York: Collier Books, 1962), 33, 69.

[315]Ibid., 52-53.

[316]Ibid., 93.

The Trilemma

In *Mere Christianity* Lewis also argued for Christ's deity. Since Jesus claimed to be God incarnate we are not justified in considering Him to be merely a great teacher or a good man. No mere good man claims to be God. Since Jesus claimed to be God, He is either a liar, a lunatic, or He is Lord. These are the only options He has given us.[317]

Lewis argued that what we know about Jesus shows us that He is not a liar who set out to deceive people. Jesus' life and character also reveal that He was not insane. Since Jesus claimed to be God and lived consistently with that claim, He must be God. He lived a life of integrity, performed miracles, and taught some of the most profound truths ever taught. Jesus of Nazareth is no liar or lunatic—He is Lord of all.[318]

Lewis said it best:

A man who was merely a man and said the sort of things Jesus said would not be a great moral teacher. He would either be a lunatic—on the level with the man who says he is a poached egg—or else he would be the Devil of Hell. You must make your choice. Either this man was, and is, the Son of God: or else a madman or something worse. You can shut Him up for a fool, you can spit at Him or kill Him as a demon; or you can fall at His feet and call Him Lord and God. But let us not come with any patronising nonsense about His being a great human teacher. He has not left that open to us. He did not intend to.[319]

---

[317] Lewis, *Mere Christianity*, 54-56.

[318] Ibid.

[319] Ibid., 56.

Cultural Apologetics: The Abolition of Man

A Christian thinker should not be content with rightly analyzing and critiquing current ideas. A true thinker should also attempt to foresee the probable future consequences of ideas. In this way, a Christian thinker performs the role of a watchman by warning his listeners of future dangers (Ezekiel 33:1-9). C. S. Lewis had the courage to fulfill this role.

Lewis, in his prophetic work *The Abolition of Man*, critiqued an English textbook, written in the 1940's, which was designed for school children. Lewis found that more than English was being taught in this book, for the authors rejected objective truth and traditional values and proclaimed a type of moral relativism.[320] Lewis expressed concern for two reasons. First, the children who read this textbook would be easy prey to its false teachings.[321] Second, this would lead to a culture built on moral relativism and the rejection of objective truth, something that, according to Lewis, has not existed in the history of mankind.[322]

Lewis not only refuted the fallacious views of the authors, but also predicted the future consequences of this type of education. He argued that teaching of this sort would produce a race of "men without chests."[323] By this he meant men without consciences. According to Lewis, this would

---

[320]C. S. Lewis, *The Abolition of Man* (New York: Collier Books, 1947), 23.

[321]Ibid., 16-17.

[322]Ibid., 28-29.

[323]Ibid., 34.

mean an entirely "new species" of man and "the abolition of man."[324]

Lewis argued that the practical result of such education would be "the destruction of the society which accepts it."[325] The rejection of all values leaves man free to recreate himself and his values.[326] When this power is placed into the hands of those who rule, their subjects will be totally at their mercy.

Lewis also saw in this rejection of traditional values a new purpose for science. In a sense, science is like magic in that both science and magic represent man's attempted "conquest of nature." However, science will become an instrument through which a few hundreds of men will rule billions of men,[327] for in man's conquest of nature, human nature will be the last aspect of nature to surrender to man.[328] Science will be used by future rulers to suppress the freedoms of the masses.

Lewis refers to the future rulers as "the man-moulders of the new age" or the "Conditioners."[329] It will be the job of the Conditioners to produce the rules, not to obey the rules.[330] The Conditioners (i.e., Nietzsche's supermen) will boldly create the laws the conditioned must obey. The role of education will become the production of artificial values

---

[324]Ibid., 77.

[325]Ibid., 39.

[326]Ibid., 62-63.

[327]Ibid., 69, 71.

[328]Ibid., 72.

[329]Ibid., 73-74.

[330]Ibid., 74.

which will serve the purposes of the Conditioners.[331] The Conditioners, through their Nietzschean "will to power" and motivated by the thirst to satisfy their own desires, will create their own new values and then force these "values" on the masses.[332]

According to Lewis, the rejection of traditional values and objective truth will lead to the same mentality in future rulers as that of "the Nazi rulers of Germany."[333] Traditional values will be replaced by the arbitrary wills of the few who rule over the billions,[334] and this will "abolish man" and bring about "the world of post-humanity."[335]

Narrative Apologetics: Lewis' Fictional Writings

C. S. Lewis understood that humans are not merely rational beings. Human beings are also creatures of imagination. Lewis realized that God not only desires that our reason be submitted to Him, but that God loves the whole man—He wants our imaginations as well. Therefore, Lewis wrote fiction in his attempt to defend the faith and lead non-believers to Christ. Lewis understood that the apologist must not only appeal to the mind of the unsaved; he must also pull at the strings of the heart. Lewis did this through arounsing the imaginations of his readers.

---

[331]Ibid.

[332]Ibid., 78, 84.

[333]Ibid., 85.

[334]Ibid.

[335]Ibid., 85-86.

It is possible that Lewis' fictional works (i.e., *Chronicles of Narnia, The Pilgrim's Regress, Out of the Silent Planet, The Screwtape Letters, That Hideous Strength,* etc.) may have won more non-believers to Christ than his rational apologetic writings. One thing is sure: Lewis was able to reach many more people than he would have been able to reach had he chosen not to write fiction as an apologetic tool.

Classifying Lewis' Apologetic Methodology

Though C. S. Lewis often argued like a classical apologist or an evidentialist, it seems that it would be more accurate to classify him as a verificationalist. His apologetic writings, taken as a whole, seem to indicate that he treated Christian Theism as a hypothesis, and that he was willing to put the Christian hypothesis to the test. Lewis seemed to be arguing that Christianity is the best explanation for the data of reality. His arguments against naturalism and for miracles fit well within the classification of verificational apologetics.

However, Lewis did not limit his defense of the faith to rational argumentation. He was also willing to do cultural apologetics and narrative apologetics. Cultural apologists argue that Christianity has a positive impact on cultures, and that any culture that forsakes its Christian heritage will suffer dire consequences. Narrative apologists are willing to appeal to the creative side of humans. Narrative apologists follow the example of Jesus when He told parables and allegories. Lewis understood that many people are not willing to read philosophical or historical works, but they might be willing to read fiction. Lewis was willing to use his fiction to try to gently persuade people to accept the Christian world view.

Hence, C. S. Lewis was a verificational apologist who was eclectic enough in his approach to use other methods. He was willing to utilize cultural and narrative apologetics in his attempt to lead others to Christ.

Chapter 9

The Classical Apologetics of Stuart Hackett

Stuart Hackett is the long time professor of philosophy of religion for Trinity Evangelical Divinity School. He received his Ph.D. from Syracuse university. His 1957 book *The Resurrection of Theism* spelled out his views on philsophical apologetics.[336] His 1984 book *The Reconstruction of the Christian Revelation Claim* completed his apologetic thought by using historical evidence to defend the Christian faith.[337] Clearly, Hackett is a classical apologist—he argues first for God's existence; then, he completes his case for Christianity by using historical evidences for Jesus and the Bible. Hackett refered to his epistemology (i.e., his theory of knowledge) and his apologetic methodology as "rational empiricism."[338]

---

[336]Stuart C. Hackett, *The Resurrection of Theism* (Grand Rapids: Baker Book House, 1957).

[337]Stuart C. Hackett, *The Reconstruction of the Christian Revelation Claim* (Grand Rapids: Baker Book House, 1984).

[338]*Resurrection of Theism*, 37.

The Resurrection of Theism—Hackett's Philosophical Case for Theism

Hackett understood that an effective defense of the faith in modern times must respond to the thought of Immanuel Kant.[339] In 1781, Kant wrote his *Critique of Pure Reason*. In this work, Kant argued that the a priori categories of the mind do not actually give us true knowledge about the world of reality. The mind impresses these categories onto the real world; the mind reads these categories into or imposes them on the world of the senses. Hence, according to Kant, the mind's categories do not give us accurate knowledge of the real world. Instead, man cannot know reality as it is (the noumena); we can only know reality as it appears to us (the phenomena).[340]

Hackett refutes Kant's skepticism by showing that Kant's claim to know that man cannot know reality as it is would actually be knowledge of reality as it is. Hence, Kant's view is self-refuting.[341] Therefore, man can know reality as it is. Still, Hackett believes that the apologist should not discard Kant's categories. Instead, Hackett believes that God has preformed the a priori categories of the human mind to enable man to attain true knowledge about the world of reality. In other words, God designed the human mind and the categories of human thought in such a way that man can really know reality. To reject Hackett's view that the categories of the mind give man true knowledge of reality leaves one with Kant's self-refuting skepticism. Hence, Hackett believes he is

---

[339]Ibid., 39.

[340]Ibid., 45-46.

[341]Ibid., 53-55.

rationally justified in assuming that the categories of the mind give us real knowledge of the real world.[342] This opens the door for Christian apologetics.

Hackett then spends the rest of his book *The Resurrection of Theism* updating some of the traditional arguments for God. He discusses the ontological, cosmological, teleological and moral arguments for God's existence.

Hackett examines the traditional ontological arguments presented by Anselm and Descartes and finds them unconvincing.[343] Still, he believes a different type of ontological argument is valid. The traditional arguments argued solely from the idea of God to the existence of God. But, Hackett's ontological argument sounds more like Cornelius Van Till's transcendental argument for God. Hackett argues that "the existence of God is concluded as an explanation for the possibility of any intelligible experience at all."[344] Hackett believed it was a mistake to use the idea of God as the a priori element in the ontological argument. Instead, the a priori element, according to Hackett, should be the mind's categorical structure that makes intelligible experience possible.[345] However, Hackett admits that this replaces the ontological argument (arguing to God from the mere idea of God) with an argument to God from the validity of human reason or from the categories of the mind.

Hackett has great respect for the traditional cosmological argument for God. The cosmological argument

---

[342]Ibid., 55.

[343]Ibid., 184-190.

[344]Ibid., 192.

[345]Ibid., 193.

argues for the universe, or something in the universe, to its uncaused Cause (i.e., God). In Hackett's 1984 book *The Reconstruction of the Christian Revelation Claim*, he spells out his cosmological argument with two premises and a conclusion:

Premise 1: If anything exists, an absolutely necessary and transcendent being exists.

Premise 2: Something (I, at least, as a thinker) exists.

Premise 3: Therefore, an absolutely necessary and transcendent being (i.e., God, as partly   defined   by theism) exists.[346]

Hackett makes a thorough and sophisticated defense of his cosmological argument in both of his works. Basically, he argues that if any finite, changing being exists, then an infinite, unchanging being must exist in order to ground the existence of the finite, changing being. If a contingent being exists then a necessary being must exist as the cause of the continuing existence of the contingent being.[347]

Hackett uses the teleological argument (the argument from design) to argue for God's existence. Hackett points to several aspects of design in reality as evidence for the existence of God, the intelligent designer[348]. First, he points to the fitness of the universe and the world to support complex life on earth. It is highly unlikely that chance accidently "produced" this fine-tuning for life. Second, he points to non-conscious things fuflilling goals or purposes (such as the eye seeing and the ear hearing). This shows evidence of these non-conscious things being designed for these purposes. Third,

---

[346]*Reconstruction*, 98.

[347]*Resurrection*, 194-203; *Reconstruction*, 90-103.

[348]*Resurrection of Theism.*, 204-242.

Hackett points to the intelligibility of the world as evidence for design. Fourth, Hackett points to the existence of the human mind as evidence for God. The mind is a nonphysical entity, and it is best explained by a nonphysical cause. It is insufficient to try to account for the presence of mind in the cosmos without appealing to an Ultimate Mind. Hackett concludes that human reason is best explained as a product of divine reason.[349]

Hackett also utilizes a moral argument for God, though he includes it as part of his teleological argument.[350] He notes that man experiences moral values that transcend subjective views and that transcend time. He argues that a transcendent, eternal moral lawgiver is the only adequate explanation for man's moral experience.[351]

Stuart Hackett not only provides strong arguments for the existence of God; he also takes the time to refute the main objections to his arguments. Hackett has provided the Christian apologists who followed him with a strong classical defense of the existence of God.

The Reconstruction of the Christian Revelation Claim

In Hackett's 1984 work, he finished his defense of Christianity. In the 1957 work, he defended theism (the belief in a personal God). In his later work, Hackett defends Christianity—he provides his readers with evidence for Jesus and the Bible.

---

[349]Ibid., 229.

[350]Ibid., 230-242.

[351]Ibid.

Hackett argues that a strong case can be made for Christianity. He provides evidence that Jesus did actually claim to be God incarnate, and that the Old Testament prophecies he fulfilled and the mighty works He performed verified this claim to be true.[352] The Jesus of history shows no sign of being deluded or psychologically impaired. He exhibits tremendous moral character, which rules out His being a liar. Unlike several others who have claimed to be God, Jesus' claims appear to be very plausible.[353] Hackett adds that acknowledging Jesus as God is at the least an exceptional starting point for a genuine spiritual life.[354]

Hackett argues that man has morally alienated himself from God, and that Jesus' death should be understood as explained in the New Testament: His death atoned for our sins and can repair our broken relationship with God. Although unbelief is still possible for man, belief in Jesus as God incarnate and man's Savior is more coherent.[355] Hackett believes that it is too incredible to believe that the early church simply invented the gospel; there was not enough time for legend to develop.[356] Hackett believes New Testament criticism, if used properly, actually supports the traditional Jesus, rather than discrediting Him.[357] Jesus is only explicable if His claims to be God and Savior are accepted. Either Jesus is the ultimate human riddle or He is God incarnate who came

---

[352]*Reconstruction*, 202-209.

[353]Ibid., 204-205.

[354]Ibid., 207.

[355]Ibid., 207-209.

[356]Ibid., 214.

[357]Ibid., 213.

to save mankind. Hackett believes it is more reasonable to accept Jesus' claims as true.[358]

Hackett next turns to the authority of the scriptures. Jesus held to the highest conceivable view of scriptural authority; He believed the Old Testament to be the divinely inspired Word of God. Jesus also promised to continue God's authoritative revelation through the writings of His apostles. Since it is reasonable to accept as true Jesus' claims to be God, it is also reasonable to accept Jesus' view of Scripture: the Bible is the inspired and inerrant Word of God.[359]

Finally, Hackett shows that the Bible does not contradict modern science.[360] First, if science is not done with an anti-religious bias, its conclusions do not contradict anything the Bible clearly teaches. Second, science has its limitations. These limitations are often overlooked by scientists who are biased against religion. Scientific theories often must be revised because science offers no guarantee to final truth. Much of scientific knowledge approximates truth. Scientific knowledge must always be open to revision. Therefore, scientists must humbly draw their conclusions. Those who claim that science has refuted the biblical portrait of reality are usually committed to an anti-Christian philosophy. Hence, it is their philosophical assumptions that contradict the bible, not their scientific findings.[361]

---

[358]Ibid., 215-217.

[359]Ibid., 262-271.

[360]Ibid., 311-329.

[361]Ibid.

139

Stuart Hackett's Apologetic Methodology

Though Stuart Hackett focused much of his early thought on the pre-conditions for human thought (i.e., the a priori categories of the mind), he is clearly a classical apologist. After clearing the way for a discussion of traditional arguments for God, Hackett presents strong philosophical arguments for God's existence. Then, he completes his case for Christianity by providing his readers with historical evidences for Jesus and the Bible.

Chapter 10

The Cumulative Case Apologetics of Paul Feinberg

Paul Feinberg earned his doctorate of theology degree from Dallas Theological Seminary. He taught theology and philosophy at Trinity Evangelical Divinity School in Derrfield, Illinois. Though Feinberg believes the traditional arguments for God are sound, he chooses to use a cumulative case for God because he believes it will be more effective in persuading non-believers of the truth of Christianity.[362]

Feinberg lists four aspects of his cumulative case. First, the cumulative case is an informal case; it does not use formal arguments. Second, it tries to explain a number of different elements in our experience. Third, no one element has any priority over the other elements. Fourth, it does not merely argue for God's existence. Instead, it seeks to make a strong case for the Christian world view, not just theism.[363]

---

[362]Steve B. Cowan, ed. *Five Views on Apologetics*. Grand Rapids: Zondervan Publishing House, 147-149.

[363]Ibid., 151-152.

In Feinberg's cumulative case, he list several tests for truth that can be applied to any world view. First, there is the test of consistency—is the world view in question internally consistent or is it contradictory.[364] Second, there is the test of correspondence or empirical fit. This test asks the question, "does the world view in question correspond to reality?"[365] Third, the test of comprehensiveness attempts to determine if the world view explains more data than other world views.[366] Fourth, the test of simplicity says that one should not needlessly multiply explanations when simpler ones will suffice.[367] Fifth, the test of livability states that true beliefs must be livable.[368] If a person cannot live consistently with their world view, it calls into question the truth of his world view. Sixth, the test of fruitfulness seeks to determine the consequences of a particular world view.[369] Does it produce positive results. And seventh, the test of conservation instructs the apologist to try to retain his world view even in the face of anomalies. One should only forsake one's world view if the weight of the evidence demands it.[370]

Feinberg points to both the internal witness of the Holy Spirit and the external witness of the Holy Spirit. The Holy Spirit internally witnesses to man by convicting him of his sin,

---

[364]Ibid., 153-154.

[365]Ibid., 154.

[366]Ibid., 154-155.

[367]Ibid., 155.

[368]Ibid.

[369]Ibid.

[370]Ibid., 155-156.

appealing to his conscience, and placing in all men an innate sense of God. Also, the Holy Spirit internally gives certitude to true believers and illuminates their minds to understand God's Word.[371]

Externally, the Holy Spirit witnesses to man in several different ways. First, there are the traditional arguments for God's existence.[372] Feinberg uses the cosmological argument (arguing from the existence of the universe to God) and the teleological argument (arguing from the design in the universe to God as its designer). Second, there is the religious experience of many people from many cultures throughout the centuries.[373] An example of these religious experiences are the many lives transformed, for the better, through faith in Jesus. Though the evidence for Christianity in religious experience is not definitive, it should be kept in mind that Feinberg is utilizing a cumulative case. Third, the external case for Christianity involves man's moral experience.[374] The most adequate explanation we have for the moral value judgments that even moral relativists make is that the moral law is real and that it comes from a Mind that is above man. Fourth, Feinberg views God's revelation in Scripture as the fourth component of the Holy Spirit's external case for Christianity.[375] From this, we find evidence for Jesus'

---

[371]Ibid., 158-160.

[372]Ibid., 160-161.

[373]Ibid., 161-163.

[374]Ibid., 163-164.

[375]Ibid., 165-166.

resurrection and deity. Feinberg also points to the evidence of the fulfilled prophecies found in the Bible.[376]

Feinberg believes that when we apply his seven tests to different world views, one finds the Christian world view to be the best explanation of reality. The cumulative case for Christianity shows Christianity to be more plausible than any other world view.

Feinberg addresses to objections to his apologetic methodology. First is the "leaky bucket objection." This objection argues that merely adding weak arguments together does not produce a strong case for Christianity. Basically, Feinberg responds to this by arguing that each of his tests or arguments, though none conclusively prove Christianity to be true on its own, show Christianity to be probably true, or at least more probably true than any of her rivals. Taken together, these arguments prove Christianity to be true with a high degree of probability. In other words, each of the so-called leaky buckets do in fact hold some water, and when combined, these arguments produce a large enough quantity of water to make the cumulative case for Christianity very probable.[377]

The second and final objection to his cumulative case is the postmodern objection. Postmodernism teaches that there is no universal truth or morality. Hence, there is no rational way to defend one's faith.[378] Feinberg points out that the postmodern critique of apologetics fails one of his tests—the test of livability. Even postmodernists cannot live like there is no uniersal truth and no universal morality. According to

---

[376]Ibid., 166.

[377]Ibid., 167.

[378]Ibid., 167-168.

Feinberg, any world view that is not livable fails as a world view.[379]

Though Feinberg has great respect for classical apologetics and evidentialism (also known as historical apologetics), he chooses to call himself a cumulative case apologist. In other words, he does not base his case for Christianity on one lone argument. Instead, he uses several tests and several arguments that, when taken together, build a strong case for Christianity.

[379]Ibid., 170-172.

Chapter 11

The Historical Apologetics of Josh McDowell

Josh McDowell's 1970's work entitled *Evidence the Demands a Verdict* may be the most influential book on evidentialism or historical apologetics written during the twentieth-century.[380] This book has helped many skeptics find faith in Jesus and has encouraged many believers to study apologetics. However, McDowell has not limited his apologetics to historical evidences; he has been very willing throughout the years to present evidence for Christianity from other disciplines as well as history.

Historical Apologetics/Evidentialism

McDowell utilizes evidence from history and archaeology to prove the historical reliability of the Bible. He then proceeds to provide evidence that the Jesus of the Bible is the true Jesus of history.

---

[380] Josh McDowell, *Evidence that Demands a Verdict* (San Bernardino: Here's Life Publishers, 1979).

McDowell provides a strong case that the sixty-six books of the Protestant Bible comprise the true canon (i.e., the true list) of Scripture. He discusses the tests each book would have to pass before being included in the Old or New Testament canon. McDowell also explains why the extra books in the Roman Catholic Bible fail these tests.[381]

McDowell argues for Old Testament reliability by showing that the scribes copying the Old Testament were meticulous in their work.[382] He then compares the recently found Dead Sea Scrolls with hand-written Hebrew copies of the Old Testament written a thousand years later, showing these manuscripts are in agreement.[383] He also turns to archaelogical finds that confirm the general historical accuracy of the Old Testament.[384]

Josh McDowell also believes establishing the reliability of the New Testament is vital to Christian apologetics. He understands that Christianity is a religion with deep historical roots. For example, if Jesus did not rise from the dead (an historical event), then the Christian Faith cannot save (1 Corinthians 15:14, 17). If He did not die on the cross for the sins of mankind (an historical event), then Christianity offers no hope (1 Peter 2:24; 3:18). Proving the New Testament can be trusted will go a long way to establishing Christianity as the one true faith. Hence, McDowell attempts to show that the New Testament documents are historically reliable.

---

[381]Ibid., 29-38.

[382]Ibid., 54-55.

[383]Ibid., 57-58.

[384]Ibid., 65-73.

Many historians mistakenly believe that one cannot know the true Jesus of history since no one no has the original writings of those who knew Him. Only copies of the originals are in existence today. Ironically, these historical scholars will often quote from Plato, as well as other ancient writers, as if they can know with certainty what Plato originally wrote. McDowell argues that this clearly unveils a double standard. Ancient secular writings can be trusted based on late copies, but the New Testament cannot be trusted since the original manuscripts are missing.

In reality, the New Testament is by far the most reliable ancient writing in existence today. There exist today over 24,000 copies (5,000 of them in the original Greek language) of the New Testament (either in whole or in part).[385] This should be compared with the fact that only seven copies presently exist of Plato's Tetralogies.[386] Homer's Iliad is in second place behind the New Testament among ancient writings with just 643 copies.[387]

The earliest copy of Plato's Tetralogies is dated about 1,200 years after Plato supposedly wrote the original.[388] Compare this with the earliest extant copy of the New Testament: the John Ryland's Papyri. It contains a portion of John 18. This fragment is dated at about 125AD, only 25 years after the original is thought to have been written.[389] Again, Homer's Iliad takes second place among ancient writings,

---

[385]Ibid., 42-43.

[386]Ibid., 42.

[387]Ibid., 43.

[388]Ibid.

[389]Ibid.

second only to the New Testament. The earliest copy of any portion of Homer's Iliad is dated about 500 years after the original writing.[390]

When the contents of the extant manuscripts of the New Testament are compared, there appears to be 99.5% agreement. There is total agreement in the doctrines taught; the corruptions are mainly grammatical.[391] Homer's Iliad once again takes second place behind the New Testament among ancient documents. Homer's Iliad has a 95% accuracy when its copies are compared.[392] Since there are so few remaining copies of Plator's writings, agreement between these copies is not considered a factor (they are probably all copies of the same copy).[393]

McDowell concludes that historical scholars should consider the extant New Testament manuscripts to be reliable and accurate representations of what the authors originally wrote. Since the New Testament is by far the most accurately and extensively copied ancient writing, to question its authenticity is to call into question all of ancient literature, something most historians are not willing to do.

McDowell lists some of the better known ancient copies of the New Testament. The John Rylands Papyri is the oldest undisputed fragment of the New Testament still in existence. It is dated between 125 and 130AD. It contains a portion of John 18.[394] The Bodmer Papyrus II contains most

---

[390]Ibid.

[391]Ibid.

[392]Ibid.

[393]Ibid.

[394]Ibid., 46.

of John's Gospel and dates between 150 and 200AD.[395] The Chester Beatty Papyri includes major portions of the New Testament; it is dated around 200AD.[396] Codex Vaticanus contains nearly the entire Bible and is dated between 325 and 350AD.[397] Codex Sinaiticus contains nearly all of the New Testament and approximately half of the Old Testament. It is dated at about 350AD.[398] Codex Alexandrinus encompasses almost the entire Bible and was copied around 400AD.[399] Codex Ephraemi represents every New Testament book except for 2 John and 2 Thessalonians. Ephraemi is dated in the 400's AD.[400] Codex Bezae has the Gospels and Acts as its contents and is dated after 450AD.[401]

The very early dates of these manuscripts provide strong evidence that the content of the current New Testament is one and the same with the original writings of the apostles. McDowell concludes that there is no logical reason to doubt the reliability of these manuscripts. Once he has established the basic reliability of the New testament manuscripts, McDowell begins to focus on the true Jesus of history. McDowell argues that Jesus claimed to be God on numerous

---

[395]Ibid., 46-47.

[396]Ibid., 47.

[397]Ibid.

[398]Ibid.

[399]Ibid., 48.

[400]Ibid.

[401]Ibid.

occassions. Since no merely good man would claim to be God, Jesus was either a liar, a lunatic, or the Lord.[402]

McDowell turns to Jesus' fulfillment of numerous Old Testament prophecies, written hundreds of years before Jesus was born, proving Him to be the Jewish Messiah (the One God anointed to rescue Israel).[403] A few examples will suffice. It was predicted that Messiah would be born to a virgin (Isaiah 7:14) and would be born in Bethlehem (Micah 5:2). He would be a descendent of Judah and David (Genesis 49:10; Jeremiah 23:5-6; 2 Samuel 7:12-16), and would be crucified (Psalm 22:14, 17) and die before 70 ad (Daniel 9:24-27). His bones would not be broken (Psalm 34:20). Lots would be cast for His garments (Psalm 22:18). He would teach in parables, perform miracles, and rise from the dead (Psalm 78:2; Isaiah 35:5-6; Psalm 60:10). He would be rejected by the Jewish people (Isaiah 53:1), yet receive a wide Gentile following (Isaiah 49:6; 60:3). He would ride into Jerusalem on a donkey and receive a King's welcome (Zechariah 9:9). McDowell presents his readers with over sixty Old Testament prophecies fulfilled by Jesus.[404]

McDowell aslo confirms Jesus' deity by providng evidence for Jesus' resurrection. He shows that the accounts of the resurrection were written by sincere eyewitnesses, and, thus, should be trusted. He makes a defense of the burial, the empty tomb, and the post-resurrection appearances of Jesus to many witnesses. He shows that the transformed lives of the apostles, the origin of the church, and the day of worship

---

[402]Ibid., 81-107.

[403]Ibid., 141-176.

[404]Ibid.

changed to Sunday by the early church (which was Jewish) are best explained by the bodily resurrection of Jesus.[405]

McDowell refutes the naturalistic alternative theories to explain away the resurrection data.[406] The swoon theory speculates that Jesus only swooned on the cross and did not actually die. The swoon theory fails because the evidence overwhelmingly indicates that Jesus was dead when taken down from the cross. The stolen body theory is rejected because men (the apostles) do not die for what they know to be a hoax. Since the apostles were willing to die for their faith, it shows they did not steal the body—they sincerely believed they saw Jesus risen from the dead. Finally, the hallucination theory fails since no two people can have the same hallucination; yet, Jesus appeared numerous times to groups of people.[407]

McDowell also provides his readers with evidence for the inspiration of the Bible. He shows that the Bible contains numerous predictions that have come true, attesting to its divine authorship. The possibility of just a sample of these Old Testament prophecies being fulfilled by chance are so small that no reasonable person should hold this thesis. McDowell has also shown that Jesus, who has proven Himself to be God, considered the Old Testament God's Word and promised to inspire the New Testament. Hence, there is strong evidence to believe the Bible is God's Word.[408]

---

[405]Ibid., 179-260.

[406]Ibid., 232-255.

[407]Ibid.

[408]Ibid., 267-320.

Testimonial Apologetics

After makinf a strong historical case for Christianity, McDowell engages in testimonial apologetics by relating the conversion stories and religious experiences of several people who have trusted in Jesus for salvation.[409] McDowell summarizes the conversion stories of criminals, police officers, professional athletes, actors, singers, authors, businessmen, politicians, and skeptics. He lists converts to Christianity from numerous countries and numerous religions. He also discusses the testimonies of people who were willing to suffer persecution (and often martyrdom) for their Christian faith.[410] He even adds his own testimony as evidence for the reality of the Christian experience.[411] Though the evidence for Christianity based on the testimonies of converts is rather subjective, when this evidence is added to other objective evidences (such as historical evidences), the case for Christianity can be strengthened.

Comparative Religious Apologetics

Josh McDowell has also been willing to write extensively on comparative religious apologetics. His work *Handbook of Today's Religions*, co-authored with Don Stewart, provides a Christian response to the world's religions, non-Christian cults, the occult, and secular religions. This work is a valuable resource for lay apologists

---

[409]Ibid., 325-359.

[410]Ibid.

[411]Ibid., 363-367.

154

who desire to dialogue with people of other faiths. He discusses the founders, histories, and beliefs of each of the major religions or cults. Then he refutes the beliefs of these non-Christian religions or cults.

JUDAISM

True Judaism is the root of Christianity; Christianity is the fulfillment of Judaism. The Old Testament is Jewish. The apostles, who wrote the New Testament, are Jewish. Jesus, who is worshipped by Christians as the incarnate God, is Jewish. Therefore, true Judaism accepts the essential truths of Christianity. The God of Israel is the God of Christianity. Unfortunately, modern Judaism has rejected Jesus as the Jewish Messiah. Therefore, modern Judaism has apostatized from the one true faith-salvation in Jesus alone.[412]

There are three main branches of modern Judaism. Orthodox Judaism continues to observe most of the ceremonial laws with the exception of temple practices—there is currently no temple in Jerusalem. Orthodox Jews accept the Old Testament as God's inspired word. They express a special reverence for the Torah (the first five books of the Bible).[413]

The Reform branch of Judaism is theologically liberal. Reform Jews reject the divine inspiration of the Old Testament. The Torah is viewed merely as an ethical guidebook. The Jewish Messiah is considered to be a mere symbol for the emancipation of the Jewish people. Still, Reform Jews are very proud of their national heritage.[414]

---

[412]Josh McDowell and Don Stewart, *Handbook of Today's religions* (San Bernardino: Here's Life Publishers, 1983), 364.

[413]Ibid., 370-371.

The Conservative branch of modern Judaism stands between the other two branches. Much emphasis is placed upon the God of Israel as the one true God. Still, Conservative Jews are more likely to reject traditional Jewish beliefs than are the Orthodox Jews.[415]

Because of this diversity within contemporary Judaism, it is impossible to utilize one apologetic approach for all Jews. Reform Jews can usually be evangelized in the same fashion as one would an agnostic or a non-Christian theist (depending on the personal beliefs of the individual). However, the Conservative and Orthodox Jews have great respect for the Old Testament. It is often possible to discuss Old Testament messianic prophecies with Conservative and Orthodox Jews. The goal in these dialogues would be to lead the Jewish person to accept Jesus as their Jewish Messiah and the Savior of mankind. This is the same approach that Paul used in the synagogues as he witnessed to Jews (Acts 17:1-2).

Christ's fulfillment of Old Testament predictions should be presented. A few examples should be noted. Micah 5:2 predicts that the Messiah would be born in Bethlehem. Zechariah 9:9 states that the Messiah would receive a king's welcome while entering Jerusalem on a donkey. Isaiah 53 prophesies that the Jews would reject their Messiah when He comes, while Isaiah 42:4 states that the Jewish Messiah would receive a large Gentile following. Daniel 9:24-27 relates that the Messiah would be executed before the destruction of the temple (which occurred in 70AD). Psalm 22 identifies the type of death the Messiah would suffer as crucifixion. Only Jesus of Nazareth fulfilled all of these prophecies.

---

[414]Ibid., 371-372.

[415]Ibid., 371.

Christian apologists must attempt to persuade Orthodox and Conservative Jews to accept Christ's death on Calvary as the fulfillment of all the Old Testament sacrifices. The Jewish person must see that Christ offered His body as a sacrifice for the sins of mankind (1 Corinthians 5:21; 1 Peter 2:24; 3:18). Many Jews believe in salvation by works. Therefore, they must be told that salvation is solely by God's grace and that it is given to all who trust in Jesus, the Jewish Messiah, for salvation (Ephesians 2:8-9; John 3:16-18; 14:6; Romans 6:23).

Christian apologists must clearly display their love for Jewish people. It is an unfortunate fact that the Christian church has not always been free from the sin of anti-Semitism. Therefore, it is only natural for Jewish people to be wary of dialogue with Christians. The Christian would do well to establish a genuine friendship with Jewish people before attempting to lead them to Christ.

ISLAM

The Islamic faith is one of the fastest growing religions in the world.[416] Islam was founded by a shepherd and trader named Muhammad (570-632AD).[417] While residing in Arabia, he rebelled against the polytheism and the superstitions of his homeland.[418] He was familiar with Judaism and Christianity (probably through word of mouth), and these religions influenced him to believe in the existence

---

[416]Ibid., 377.

[417]Ibid., 378.

[418]Ibid., 379.

157

of only one God.[419] Muhammad called this one God, "Allah." He supposedly received several visions and recorded them into what later became the Muslim holy book, the Koran.[420]

It was Muhammad's goal to unite the Arab tribes under Allah's rule.[421] To accomplish this goal, he often used militaristic acts to "convert" cities to Islam.[422] Since Muhammad died without choosing his successor, divisions arose within Islam.[423]

Today, Islam is split into three main groups: the Sunnis, the Shi'ites, and the Sufis.[424] Most Muslims are Sunnis. They consider themselves the true followers of their prophet Muhammad's teachings.[425] Shi'ite Muslims are Muslims who believe their leader (called the "Ayatollah") speaks for God. Shi'ite Muslims believe that the Ayatollah can infallibly call for a holy war (a jihad).[426] (Islamic terrorist groups can be found in both Sunni and Shi'ite Islam.) The Sufis are Islamic mystics who seek personal experiences of God.[427] It should be added that the Black Muslim movement

---

[419]Ibid.

[420]Ibid.

[421]Ibid., 381.

[422]Norman L. Geisler and Abdul Saleeb, *Answering Islam* (Grand Rapids: Baker Book House, 1993), 76-79.

[423]McDowell and Stewart, 381.

[424]Ibid., 382-384.

[425]Ibid., 382.

[426]Ibid., 382-384.

[427]Ibid., 383-384.

in America is considered by traditional Muslims to be a heretical offshoot of historical Islam.[428]

Muslims believe that there is only one God and that He is called Allah. They accept the Torah of Moses, the Psalms of David, the Gospels of Christ, and the Koran as inspired works of God.[429] Still, Muslims believe that the Koran is the final and most authoritative word God has given to man.[430] Hence, if there is any disagreement between a sacred book and the Koran concerning any teaching, the Muslim will accept the teaching found in the Koran. The Old or New Testament teaching called into question is usually attributed to copyist errors. The six greatest prophets are listed as Adam, Noah, Abraham, Moses, Jesus, and Muhammad. However, Muhammad is considered to be the greatest of these prophets.[431] Islam teaches that there will be a resurrection and time of judgment in the last days. Hell will be the final destiny of all those who have opposed the work of Muhammad and Allah. Heaven will be populated by those who obeyed Allah and His prophet.[432]

To become a Muslim, a person must publicly recite the creed: "There is no God but Allah, and Muhammad is the prophet of Allah." Muslims must pray five times a day facing Mecca, one of their holy cities. Muslims are required to give alms and to follow prescribed fasts. Each Muslim must make

---

[428]Robert Morey, *The Islamic Invasion* (Eugene: Harvest House Publishers, 1992), 161.

[429]McDowell and Stewart, 390.

[430]Ibid.

[431]Ibid.

[432]Ibid.

a pilgrimage to the city of Mecca at least once. These practices are called "the Five Pillars of Islam."[433]

Muslims deny the doctrine of the Trinity; they believe that God is only one Person. Muslims deny the deity of Christ, lowering His status to that of a mere man, though a great prophet. Muslims deny that Jesus died for the sins of mankind and that salvation comes through Him. In fact, they deny even that He died on the cross. Muslims also reject that Jesus rose from the dead. They teach that Jesus was a sinless prophet, but that He was not as great as Muhammad. Muslims believe that man can be saved through human effort-obedience to the commands of Allah (as given through His prophet Muhammad).[434]

There are numerous contradictions in the Koran. The Koran teaches that Jesus ascended to heaven without dying (Surah 4:157-158), but it also teaches that Jesus predicted His own death and resurrection (Surah 19:33). In Surah 2:256, Muhammad proclaims religious tolerance, but, in Surah 9:5, he commands Muslims to slay all who refuse to worship Allah alone. One passage in the Koran states that Allah created the universe in six days (Surah7:54), while another passage speaks of eight days of creation (Surah 4:8-15). It appears that Muhammad learned about the Bible through secondary sources that were unreliable, for he mistakenly credits Haman, who lived around 500BC, with building the Tower of Babel, which was built around 2300BC (Surah 28:37-38). Muhammad also wrongly considered Haman to be a contemporary of Moses, who lived from about 1525BC to 1400BC (Surah 29:39). Many other contradictions found in the Koran could be identified by the Christian apologist in

---

[433]Ibid., 390-392.

[434]Ibid., 393-397.

order to show that the Koran could not possibly be the infallible word of God.[435] However, this is a sensitive subject for many devout Muslims. Hence, the Christian apologist is encouraged to first build a strong friendship with the Muslim before dealing with issues such as contradictions in the Koran or the moral character of Muhammad.

Besides critiquing the Koran, the Christian apologist should also defend the historicity of the Gospel accounts of Christ. The Christian apologist should present historical evidences for the death, resurrection, and deity of Christ. For example, ancient evidence for Christ's death by crucifixion abounds. There is solid manuscript evidence for Christ's death found in the Bodmer Papyrus II (150-200AD-contains most of John's Gospel), the Chester Beatty Papyri (200AD-contains most of the New Testament), and the Vaticanus and Sinaiticus (350AD-each contains most of the New Testament).[436] There are even ancient non-Christian sources dated between 52AD and 200AD which speak of Christ's death by crucifixion (Thallus, Josephus, Tacitus, and the Jewish Talmud).[437] There is much historical evidence for the Jesus of the Bible. This evidence predates the origin of Islam by several hundred years. This evidence should be utilized to persuade Muslims that their Jesus is not the Jesus of the Bible, and that only the true Jesus of the Bible can save mankind from its sins.

---

[435] *The Koran*, trans. By N. J. Dawood (New York: Penguin Books, 1990).

[436] McDowell, *Evidence the Demands a Verdict*, 46-48.

[437] Gary R. Habermas, *Ancient Evidence for the Life of Jesus* (Nashville: Thomas Nelson Publishers, 1984), 87-98.

HINDUISM

Hinduism is one of the oldest religions in the world. It is also one of the most complex religious systems. It is actually a family of religions since it has many diverse sects. A Hindu can be a pantheist, a polytheist, a monotheist, an agnostic, or even an atheist. Hinduism claims to be tolerant of all faiths and teaches there are many paths to God.[438]

The Hindus have a variety of sacred writings written between 1400BC and 500AD. Among these are the Vedas, the Upanishads, Ramayana, Mahabharata, and the Puranas. The most sacred of all Hindu writings is the Bhagavad Gita. The Bhagavad Gita dates to the first century AD; it is found in the Mahabharata. This work teaches that devotion to the god of one's choice brings salvation. This writing also speaks of Krishna, a supposed manifestation of the god called Vishnu.[439]

There is a common core of Hindu beliefs despite the diversity within Hinduism. Brahman is the ultimate reality for the Hindu. God is everything (pantheism). The Hindu god is a three-in-one god; Brahman is the creator, Vishnu the preserver, and Shiva the destroyer. (This three-in-oneness is not to be mistaken with the Christian doctrine of the Trinity, for the three are only manifestations of the Hindu god; they are not three eternal persons.) The soul of each human is part of Brahman (god), and the physical world is thought to be an illusion (called Maya).[440]

---

[438]McDowell and Stewart, 283-284.

[439]Ibid., 284-287.

[440]Ibid., 287-289.

Karma is the Hindu belief that the consequences from a person's actions of a previous life determine his present state of existence. Negative karma must be worked off through suffering and multiple reincarnations before Nirvana (eternal bliss) can be achieved. Nirvana is when a person is freed from the long cycle of reincarnation and becomes one with Brahman.[441]

Hindus believe that salvation (freedom from the cycle of reincarnations) can be achieved in one of three ways. The first way is through works and rituals. The second way is through the attaining of knowledge. The third way is through devotion to a deity of one's choice. Usually, Hindu meditation is an essential aspect of this third way.[442]

Christianity and Hinduism are not compatible. The god of Hinduism is usually considered to be an impersonal god. Brahman is an indefinable concept; it is not the personal, loving God of the Bible (John 3:16).[443] Negative karma is not to be equated with the Christian concept of sin, for, in Hinduism, ultimate reality is beyond the concepts of right and wrong.[444] As Francis Schaeffer pointed out, if the universe had an impersonal beginning, then the universe is "totally silent" concerning moral values.[445] Hinduism also rejects Christ's unique claim to deity. At most, Hindus will accept Jesus as

---

[441]Ibid., 289.

[442]Ibid., 290-291.

[443]Ibid., 290-292.

[444]Ibid., 292-293.

[445]Francis A. Schaeffer, *Trilogy* (Wheaton: Crossway Books, 1990), 293.

163

one of many manifestations of their god.[446] In Hinduism salvation is through human effort, not through the grace of God. Hindus believe in reincarnation, not a future resurrection.[447] On each of these vital points, Hinduism is opposed to Christianity. They cannot both be true.

The Christian apologist should be prepared to refute pantheism, as well as polytheism, when evangelizing Hindus. Historical apologetics may be useful in showing the Hindu the uniqueness of Christ. Since Hinduism collapses into moral relativism, the Christian apologist must be prepared to argue for absolute moral laws (moral values that are universally valid). Dialogue between Hindus and Christians is very difficult due to the vast gulf between these two schools of thought. Nevertheless, God has called His followers to preach His Gospel to all people.

BUDDHISM

Buddhism came into existence about 500BC. At that time, many people in India were disillusioned with Hinduism (due to the vicious Hindu caste system and a corrupt priesthood). Because of this disillusionment, many different sects arose from Hinduism. Of these offshoots, Buddhism was the most successful.[448]

Buddhism was founded by Siddhartha Gautama, who later became known as Buddha. Buddha was married and had a son. He was a prince who lived a sheltered and pleasurable life. One day, he left the palace to see life in the outside world.

---

[446]McDowell and Stewart, 292-293.

[447]Ibid., 289, 293.

[448]Ibid., 304.

This experience taught him about sickness, old age, death, hunger, and poverty. Eventually, Buddha left the palace and his family to seek "enlightenment." While meditating under a fig tree, he reached nirvana (the state of spiritual enlightenment). He decided to proclaim the truth he had learned while meditating under the tree. This truth can be summed up under the four noble truths and the eightfold path.[449]

The four noble truths are: 1) the existence of suffering, 2) the cause of suffering is one's desire for the pleasures of the senses, 3) the extinguishing of one's desires will end suffering, and 4) the extinguishing of one's desires can be accomplished through the eightfold path.[450]

The eightfold path is: 1) right views, 2) right attitude, 3) right speech, 4) right conduct, 5) right livelihood, 6) right effort, 7) right mindfulness, and 8) right contemplation or meditation. Through the eightfold path, one can attain nirvana, the cessation of all desire.[451]

Although Buddha was himself deified by some of his followers many years after his death, he himself was an agnostic concerning the existence of God and the afterlife.[452] Both pantheists and atheists can be found within Buddhism. Buddhism holds to the teaching of reincarnation, with nirvana as the ultimate escape from the cycle of reincarnation. Evil is merely an illusion caused by ignorance. As in Hinduism, moral values in Buddhism are ultimately relative since there

---

[449]Ibid., 305-306.

[450]Ibid., 307.

[451]Ibid.

[452]Ibid., 307-308.

is no belief in a personal, moral God. Still, in a contradictory fashion, Buddhism forbids certain behavior such as the killing of living things (including insects), adultery, stealing, telling falsehoods, and the drinking of intoxicants.[453]

Buddhism is obviously opposed to the Christian Faith. The Christian believes that God created the universe (Genesis 1:1), while Buddhists are monists—they believe all reality is one. Buddhists reject the personal, loving God of the Bible (John 3:16; Romans 5:8). Buddhism denies the reality of sin against God (Romans 3:10, 23; 5:12; 6:23) and the need for a Savior (John 3:16-18; 14:6; 1 Peter 2:24; 3:18). Buddhists also deny the unique deity of Christ (John 1:1, 14; Titus 2:13). Therefore, the Christian apologist must present a persuasive case for the truth of Christianity, while also refuting the major premises of Buddhism.

JAINISM

Jainism (an offshoot of Hinduism) was founded in India by Mahavira, a contemporary of Buddha. Mahavira lived a life of self-denial for twelve years. During that time, he did not speak; he wandered naked and unwashed, meditating daily, throughout India until he found nirvana. At that point, he accepted followers and began to teach his beliefs. Mahavira refused to acknowledge or worship any god. Despite his atheism, however, he (like Buddha) was deified years after his death by his followers. Jainism teaches the equality of all people. It renounces the killing of any living thing, sexual pleasures, and worldly goods. Jainism teaches

---

[453]Ibid., 309-311.

reincarnation, non-violence, and strict vegetarianism. Jainism encourages its adherents to flee from both hate and love.[454]

When witnessing to Jainists, Christian apologists should provide evidence from nature for God's existence and historical evidences for the deity and resurrection of Christ. Christ's command to love God with all one's being and to love one's neighbor as oneself (Mark 12:30-31) directly contradicts the Jainist belief that man is to renounce both hate and love. The Jainist acceptance of reincarnation is also unbiblical (Hebrews 9:27; Luke 16:19-31). Reincarnation teaches that salvation is attainable through human effort; whereas, the Bible clearly states that man can only be saved by God's grace through faith alone in Jesus alone (Ephesians 2:8-9; Romans 3:20-24).

CONFUCIANISM

Confucianism was founded by Confucius (another contemporary of Buddha) in China. Confucius was a moral reformer and a government official. In its purest form, Confucianism is more of an ethical system than a religion. Its founder is famous for his moral philosophy of life. Confucianism is agnostic about the spiritual realm. Man is viewed as basically good in this system of thought. Confucius (like Buddha and Mahavira) was later worshiped as a god by his followers.[455]

Christian apologists should argue for the biblical view of man as sinful in nature (Romans 3:10, 23; Jeremiah 17:9). Confucius misdiagnosed man, for man is not basically good. Man is sinful and in desperate need of salvation (Matthew

---

[454]Ibid., 296-301.

[455]Ibid., 325-338.

19:25-26). Only through Jesus can man be saved (John 14:6). Christians should also counter Confucius' lack of emphasis on the spiritual realm and the hereafter. If there is no life after death, then life on earth is meaningless, for a million years from now it would not make any difference how one lived their life. Confucius' preoccupation with morality and government issues is inconsistent with his agnosticism concerning the hereafter.

TAOISM

Taoism is a Chinese religion supposedly founded by Lao-tzu. (Some scholars doubt that he ever existed.) Lao-tzu was thought to have been born around 600BC. Lao-tzu opposed tyranny and the idea of government itself. His philosophy is called the "Tao," which means the way or path of ultimate reality. The Tao is the way of the universe—the way one should order one's life. Man is to live a passive life of inactivity, indifference, and irresponsibility. Avoidance of all stress and violence is emphasized. This will enable men to live in harmony with the universe. Taoism teaches that all things emanate from the Tao, including the Yin and the Yang. The Yin represents the negative side of the universe (the female, evil, darkness, death, winter, passive). The Yang represents the positive side of the universe (the male, good, light, life, summer, active). Taoism's god is an impersonal force.[456]

The Christian, when dealing with a Taoist, should provide evidence from nature for the personality of God. The design and complexity of the universe reveals that God is an intelligent designer, and the moral judgments that people

---

[456]Ibid., 339-348.

make show that the Cause of the universe is a moral Being. The Christian ethic is opposed to the ethic of the Tao—an ethic of inactivity, indifference, and irresponsibility. Christianity teaches its adherents to stand up for that which is good, to fight the good fight of faith, to press on in service for God, and to oppose that which is evil (Ephesians 6:13; 1 Timothy 6:12; Philippians 3:14; James 4:7). Man's ultimate goal should not be to live at harmony with the universe. Man's ultimate goal should be to live in harmony with the personal God of the Bible, and this harmony with God can only be received through Jesus (Romans 5:1; 2 Corinthians 5:18; 1 Timothy 2:5).

SHINTOISM

Shintoism is purely a Japanese religion. It is one of the world's oldest religions. It is not really a system of beliefs. Shintoism teaches that the Japanese islands were the first divine creation and that Japanese emperors were descendants of the sun-goddess, Amaterasu. Even as late as World War II, Shintoism was still being taught in Japanese schools. Between the two world wars the Japanese Emperor was worshiped. The essential beliefs of Shintoism are: 1) Japan is the country of the gods, 2) her people are descendants of the gods, and 3) the Japanese people are superior in intelligence and courage.[457]

The Christian can respond to Shintoism by stating that all people are equal in God's eyes since all bear His image (Genesis 1:26-27; 9:6). All mankind is related since all people are descendants of Adam and Eve (Acts 17:26; Genesis 3:20). The Christian must also attempt to persuade the Shintoist that

---

[457]Ibid., 349-355.

all people are sinners who can only be saved by Jesus (Romans 3:10, 23; John 3:16-18).

ZOROASTRIANISM

Zoroastrianism was founded by Zoroaster in Persia (modern Iran) several hundred years before Jesus was born. At that time, the Persians were polytheistic. Zoroaster protested against polytheism and taught there is only one God. Still, many Zoroastrians (and several offshoot religions of Zoroastrianism) teach dualism, the belief in two gods. Ahura-Mazda is the perfect and all-knowing creator; Angra Mainyu is co-eternal with Ahura-Mazda. Angra Mainyu is the evil spirit of destruction that has been at war with the Ahura Mazda throughout all eternity. Zoroastrianism teaches that good will ultimately triumph over evil. Today, Zoroastrianism has only about 100,000 adherents.[458]

Dualism must be refuted when dealing with Zoroastrians who believe there are two gods. If two equally powerful gods—one good and one evil—exist, then there is no guarantee that evil will be defeated. All finite existence must depend on infinite existence for its being, but two equal gods cannot be infinite, for they limit each other. Therefore, if the two finite gods of Zoroastrianism exist, there must also exist an infinite God who is the Cause of their existence.

Zoroastrians who already acknowledge only one God must be shown that the one true God has manifested Himself in the God-man, the Lord Jesus. Jesus died for our sins and rose from the dead. There is salvation in no one else.

---

[458]Ibid., 356-363.

SIKHISM

Sikhism attempts to harmonize the beliefs of Hinduism and Islam. It was founded by Nanak in India around 1500AD. Sikhism teaches the existence of one impersonal god called "Sat Nam." Salvation is achieved through knowing this god and being absorbed into him (the merging of the individual soul with the world soul). Hindu polytheism is rejected, while the Islamic belief in one god is affirmed. Sikhism retains the Hindu belief in reincarnation.[459]

Sikhism can be refuted by providing evidence from nature for the personality of God, and by disproving reincarnation. The need for personal salvation through Christ must be proclaimed and defended.

Cultural Apologetics

Besides utilizing historical evidences, testimonial apolgetics, comparative religious apologetics, Josh McDowell also defends the faith from a cultural standpoint by refuting "the new tolerance." The traditional view of tolerance encouraged the freedom of religious expression and the freedom of speech.[460] The Christian had the right to believe and proclaim that anyone who rejects Jesus as Savior will spend eternity in torment The Muslim had the right to preach that only good Muslims will go to heaven. The traditional view of tolerance promoted dialogue between people who disagreed on religious, political, or moral issues. It upheld a person's right to disagree with others without fear of

---

[459]Ibid., 499-405.

[460]Josh McDowell and Bob Hostetler, *The New Tolerance* (Wheaton: Tyndale House Publishers, 1998), 18.

imprisonment or censorship; it respected the views of others even when they disagreed with your own beliefs.

The traditional view of tolerance has been replaced by a new definition of tolerance. Josh McDowell and Bob Hostetler explain the difference between the traditional view and the new view:

> In contrast to traditional tolerance, which asserts that everyone has an equal right to believe or say what he thinks is right, the new tolerance—the way our children are being taught to believe—says that what every individual believes or says is equally right, equally valid. So not only does everyone have an equal right to his beliefs, but all beliefs are equal. All values are equal. All lifestyles are equal. All truth claims are equal.[461]

In the name of tolerance, traditional beliefs are no longer tolerated. The goal of the new tolerance is not to get people to respect and tolerate the lifestyles and beliefs of all people. Instead, the goal of the new tolerance is to attempt to force everyone to "approve of and participate in" the attitudes and activities of the new morality.[462] This new "tolerance" is rapidly becoming a religion of tolerance; however, it has the potential to be the most intolerant religion in the history of mankind. Those who choose to reject the new tolerance (also known as "the new morality" or "political correctness") are often "branded as narrow-minded bigots, fanatics, extremists,

---

[461]Ibid., 19-20.

[462]Ibid., 31.

and hatemongers and subjected to public humiliation and indoctrination."[463]

Whereas the traditional view of tolerance promoted freedom of religion and freedom of speech, the new tolerance only allows for those freedoms if you are an adherent of the new tolerance. The new tolerance proclaims, "I am all for your freedoms of speech and religion so long as your share my views and my religion. Any other views are unacceptable and cannot be tolerated." In other words, the new tolerance is intolerant with a vengeance.

McDowell points out that, unfortunately, this new tolerance is not limited to American soil. The United Nations also adheres to the new tolerance. The United Nations *Declaration of Principles on Tolerance* states that "Tolerance . . . involves the rejection of dogmaticism and absolutism."[464] Obviously, this is a self-contradictory statement, for the rejection of dogmaticism is itself a dogma, and the rejection of absolutism is itself an absolute.

In the name of the new tolerance, traditional Americans, in some cases, have been denied "schooling, scholarships, and employment."[465] In 1995, a US District judge from Texas "ruled that any student mentioning the name of Jesus in a graduation prayer would be sentenced to a six-month jail term."[466] It seems that anyone who holds to absolute standards (God's moral absolutes) will eventually

---

[463]Ibid., 32.

[464]Ibid., 43.

[465]Ibid., 32.

[466]Ibid., 53.

lose their freedom of speech and be silenced so that politically-correct "progress" may continue.[467]

Classifying McDowell's Apologetic Methodology

Clearly, Josh McDowell is an evidentialist or a historical apologist. Still, he is willing to use other evidences for the truth of Christianity as well. Besides using historical evidence for Christianity, McDowell delves into testimonial apologetics, comparative religious apologetics, and cultural apologetics. McDowell has shown that the case for Christianity can be greatly strengthened when the apologist does not restrict himself to one or two fields of evidence.

---

[467]Ibid., 56.

Chapter 12

The Historical Apologetics of John Warwick Montgomery

John Warwick Montgomery is a great Lutheran scholar and a world class apologist. He has been defending the faith sine the early 1960's. He holds doctorate degrees from the University of Strasbourg, France, and the University of Chicago. He is a noted theologian, historian, apologist, and expert on international law. In the 1960's and the 1970's he debated some of the leading anti-Christian thinkers. Montgomery is primarily a historical apologist. A prolific author, three of his main works on historical apologetics are: *History and Christianity*, *Faith Founded on Fact*, and *The Shape of the Past*.[468]

---

[468]John Warwick Montgomery, *History and Christianity: A Vigorous, Convincing Presentation of the Evidence for a Historical Jesus* (Minneapolis: Bethany House Publishers, 1964); John Warwick Montgomery, *Faith Founded on Fact: Essays in Evidential Apologetics* (Nashville: Thomas Nelson Publishers, 1978); John Warwick Montgomery, *The Shape of the Past: A Christian Response to Secular Philosophies of History* (Minneapolis: Bethany House Publishers, 1975).

175

A Common Critical Attack on the Historical Jesus

In 1964, John Warwick Montgomery wrote *History and Christianity: A Vigorous, Convincing Presentation of the Evidence for a Historical Jesus.* This book is based upon two lectures Montgomery gave in response to a lecture given by professor Avrum Stroll at a philosophy club meeting at the University of British Columbia. Stroll, during this lecture, argued that Jesus probably did exist, but little can be known about Him since the four Gospels were written long after the crucifixion. Montgomery quickly came to the defense of the historical Jesus.[469]

Montgomery argued that Stroll's thesis committed four common errors.[470] First, Stroll mistakenly relies almost exclusively on modern "authorities" when assessing the reliability of the New Testament manuscripts. The proper approach, writes Montgomery, would be to apply the standard rules historians and literary experts use when assessing any ancient manuscript. Instead, Stroll appeals to the work of modern scholars who are biased against the New Testament *before* they examine the evidence.[471]

Second, Stroll ignores the primary or earliest documents we have concerning Jesus. According to current New Testament scholarship, Paul wrote many (if not all) of his letters before the Gospels were written. Stroll neglects to look at the portrait of Jesus painted by the Apostle Paul. No

---

[469]Montgomery, *History and Christianity*, 11.

[470]Ibid., 17-22.

[471]Ibid., 17-18.

serious historian should ignore the earliest sources available; but, this is exactly what Stroll does.[472]

Third, Montgomery accuses Stroll of committing the logical fallacy of "begging the question," for, Stroll argues in a circle—he assumes what he is supposed to prove. Stroll rejects the Gospels' depiction of Jesus because he has already ruled out the possibility of miracles. In other words, he argues that miracles are impossible; therefore, the Jesus of the Bible cannot be the true Jesus of history because the Jesus of the Bible was a miracle worker.[473] Montgomery points out that Hume's argument against miracles has been thoroughly refuted by C. S. Lewis and others, and that the historian has no right to ignore documentary evidence merely because it does not line up with his philosophical assumptions.

Fourth, Stroll assumes that there existed an irrational "messianic fever" during the time of Christ, and that this impeded the judgment of Jesus' followers. Stroll views the Essene messiahs of the Dead Sea Scrolls as parallels of Jesus, thus making it easier for the apostles to deify Jesus and attribute messianic status to Him.[474] But, Montgomery shows this was not the case. Jesus' conception of Himself as Messiah differered greatly with the "Teacher of Righteousness" found in the Dead Sea Scrolls. Montgomery reminds his readers that Jesus did not meet the stereotypical messianic expectations of the first-century Jewish community—no one expected a suffering and dying Messiah. And, no first-century Jew expected a divine Messiah either. The portrait of Jesus found

---

[472]Ibid., 18-19.

[473]Ibid., 19-21.

[474]Ibid., 21.

in the New Testament is not something that first-century Jews would have invented.[475]

After pointing out these four errors in Stroll's thought, Montgomery goes on to build his historical case for Jesus. He argues for the reliability of the New Testament manuscripts, that Jesus claimed to be God, and that He bodily rose from the dead to prove this claim true. This line of argumentation offers a good overview of Montgomery's apologetic methodology.

The Reliability of the New Testament

Montgomery reasons that historians should treat the New Testament documents the same way they treat other historical materials. This means that three basic tests should be utilized to determine the reliability, or lack thereof, of the New Testament manuscripts. The three tests are: the bibliographical test, the internal evidence test, and the external evidence test.[476]

The bibliographical test examines the copies of ancient writings to ascertain how reliably they represent the originals.[477] When this test is applied to the New Testament, it shows itself to be the most reliable of all ancient writings. The New Testament has far more copies than any other ancient writing. The gap between the oldest extant copies and when the originals were written is smaller with the New Testament than the gap with any other ancient writing. Even apart from the ancient copies of the New Testament, nearly the entire New Testament can be reproduced from quotations

---

[475]Ibid., 22.

[476]Ibid., 26.

[477]Ibid., 26.

178

of the New Testament found in the writings of the early church fathers.[478]

The internal evidence test rests upon Aristotle's principle that the benefit of the doubt is given to the document itself. The historian is not to assume fraud or error in the document. If the historian believes the document to be in error or inaccurate, he must produce evidence for his claims. Otherwise, the document should be considered reliable without evidence to the contrary.[479] All other ancient literature is treated this way; scholars should not invoke a double standard when it comes to the New Testament.

The external evidence test asks if other ancient writings or archaeological evidence contradicts or affirms the document in question. Montgomery refers to the work of world renown archaeologists Sir William M. Ramsay and William F. Albright to show that the external confirmation for the reliability of the New Testament documents is excellent.[480] Whether one is looking at other ancient documents or archaeological finds, the external confirmation of the New Testament books is strong. No unbiased historian or New Testament scholar should doubt the reliability of the New Testament documents. The New Testament has more internal and external confirmation for its relaibility than can be found for any other ancient writing. There is no reason to reject the reliability of the New Testament books.

Montgomery also refutes critical attempts to find a Jesus of history who differs from the biblical Jesus. He notes that the time interval between the writing of the New

---

[478]Ibid., 26-29.

[479]Ibid., 29-31.

[480]Ibid., 31-35.

Testament and the events of Jesus' life which they record is too brief to allow for any legendary changes to the true portrait of Jesus. The entire New testament was written while the eyewitnesses who knew Jesus were still alive.[481] Plus, the Jews considered the teachings of their rabbis to be so important that they would memorize the main doctrines.[482] Everything the historian knows about first-century Judaism makes it extremely unlikely the early church was willing to change the teachings of Christ and fabricate the events of His life.

Jesus's Claims to be God

Montgomery shows that Jesus clearly considered Himself to be God incarnate. Modern scholars have no right to assume a merely human Jesus. They have no right to explain away all the New Testament data that points to His claiming to be deity. Montgomery argues that the New Testament shows that Jesus claimed to be God incarnate and His disciples came to accept Him as God. Montgomery surveys the New Testament and shows that Jesus is presented as God in Paul's writings, the Gospels, and Acts.[483]

Since Jesus claimed to be God, the deity of Christ is not a legend. The reliability of the New Testament argues against this. Jesus actually considered Himself to be God and claimed to be God on numerous occassions and in numerous ways.

---

[481]Ibid., 37.

[482]Ibid.

[483]Ibid., 49-58.

But, Montgomery argues that the character and teachings of Jesus show that He was not a charlaton (i.e., a liar) or a lunatic (i.e., a deranged individual who thought He was God but was not). No insane man or deceiver would have preached the Sermon on the Mount.[484]

Montgomery adds that there are three reasons why the disciples would not themselves deify Jesus. First, the messianic expectation of first-century Jews differed greatly from the New Testament portrait of Jesus as a suffering and dying Messiah who happens to be God. The disciples were not expected either a suffering Messiah or a divine Messiah. They also did not expect and would never invent a Messiah who would freely offer salvation to Gentiles. In fact, if Jesus had fulfilled the messianic expectations of the first-century Jewish people, He would never have been crucified.[485] Second, the psychological, ethical, and religious (i.e., ancient Jewish monotheism) makeup of the disciples made them incapable of deifying a person who was not God. As first-century monotheistic Jews, the disciples would never have chosen to deify Jesus on their own.[486] Instead, they taught He was God because He claimed He was God and He proved he was God. And third, Montgomery argues that the historical evidence for Jesus' resurrection could not have been manufactured by the disciples.[487]

---

[484]Ibid., 61-72.

[485]Ibid., 70-72.

[486]Ibid., 71.

[487]Ibid., 72.

Evidence for Jesus' Resurrection

Montgomery notes that it was Jesus' bodily resurrection from the dead that finally convinced the disciples that Jesus was God incarnate. The disciples present themselves as people who could discern between myth and fact. They reported the resurrection as fact—Jesus actually rose from the dead in history. When false messiahs of the first-century died, their claims to be messiah died with them. But, Jesus' messianic movement did not die—in fact, His movement came back to life after His death because he rose from the dead. Hence, the origin and early growth of the church points to Jesus' bodily resurrection being factual.[488] And, Jesus' resurrection convinced the disciples that Jesus' claims to be God, Savior, and Messiah were true.

Montgomery chides New Testament scholars for a priori ruling out the resurrection because miracles are impossible. Now that the closed and mechanical universe of Newtonian Physics has given way to Einstein's thought, the world in which man finds himself is not as predictable as man once thought. Therefore, Montgomery states, "The problem of 'miracles,' then, must be solved in the realm of historical investigation, not in the realm of philosophical speculation."[489] The statement that miracles are impossible is a philosophical statement which is lacking in evidence; it is not a historical statement. The historian must look at the historical evidence—he must not bring his philosophical assumptions to the table. The historian must go where the historical evidence leads. He has no right to throw out primary, reliable sources simply because they do not fit his

---

[488]Ibid., 74-75.

[489]Ibid., 75.

philosophical world view.[490] Also, if God exists, then He has power over death and power to supercede the laws of nature. If God exists, miracles are possible.[491]

Montgomery refutes the naturalistic attempts to explain away the resurrection data. The swoon theory failed because Jesus died by crucifixion. The Roman executioners knew how to do their job—they knew how to kill. Assuming Jesus had only passed out on the cross and had not died (a wild, groundless assumption at best), He would not have had the strength to remove the stone from the tomb and present Himself to His disciples as the one who has conquered death.[492]

The stolen body theory fails as well. Montgomery argues that neither friend nor foe had the motivation to steal the body. Plus, the stolen body would only explain the empty tomb—not the post-resurrection appearances of Jesus. Yet, Paul, while writing to the Corinthians in about 56 ad, wrote that over 500 people had seen Jesus alive after His death. He added that most of these witness were still alive and could be interrogated. Why would the leaders of the early church fabricate such a lie? The enemies of the church could so easily refute this lie by producing the rotiing corpse of Christ.[493]

Montgomery concludes that Jesus did actually claim to be God, and that He rose from the dead to prove this claim to be true. This is the conclusion when all the available primary evidence is taken seriously. The historical evidence

---

[490]Ibid., 75-76.

[491]Ibid., 76.

[492]Ibid., 77.

[493]Ibid., 77-78.

points to Jesus as God incarnate and as risen from the dead.[494] The historian may not like this conclusion; but, that is what the historical evidence indicates.

Classifying Montgomery's Apologetic Methodology

Obviously, John Warwick Montgomery should be classified as a historical apologist (also known as an evidentialist). Still, it should be noted that he had great respect for other approaches to defending the faith. For instance, he was a fan of C. S. Lewis' narrative approach to defending Christinaity through his fiction. Still, Montgomery set a very high standard for future historical apologists (i.e., McDowell, Habermas, Licona, etc.) to follow.

---

[494]Ibid., 79.

Chapter 13

The Historical Apologetics of Gary Habermas

Gary Habermas is the distinguished professor of philosophy and theology at Liberty University. Many consider him to be the world's leading expert on the historical evidence for Jesus' resurrection from the dead. Habermas provides historical evidence to show that Jesus really did claim to be God and that He physically rose from the dead. Jesus' resurrection from the dead in history provides strong proof for the truth of His claim to be God incarnate.

THE APOSTOLIC FATHERS: EVIDENCE FOR JESUS

Habermas finds evidence for the historical Jesus in numerous ancient sources. The primary evidence Habermas utilizes to build his case for Jesus is the core data, found in the New Testament, which is accepted as historical by the vast majority of New Testament critical scholars today. Still, Habermas is willing to use ancient extra-biblical sources to find evidence for the true Jesus of history. These sources include the writings of the apostolic fathers, other early Christian literature, and ancient secular writings.

The apostolic fathers were leaders in the early church who personally knew the apostles and their doctrine.[495] Most of their writings were produced between 95 and 150AD.[496] There were also other prominent Christian thinkers who wrote about Jesus during this time period.

Radical New Testament scholars have attempted to find the so-called true Jesus of history, but it was their goal to find a non-supernatural Jesus who never claimed to be God. These scholars believe that Christ's claim to be God and Savior, and His miraculous life (especially His bodily resurrection from the dead) are merely legends—distortions of the true historical accounts. In the view of these critics, the true Jesus of history was a great teacher; still, He was merely a man.[497] Therefore, if it can be shown that early church leaders, who personally knew the apostles or their colleagues, taught that the miraculous aspects of Christ's life actually occurred and that Jesus did in fact make the bold claims recorded in the New Testament, then this legend hypothesis fails.

A legend is a ficticious story that, through the passage of time, many people come to accept as historically accurate. A legend is able to wipe out core historical data only if the eyewitnesses and those who knew the eyewitnesses are already dead. Otherwise, the eyewitnesses or those who knew them would refute the legend. Therefore, a legend usually

---

[495]Earle E. Cairns, *Christianity Through the Centuries*(Grand Rapids: Zondervan Publishing House, 1981), 73.

[496]Ibid.

[497]Gary R. Habermas, *Ancient Evidence for the Life of Jesus* (Nashville: Thomas Nelson Publishers, 1984), 42.

begins to replace accurate historical data a generation or two after the event or person in question has passed. If a written record compiled by eyewitnesses is passed on to future generations, legends can be easily refuted. If those who knew the apotles or their colleagues passed on to us accounts of Jesus, their accounts would hold great evidential weight. And, if these accounts were in general agreement with the New Testament accounts, then our confidence in the reliability of the New Testament portrait of Jesus should increase greatly.

Habermas examines the work of several apostolic fathers and their contemporaries: Clement of Rome (95AD), Ignatius (110-115AD), Polycarp (110AD), Papias (110AD), Quadratus (125AD), Barnabas (135AD), and Justin Maryr (150AD). Habermas notes that these early sources give us vital information concerning the life, teachings, death, and resurrection of Jesus.[498] Just a sample of the facts that Habermas gleaned from their writings include: 1) Jesus really did live, 2) He was born of a virgin in the city of Bethlehem, 3) He was from the tribe of Judah, 4) He was a descendant of David, 5) He was visited by Magi, 6) He was baptized by John, 7) He performed miracles and fuflilled Old Testament prophecies, 8) He preached the good news concerning the Kingdom of God, 9) He was crucified by order of Pontius Pilate, 10) He was temporarily forsaken by His friends, 11) He bodily rose from the dead, and 12) after His death, He appeared alive to His disciples on numerous occassions.[499] Several of these early church leaders also attributed deity to

---

[498]Gary R. Habermas, *The Historical Jesus: Ancient Evidence for the Life of Christ* (Joplin: College Press, 1996), 229-242, 111-114.

[499]Ibid., 239-241.

Jesus,[500] and wrote of the saving value of His sacrifical death.[501]

The testimony of the early second century church should be considered extremely important. Many of these early Christians were martyred for their beliefs. Since people will only die for what they truly believe, it is reasonable to conclude that the early church sincerely believed they were protecting the true apostolic faith from possible perversions. If they had tampered with the teachings of the apostles, they certainly would not have died for their counterfeit views. The apostolic fathers and early church leaders taught essentially the same things about Jesus as that taught in the New Testament, thus confirming the portrait of Jesus found on the pages of the New Testament.

ANCIENT SECULAR WRITINGS

Besides references to Christ in Christian literature which dates back to the first and second centuries AD, Habermas also refers to ancient secular writings which refer to Christ from that same time period. The significance of these non-Christian writings is that, though the secular authors themselves did not believe the early church's message, they stated the content of what the early church actually taught.

In 52AD, Thallus recorded a history of the Eastern Mediterranean world. In this work, he covered the time period from the Trojan War (mid 1200's BC) to his day (52AD). Though no manuscripts of Thallus' work are known to currently exist, Julius Africanus (writing in 221AD) referred

---

[500]Ibid., 245.

[501]Ibid., 233.

to Thallus' work. Africanus stated that Thallus attempted to explain away the darkness that covered the land when Christ was crucified. Thallus attributed this darkness to an eclipse of the sun.[502] This reveals that about twenty years after the death of Christ, non-believers were still trying to give explanations for the miraculous events of Christ's life.

In 115AD, a Roman historian named Cornelius Tacitus wrote about the great fire of Rome which occurred during Nero's reign. Tacitus reported that Nero blamed the fire on a group of people called Christians, and he tortured them for it. Tacitus stated that the Christians had been named after their founder "Christus." Tacitus said that Christus had been executed by Pontius Pilate during the reign of Tiberius (14-37AD). Tacitus related that the "superstition" of the Christians had been stopped for a short time, but then once again broke out, spreading from Judaea all the way to Rome. He said that multitudes of Christians (based on their own confessions to be followers of Christ) were thrown to wild dogs, crucified, or burned to death. Tacitus added that their persecutions were not really for the good of the public; their deaths merely satisfied the cruelty of Nero himself.[503]

These statements by Tacitus are consistent with the New Testament records. Even Tacitus' report of the stopping of the "superstition" and then its breaking out again appears to be his attempt to explain how the death of Christ stifled the spreading of the gospel, but then the Christian message was once again preached, this time spreading more rapidly. This is perfectly consistent with the New Testament record. The New Testament reports that Christ's disciples went into hiding during His arrest and death. After Jesus rose from the dead

---

[502]Habermas, *Ancient Evidence*, 93.

[503]Ibid., 87-88.

189

(three days after the crucifixion), He filled His disciples with the Holy Spirit (about fifty days after the crucifixion), and they fearlessly proclaimed the gospel throughout the Roman Empire (Acts 1 and 2).

Suetonius was the chief secretary of Emperor Hadrian who reigned over Rome from 117 to 138AD. Suetonius refers to the riots that occurred in the Jewish community in Rome in 49AD due to the instigation of "Chrestus." Chrestus is apparently a variant spelling of Christ. Suetonius refers to these Jews being expelled from the city.[504] Seutonius also reports that following the great fire of Rome, Christians were punished. He refers to their religious beliefs as "new and mischievous."[505]

Pliny the Younger, another ancient secular writer, provides evidence for early Christianity. He was a Roman govenor in Asia Minor. His work dates back to 112AD. He states that Christians assembled on a set day, sangs hymns to Christ as to a god, vowed not to partake in wicked deeds, and shared "ordinary" food.[506] This shows that by 112AD, it was already common knowledge that Christians worshiped Christ, sang hymns to Him, lived moral lives, assembled regularly, and partook of common food (probably a reference to the celebration of the Lord's Supper).

The Roman Emperor Trajan also wrote in 112AD. He gave guidelines for the persecution of Christians. He stated that if a person denies he is a Christian and proves it by

---

[504] Ibid., 90.

[505] Ibid.

[506] Ibid., 94.

worshiping the Roman gods, he must be pardoned for his repentance.[507]

The Roman Emperor Hadrian reigned from 117 to 138AD. He wrote that Christians should only be punished if there was clear evidence against them. Mere accusations were not enough to condemn a supposed Christian.[508] The significance of these passages found in the writings of Trajan and Hadrian is that it confirms the fact that early Christians were sincere enough about their beliefs to die for them.

The Talmud is the written form of the oral traditions of the ancient Jewish Rabbis. A Talmud passage dating back to between 70 and 200AD refers to Jesus as one who "practised sorcery" and led Israel astray. This passage states that Jesus (spelled Yeshu) was hanged (the common Jewish term for crucifixion) on the night before the Passover feast.[509] This is a very significant passage, for it reveals that even the enemies of Christ admitted there were supernatural aspects of Christ's life by desribing Him as one who "practiced sorcery." This source also confirms that Jesus was crucified around the time of the Passover feast.

Another anti-Christian document was the Toledoth Jesu, which dates back to the fifth century AD, but reflects a much earlier Jewish tradition. In this document, the Jewish leaders are said to have paraded the rotting corpse of Christ through the streets of Jerusalem.[510] This obviously did not occur. The earliest preaching of the gospel took place in

---

[507]Ibid., 96.

[508]Ibid., 97.

[509]Ibid., 98.

[510]Ibid., 99-100.

Jerusalem. Therefore, parading the rotting corpse of Christ through the streets of Jerusalem would have crushed the Christian faith in its embryonic stage. However, some of the other non-Christian authors mentioned above stated that Christianity spread rapidly during the first few decades after Christ's death. The preaching of Christ's resurrection would not have been persuasive if His rotting corpse had been publicly displayed.

It is also interesting to note that the Jewish religious leaders waited quite a long time before putting a refutation of the resurrection into print. Certainly, it would have served their best interests to disprove Christ's resurrection. But as far as written documents are concerned, the first century Jewish authorities were silent regarding the resurrection of Jesus.

Lucian was a Greek satirist of the second century. He wrote that Christians worshiped a wise man who had been crucified, lived by His laws, and believed themselves to be immortal.[511] Thus, this ancient secular source confirms the New Testament message by reporting the fact that Jesus was worshiped by His earliest followers.

Probably the most interesting of all ancient non-Christian references to the life of Christ is found in the writings of the Jewish historian named Josephus. Josephus was born in 37 or 38AD and died in 97AD. At nineteen, he became a Pharisee (a Jewish religious leader and teacher).[512] The following passage is found in his writings:

> Now there was about this time Jesus, a wise man, if it be lawful to call him a man; for he was a doer of wonderful works, a teacher of such men as receive the

---

[511]Ibid., 100.

[512]Ibid., 90.

truth with pleasure. He drew over to him both many of the Jews and many of the Gentiles. He was (the) Christ. And when Pilate, at the suggestion of the principal men amongst us, had condemned him to the cross, those that loved him at the first did not forsake him; for he appeared to them alive again the third day; as the divine prophets had foretold these and ten thousand other wonderful things concerning him. And the tribe of Christians, so named after him, are not extinct at this day.[513]

Since Josephus was a Jew and not a Christian, many scholars deny that this passage was originally written by him. These scholars believe this text was corrupted by Christians. Gary Habermas dealt with this problem in the following manner:

> There are good indications that the majority of the text is genuine. There is no textual evidence against it, and, conversely, there is very good manuscript evidence for this statement about Jesus, thus making it difficult to ignore. Additionally, leading scholars on the works of Josephus have testified that this portion is written in the style of this Jewish historian. Thus we conclude that there are good reasons for accepting this version of Josephus' statement about Jesus, with modifications of questionable words. In fact, it is possible that these modifications can even be accurately ascertained. In 1972 Professor Schlomo Pines of the Hebrew University in Jerusalem released the results of a study on an Arabic manuscript containing Josephus' statement about Jesus. It includes a different and briefer

---

[513]Flavius Josephus, *The Works of Josephus*, William Whiston, trans. (Peabody: Hendrickson Publishers, 1987), 480.

rendering of the entire passage, including changes in the key words listed above. . .[514]

Habermas goes on to relate the Arabic version of this debated passage. In this version, Jesus is described as being a wise and virtuous man who had many followers from different nations. He was crucified under Pontius Pilate, but His disciples reported that, three days later, He appeared to them alive. Josephus added that Jesus may have been the Messiah whom the prophets had predicted would come.[515]

It is highly unlikely that both readings of this controversial passage are corrupt. One of these two readings probably represents the original text. The other reading would then be a copy that was tampered with by either a Christian or a non-Christian. Whatever the case may be, even the skeptic should have no problem accepting the Arabic reading. Still, even if only this reading is accepted, it is enough. For it is a first century testimony from a non-Christian historian that declares that those who knew Jesus personally claimed that He had appeared to them alive three days after His death by crucifixion under Pilate.

Several things can be learned from this brief survey of ancient non-Christian writings concerning the life of Christ. First, His earliest followers worshiped Him as God. The doctrine of Christ's deity is therefore not a legend or myth developed many years after Christ's death (as was the case with Buddha). Second, they claimed to have seen Him alive three days after His death. Third, Christ's earliest followers faced persecution and martyrdom for their refusal to deny His deity and resurrection. Therefore, the deity and resurrection of

---

[514]Habermas, *Ancient Evidence*, 91.

[515]Ibid., 91-92.

Christ were not legends added to the text centuries after its original composition. Instead, these teachings were the focus of the teaching of Christ's earliest followers. They claimed to be eyewitnesses of Christ's miraculous life and were willing to die horrible deaths for their testimonies. Therefore, they were reliable witnesses of who the true Jesus of history was and what He taught.

EVIDENCE JESUS CLAIMED TO BE GOD

Habermas builds a strong historical case that Jesus did actually consider Himself to be God incarnate. He notes that many New Testament scholars acknowledge the "Son of Man" sayings as authentic sayings of Jesus. This is because of the critical principle called "discontinuity." This principle says that a saying attributed to Jesus in the Gospels was probably actually uttered by Jesus if it was disimilar to what first-century AD Jews taught, and disimilar to what the early church taught. The reasoning of critical scholars is that if the early church taught something, then they would place those words on Jesus' lips to give authority to their beliefs. But, this cannot apply to the "Son of Man" sayings. For, though the phrase comes from Daniel chapter seven, it was not in common use by the Jews of the first century AD. Also, the church almost never used the title of Jesus, not even in New Testament times. Yet, it was the most common title Jesus used of Himself. Hence, the principle of discontinuity shows that the "Son of Man" sayings were probably uttered by Jesus Himself.[516]

---

[516]Gary Habermas, *The Risen Jesus and Future Hope* (Lanham, MD: Rowman and Littlefield Publishers, 2003), 100-106.

But, when we look at the Son of Man sayings, we see several things that Jesus taught about Himself. Jesus predicted His death and resurrection numerous times (Mark 8:31; 9:31; 10:32-34). He claimed to be equal to God and have the power to forgive sins (Mark 2:5-12). Also, He claimed to be the Son of God and the Jewish Messiah, and He said that He would return to judge the world (Mark 14:61-64). He also claimed He came to earth to die "to give His life a ransom for many" (Mark 10:45).

Habermas also notes that when Jesus called God "Abba," He claimed to have a closeness or intimacy with the Father that no one else had.[517] When He claimed that God was His "Abba" (something as intimate as "daddy," yet more respectful), the Jews understood Jesus to be claiming to be "the Son of God" and equal to God (John 5:17-18). Some modern critics reject the passages where Jesus called Himself the Son of God. But, it is hard for New Testament critics to deny the authenticity of Mark 13:32. For, in this passage, Jesus, while calling Himself "the Son," admits that, in His human nature, He did not know the day or the hour of His return. This is an excellent example of the principle of embarrassment. The Apostles would never place these words on the lips of Jesus if He did not actually say them, for they imply a limitation of Jesus' knowledge. Hence, Jesus did make this statement, and He did think of Himself as the Son of God.

EVIDENCE JESUS ROSE FROM THE DEAD

Gary Habermas has researched the issue of Jesus' resurrection probably more than any other contemporary scholar. He has read everything in print, in English, German,

---

[517]Ibid., 107.

and French, from the world's leading New Testament scholars, written from 1975 to nearly the present day. Habermas was able to chart their views concerning the resurrection.[518]

However, before discussing the historical data found in the New Testament that is nearly universally accepted by current New Testament critical scholarship, Habermas understands that he must answer the Scottish philosopher David Hume's objection to miracles. Hume argued that no wise man would accept the historicity of a miracle claim because the probability of a natural event will always be higher than the probability of a supernatural event. Hume believed that common experience of uninterrupted natural laws will always outweigh any supposed evidence for a miracle claim.[519]

Habermas responds by making several points. First, Hume is arguing in a cricle—he is assuming what he is supposed to prove. Hume is assuming (without argument) that common human experience is against miracles. But, there is no way to know this unless Hume already knows that no human has ever actually experienced a miracle. Second, Hume has an outdated Newtonian misunderstanding of the laws of nature—he acts as if the laws of nature prescribe what can or cannot occur. Actually, most contemporary scientists and philsoophers now understand the laws of nature to be descriptive, not prescriptive. The laws of nature describe the way nature generally operates; they do not prescribe what can or cannot occur. Third, if a theistic God exists, then miracles are possible. In other words, if a personal God exists and He is the author of the laws of nature (the way nature generally

---

[518]Ibid., vii.

[519]Ibid., 25.

operates), then He can interrupt or supersede these laws whenever He chooses to do so. In short, Hume's a priori bias against miracles is unjustified.[520] One should not rule out miracles without examining the supposed evidence for the specific miracle claim. Having responded to Hume's objection, Habermas now turns to the historical evidence for Jesus' bodily resurrection.

His work shows that the vast majority of New Testament scholars (i.e., over 97%) acknowledge, based on the New Testament evidence, that 1) Jesus died by crucifixion, 2) his apostles' lives were transformed by what they believed were appearances to them of the resurrected Jesus, 3) Paul's life was transformed by what he believed was a post-resurrection appearance of Jesus, and 4) James' life was somehow transformed from being a mocker of His brother to being one of the key leaders in the early church. Habermas also shows that over 70% of the world's leading New Testament scholars acknowledge that the tomb was found empty early Sunday morning after Christ's crucifixion.[521]

---

[520]Ibid., 5-8.

[521]Gary R. Habermas and Michael R. Licona, *The Case for the Resurrection of Jesus* (Grand Rapids: Kregel Publications, 2004), 48-75. In *The Risen Jesus and Future Hope*, pages 9-10, Habermas actually lists twelve facts accepted as historical by virtually all the world's leading New Testament critics today. The twelves facts are as follows: 1) Jesus died by Roman crucifixion, 2) He was buried in a private tomb, 3) the disciples lost hope, 4) Jesus' tomb was found empty, 5) the disciples had experiences in which they believed they actually saw the risen Christ, 6) due to these experiences, the lives of the apostles were transformed to the point of being willing to suffer and die for Jesus, 7) the church proclaimed the resurrection from the earliest days, 8) the earliest preaching of the resurrection took place in Jerusalem, 9) the Gospel message focused on Jesus' death and resurrection, 10)

Habermas believes that the best explanation of the accepted data is that Jesus did in fact rise from the dead and appear to His disciples.

The strength of Habermas' argument for Jesus' resurrection is in the fact that he uses what the world's leading critical New Testament scholars accept to build his case for the historicity of Jesus' bodily resurrection. Most of these critics start their research with a strong bias against the resurrection. Using highly critical principles (i.e., mutiple attestation, embarrassment, discontinuity, enemy attestation, etc.), these scholars have uncovered solid historical data that they feel compelled to accept. That is the data that Gary Habermas uses to prove Jesus' resurrection.

In the case of *the empty tomb*, further argumention is needed. This is because only just over 70% of New Testament scholars accept the empty tomb, rather than the near universal support for the other four pieces of data. There are several reasons which show that the accounts of the empty tomb are probably historical. First, the first eyewitnesses of the empty tomb (and the resurrected Christ) were women. This is something the apostles would not have made up, for a woman's testimony was held highly suspect in the first-cenutry ad. It offered practically no evidential value to

---

Sunday became the primary day for worship, 11) Jesus' brother James was converted from skepticism to Christianity by what he believed was an appearance of Jesus to him, and 12) a leading persecutor of the early church, Saul of Tarsus (Paul), became a believer when he had an experience in which he believed he saw the risen Christ. Still, despite the near unanimous acceptance of these twelve facts, Habermas chooses to limit his case for the resurrection to the five facts listed in the text of this chapter. If Habermas' case for Jesus' resurrection based on the five core facts is successful, then it can only be strengthened by utilizing the additional seven facts.

fabricate a story of women being the first witnesses.[522] Plus, the principle of embarassment applies here. For, it would have been very embarassing for the two leading apostles, Peter and John, to have been proven wrong by ladies. This would be horrible public relations for the early church. The only reason for reporting that women were the first witnesses of the empty tomb would be if it was actually true.

Second, if Jesus did not rise from the dead, then the Jewish religious authorities would have produced the rotting corpse of Christ, thus refuting Christianity and stifling its growth at its earliest stage. But this did not happen— Christianity grew at a tremendous rate in the early 30's ad in the Jerusalem area. This would not be the case if Jesus' body was still in the tomb.

Third, New Testament scholars agree that the sermons of Acts chapter 1 through 12 are the earliest sermons of the church—they date back to the early 30's ad. Their antiquity is accepted by scholars because these sermons show no signs of theological development (this type of theological development is found in Paul's letters which were written twenty years later).[523] These sermons seem to report the events of the resurrection at the earliest stage of the church. One of the main themes of these early sermons was the resurrection of Jesus. Hence, the resurrection of Jesus was reported shortly after Christ's crucifixion by people who claimed to be eyewitnesses and who were willing to suffer and die for their

---

[522]Ibid., 70-73.

[523]J. P. Moreland, *Scaling the Secular City* (Grand Rapids: Baker Book House, 1987), 155-156.

proclamation. Men do not die for what they know to be a hoax—they sincerely believed they saw the risen Christ.[524]

Fourth, Jesus was buried in the tomb of a well-known man—Joseph of Arimathea. It would have been easy to locate the tomb to ascertain if it was empty. Many critics acknowledge the reliability of the account of Jesus being buried in Joseph's tomb.[525] For, if there was no real Jospeh of Arimathea on the Jewish Ruling Council, then this account would be easily refuted by the enemies of the early church. However, once we admit that there existed a man named Jospeh of Arimathea on the Jewish Ruling Council, then it is highly unlikely the apostles fabricated this account. Joseph would have been easy to find—there were only 70 members on the Sanhedrin and they met regularly in Jerusalem. If the apostles lied about the burial, then one could interview Joseph of Arimathea to check the account to disprove it. But, once we admit Jesus was buried in the tomb of a famous man, then we must acknowledge how easy it would have been to prove the corpse was still in the tomb, had it actually been there. But, this did not happen. Hence, the tomb was empty.

Habermas believes the ancient creed found in 1 Corinthians 15:3-8 also provides strong evidence of the post-resurrection appearances of Jesus to His followers. In the Apostle Paul's First Letter to the Corinthians, we find excellent eyewitness testimony concerning the resurrection that nearly dates back to the event itself. The Apostle Paul wrote:

> For I delivered to you as of first importance what I also received, that Christ died for our sins according to the Scriptures, and that He was buried, and that He

---

[524]Habermas and Licona, 98.

[525]Habermas, *Historical Jesus*, 152-157.

was raised on the third day according to the Scriptures, and that He appeared to Cephas, then to the twelve. After that He appeared to more than five hundred brethren at one time, most of whom remain until now, but some have fallen asleep; then He appeared to James, then to all the apostles; and last of all, as it were to one untimely born, He appeared to me also (1 Corinthians 15:3-8).

Most New Testament scholars, liberal and conservative alike, agree that this passage is an ancient creed or hymn formulated by the early church.[526] In our task of ascertaining when the creed of 1 Corinthians 15 was created, it is first necessary to determine when Paul wrote 1 Corinthians. In this way, we will establish the latest possible date for the creed. We can then work our way back in time from that date, following any clues based upon the internal evidence found in the creed itself.

Christian philosopher J. P. Moreland, one of Habermas' colleagues, has correctly stated that for the past one hundred years almost all New Testament critics have accepted the Pauline authorship of 1 Corinthians.[527] A comparison of 1 Corinthians 16 with Acts 18, 19, and 20 provides strong evidence that 1 Corinthians was written by Paul in 55AD while in Ephesus. Scholars such as John A. T. Robinson, Henry C. Thiessen, A. T. Robertson, Douglas Moo, Leon Morris, and D. A. Carson all concur that 1 Corinthians was written in the mid 50's AD.[528]

---

[526]Moreland, 148.

[527]Henry Thiessen, *Introduction to the New Testament* (Grand Rapids: William B. Eerdmans Publishing Company, 1987), 205.

[528]John A. T. Robinson, *Redating the New Testament* (SCM Press, 1976), 54. Thiessen,

If 55AD is the approximate date for the composition of 1 Corinthians, then the ancient creed quoted by Paul in 1 Corinthians 15:3-8 had to originate before this date. However, there is strong evidence found in the creed itself that points to its development at a much earlier time.

Habermas discusses at least eight pieces of evidence from within the creed that indicate a very early date.[529] First, the terms "delivered" and "received" have been shown to be technical rabbinic terms used for the passing on of sacred tradition. Second, Paul admitted that this statement was not his own creation and that he had received it from others. Third, scholars agree that some of the words in the creed are non-Pauline terms and are clearly Jewish. These phrases include "for our sins," "according to the Scriptures," "He has been raised," "the third day," "He was seen," and "the twelve." Fourth, the creed is organized into a stylized and parallel form; it appears to have been an oral creed or hymn in the early church. Fifth, the creed shows evidence of being of a Semitic origin and, thus, points to a source that predates Paul's translation of it into Greek. This can be seen in the use of "Cephas" for Peter, for "Cephas" is Aramaic for Peter (which is Petros in the Greek). Moreland notes additional evidence for the Semitic origin of this creed by relating that the poetic style of the creed is clearly Hebraic.[530] Sixth, Habermas reasons that Paul probably received this creed around 36-38AD, just three years after his conversion, when he met with

---

205. A. T. Robertson, *Word Pictures in the New Testament*, vol. 4. (Grand Rapids: Baker Book House, 1931), 16. D. A. Carson, Douglas J. Moo, and Leon Morris, *An Introduction to the New Testament* (Grand Rapids: Zondervan Publishing House, 1992), 283.

[529]Habermas, *Historical Jesus*, 152-157.

[530]Moreland, 150.

Peter and James in Jerusalem (as recorded by Paul in Galatians 1:18-19). Jesus' death occurred around 30AD, and Paul was converted between 33 and 35AD. Seventh, Habermas states that, due to the above information, "numerous critical theologians" date the creed "from three to eight years after Jesus' crucifixion."[531] Eighth, since it would have taken a period of time for the beliefs to become formalized into a creed or hymn, the beliefs behind the creed must date back to the event itself.

As mentioned above, the antiquity of this creed is almost universally accepted across the theological spectrum of New Testament scholarship. A brief list of some of the world's leading New Testament scholars, past and present, who date the origin of this creed to the early 30's AD (just a few years after the crucifixion) will suffice: Gerd Luedemann, Marcus Borg, Reginald Fuller, Oscar Cullman, Wolfhart Panneberg, Martin Hengel, Hans Conzelman, C. H. Dodd, A. M. Hunter, James Dunn, N. T. Wright, Richard Bauckham, Rudolph Bultmann, Raymond E. Brown, Larry Hurtado, Joachim Jeremias, Norman Perrin, George E. Ladd, and Willi Marxsen.[532] Again, this list of New Testament scholars covers the theological spectrum. Some are evangelical, or at least fairly conservative in their theology and view of the Bible, while others are rather liberal in their theological and biblical perspective. Virtually, all the world's leading New Testament scholars, despite their theological perspectives, date this creed to the early 30's AD.

Habermas has provided strong evidence that the creed of 1 Corinthians 15:3-8 originated between three to eight years after Christ's crucifixion, and that the beliefs which underlie

---

[531]Habermas, *Historical Jesus*, 154.

[532]Ibid., 154-155.

this creed must therefore go back to the event itself. Next, Habermas examines the content of this ancient creed.

First, the creed, as stated in this passage, mentions the death and burial of Christ. Second, it states that Christ was raised on the third day. Third, it lists several post-resurrection appearances of Christ. These include appearances to Peter, to the twelve apostles, to over 500 persons at one time, to James (the Lord's brother), to all the apostles, and, finally an appearance to Paul himself.

It should be noted that scholars differ as to the exact contents of this ancient creed in its most primitive form. Habermas believes that Paul added verse eight (detailing his own eyewitness account) to the original creed, as well as a portion of verse six (a reminder that most of the 500 witnesses were still alive). This in no way lessons the force of this ancient creed. In fact, it strengthens it as evidence for the resurrection, for Paul adds his own testimony and encourages his readers to question the many eyewitnesses still living in his day. Even scholars who disagree with this view still accept a large enough portion of the creed for it to be considered a valuable piece of eyewitness evidence for the resurrection of Christ from the dead.

The early date of the 1 Corinthians 15 creed proves that the resurrection accounts found in the New Testament are not legends. Christian philosopher William Lane Craig, another colleague of Gary Habermas, appealed to the work of the great Roman historian A. N. Sherwin-White and stated that "even two generations is too short a time span to allow legendary tendencies to wipe out the hard core of historical facts."[533] If two generations is not enough time for legends to

[533]William Lane Craig, *Reasonable Faith* (Wheaton: Crossway Books, 1984), 285.

develop, then there is no way that a resurrection legend could emerge in only three to eight years.

It should also be noted that, in this creed, Paul is placing his apostolic credentials on the line by encouraging his Corinthian critics to check out his account with the eyewitnesses who were still alive. These eyewitnesses not only included over 500 people, but also Peter, James, and the other apostles—the recognized leaders of the early church (Galatians 2:9). It is highly improbable that Paul would fabricate the creed and jeopardize his own position in the early church.

Finally, it should be obvious to any open-minded person who examines the evidence that Paul was a man of integrity. He was not lying. Not only did he put his reputation and position in the early church on the line, but he was also willing to suffer and die for Christ. Men do not die for what they know to be a hoax. Paul was a reliable and sincere witness to the resurrection of Christ.

Hence, the creed of 1 Corinthians 15:3-8 provides us with reliable eyewitness testimony for the bodily resurrection of Jesus Christ. Not only did Paul testify that he had seen the risen Christ, but he also identified many other witnesses to the resurrection that could have been interrogated. Contrary to the futile speculations of radical scholars, Paul was not devising myths behind closed doors. No, from the beginning he was preaching a risen Savior who had conquered death and the grave, a risen Savior who had met him on the road to Damascus and changed his life forever.

Habermas notes that the ancient creed of 1 Corinthians 15:3-8 is an example of the type of evidence that has convinced virtually all the world's leading New Testament scholars that the lives of the apostles, Paul, and James (the brother of Jesus) were radically transformed by what they believed were post-resurrection appearances of Jesus.

Scholars agree that the apostles were transformed from cowardly men who fled and hid on the night Jesus was executed to courageous men willing to suffer and die for Christ. They proclaimed Jesus as the Jewish Messiah; yet, Jesus died before Israel was delivered from her pagan enemies—the Romans. When a self-proclaimed Messiah dies, his movement dies with him. When Jesus died, His Messiah movement died as well. Yet, fifty days later, at the Feast of Pentecost, it came back to life. Since a dead Messiah cannot rescue Israel from her enemies, the Messiah must have come back to life as well. The resurrection strengthened the faith of the apostles to the point that they were willing to suffer and die for Jesus.

New Testament scholars agree that Paul was a leading persecutor of the early church. However, within a few years of the crucifixion, he was radically changed. The persecutor of the church became its greatest missionary and theologian, and one of its greatest leaders. Only Jesus' post-resurrection appearance to Paul on the Road to Damascus (Acts 9) adequately explains this radical transformation, a transformation that led to much suffering and, eventually, martyrdom.

James was an orthodox Jew and one of Jesus' brothers. During Jesus' public ministry, James was not a believer. In fact, he mocked his brother and may have even questioned his brother's sanity (John 7:3-5; Mark 3:31-35; 6:3; Matthew 13:55). This is embarassing material—the Gospels would not report this rejection of Jesus by His brothers unless it were true. Yet, in less than fifty days after the crucifixion, James became one of the most respected leaders in Jesus' church (Acts 1:14; Galatians 1:18-19; 2:9). What brought about such a drastic and abrupt change? Only Jesus' resurrection and appearance to James adequately explains how the mocking brother became a bold and courageous follower of his brother.

In 62 AD, James was stoned to death for preaching his brother Jesus was the Jewish Messiah.

We must also remember that when we speak of Jesus' resurrection, we are talking about a *bodily resurrection*. Many people misunderstand Paul's phrase "spiritual body" in 1 Corinthians 15. They mistake this phrase for signifying some type of immaterial spirit. However, this is not the case. In the Greek, the phrase is "soma pneumatikon." The word soma almost always refers to a physical body. Still, in this passage this physical body is somehow described as being "spiritual" (pneumatikon). But, the spiritual body is contrasted with the natural body. The natural body refers to the physical body before physical death. The Greek words for natural body are "soma psuchikon." Literally, this phrase means a "soulish body." The word soul usually carries with it the idea of immateriality, but, in this passage, it cannot. It is referring to the human body before death, and, the human body is of course physical, despite the adjective "soulish." Therefore, if the "soulish body" is physical, then there should be no difficulty viewing the "spiritual body" as also being physical. The soulish body is sown (buried) at death, but, this same body is raised as a spiritual body; it receives new powers. It is no longer a natural body; it is a supernatural body. The body is changed, but it is still the same body. For, the body that was sown (buried) is the same body that will be raised. Gary Habermas discussed Christ's spiritual body in the following words:

> . . . the Gospels and Paul agree on an important fact: the resurrected Jesus had a new spiritual body. The Gospels never present Jesus walking out of the tomb. . . when the stone is rolled away, Jesus does not walk out the way He does in apocryphal literature. He's already gone, so He presumably exited through

the rock. Later He appears in buildings and then disappears at will. The Gospels clearly say that Jesus was raised in a spiritual body. It was His real body, but it was changed, including new, spiritual qualities.[534]

Paul is using the term spiritual body to contrast it with the natural body. He is making the point that Christ's body after the resurrection (and ours too) has different characteristics to it than it did before. . . But the point is made very clearly that what is being talked about is the same body, the contrast here is not between physical body and spiritual body, but rather between the same body in different states or with different characteristics.[535]

Walter Martin, the foremost authority on non-Christian cults during his lifetime, also discussed Christ's spiritual body in his greatest work, *Kingdom of the Cults*:

However, Christ had a "spiritual body" (1 Corinthians 15:50, 53) in His glorified state, identical in form to His earthly body, but immortal, and thus capable of entering the dimension of earth or heaven with no violation to the laws of either one.[536]

---

[534]Gary R. Habermas and Antony Flew, *Did Jesus Rise From the Dead?* (San Francisco: Harper and Row Publishers, 1987), 58.

[535]Ibid., 95.

[536]Walter Martin, *Kingdom of the Cults* (Minneapolis: Bethany House Publishers, 1977), 86.

Therefore, Christ rose in the same body in which He lived and died. However, His body had been changed in the "twinkling of an eye" (1 Corinthians 15:50-53) so that His mortal body (a body capable of death) was glorified and became immortal (incapable of death). In His spiritual body, He can apparently travel at the speed of thought, unhindered by distance. The Bible teaches that in the first resurrection all believers will receive glorified bodies. Believers' bodies will be changed into glorified and immortal bodies. The presence of sin will be totally removed from them (1 Corinthians 15:50-53).

There are several good arguments that Jesus' resurrection was bodily—it was not merely a spiritual resurrection. First, as the British New Testament scholar N. T, Wright points out, the Greek words for resurrection (anistemi, anastasis, eigero, etc.), in the first century ad, always meant a reanimation of a corpse, the raising back to life of a dead body. Even those who denied the reality of resurrection always used these words to refer to bodily resurrection when denying the reality of resurrection.[537]

Second, Paul was a Pharisee (Philippiand 3:5). The Pharisees believed in the concept of physical resurrection—they believed that the children of God would be bodily raised from the dead on the last day. A non-bodily resurrection is an oxymoron.

Third, Paul believed in life after death, and that life after death started immediately following death for the believer (2 Corinthians 5:8; Philippians 1:23). But, resurrection is something that occurred *after* life after death. For instance, the creed of 1 Corinthians 15:3-8 states that

---

[537]N. T. Wright, *The Resurrection of the Son of God* (Minneapolis: Fortress Press, 2003), 31, 147-148.

Jesus died, was buried, and then was raised "on the third day" (vs. 4). So, as N. T. Wright says, resurrection is "life after life-after-death." The difference between life after death and "life after life-after-death" is that the former is non-bodily existence, while the latter is bodily existence. Hence, the first-century AD concept of resurrection was bodily.[538]

Fourth, the Old Testament concept of resurrection (Daniel 12; Ezekiel 37; Isaish 26:19), which was inherited by the early church, was clearly that of bodily resurrection. Fifth, Paul's writings reveal that when he spoke of resurrection he meant bodily resurrection (1 Thessalonians 4:13-18; Philippians 3:21). Sixth, 1 Corinthains 15:42-44, speaking about the resurrection body, says that that which is sown or buried is that which is raised—the same thing that is buried (i.e., the body) is the same thing that is raised (i.e., the body). Seventh, if Paul denied the bodily resurrection and was trying to proclaim a spiritual resurrection, why not say "it is sown a soma (body), but it is raised a pneuma (spirit)?"

And, finally, the Gospel accounts of Jesus post-resurrection appearances, according to N. T. Wright, are not very theologically developed. These accounts are certainly much less theologically developed than Paul's discussions of Jesus' resurrection in his letters. Paul draws a lot of theological data from Jesus' resurrection—this implies he thought deeply about the theological implications of Jesus' resurrection. This is not the case in the Gospels—the resurrection and appearances are merely reported as historical incidents. Wright argues that this shows that the resurrection accounts in the Gospels predate Paul's writings. Since Paul began to write around 50 AD, the Gospel accounts of Jesus'

---

[538]Ibid., 31.

resurrection and appearances must predate 50 AD.[539] Yet, in these early accounts, Jesus is reported to have bodily appeared to His disciples. He still had the scars in His hands, feet, and side. He encouraged the apostles to touch Him; He even ate food with them (John 20:26-29; Luke 24: 36-43). Together, these eight points make it clear that the early church proclaimed and believed that Jesus bodily rose from the dead.

THE FAILURE OF NATURALISTIC THEORIES

One final issue needs to be mentioned to seal Habermas' case for Christ's bodily resurrection: the failure of naturalistic theories. All alternative, non-supernatural explanations of the resurrection data fail to explain the almost universally accepted data we have mentioned. This is why the naturalistic theories of Jesus' resurrection are not popular today—they fail to explain the agreed-upon data.

The stolen body theory fails because the disciples were sincere enough in their belief that Jesus rose from the dead that they were willing to die for that belief. Men do not die for what they know to be a hoax; hence, the disciples did not steal the body and fabricate the resurrection accounts.[540]

But what if others stole the body without the disciples knowledge? This would explain the empty tomb, but not the experiences the apostles had in which they believe they saw the risen Christ numerous times. The stolen body theory simply does not adequately explain the historical data accepted by the vast majority of New Testament scholars.[541]

---

[539]Antony Flew, *There is a God* (New York: Harper Collins Publishers, 2007), 202-209.

[540]Habermas and Licona, 93-95.

[541]Ibid., 95-97.

The wrong tomb theory fails. This alternative "explanation" speculates that maybe the women went to the wrong tomb and found it empty. They then told the disciples, who visited the same wrong tomb, also finding it empty. As a result, the disciples mistakenly proclaimed Jesus as risen from the dead. This alternative explanation fails due to the fact that the empty tomb alone did not convince the disciples that Jesus rose. They were persuaded that Jesus rose from the dead when they had experiences in which they believed He appeared to them alive from the dead. The wrong tomb theory does not explain the apostles' experiences of the post-resurrection Christ.[542]

The swoon theory is the idea that maybe Jesus merely passed out on the cross; He did not actually die. Maybe, He was revived in the tomb and was some how able to remove the large stone covering the mouth of the tomb. He then somehow travelled on scarred feet on rocky ground and appeared to His disciples. They mistook Him for risen and proclaimed Him as the Lord. This explanation fails for several reasons. First, the Roman soldier confirmed Jesus was dead with his spear thrust to Jesus' side. The Romans would confirm death before removing bodies from crosses. Second, due to the rigors of the Roman scourging and crucifixion, assuming Jesus was alive in the tomb, He would have almost certainly died due to His wounds while staying in a cold, damp tomb. Third, John records that when Jesus' side was pierced, blood and water flowed from His side. Modern medical science has proven that this only happens when the side of a corpse has been punctured—Jesus was already dead when His side was pierced. This was confirmed in the March, 1986 edition of the *Journal of the American Medical Association*. Fourth, even if

---

[542]Ibid. 97-98.

we ignore all the above evidence against the swoon theory, it is hard to believe that the apostles would have seen Jesus in His dire, unhealthy state, and then proclaim Him as the risen Savior who has conquered death! No, they would have sought medical attention for a severely beaten, dying friend. For these reasons and others, virtually no scholars promote the swoon theory today.[543]

Finally, the hallucination theory also fails to adequately explain the resurrection data. This view supposes that the apostles never saw the risen Christ; they merely hallucinated on numerous occassions, thinking they had seen Jesus alive from the dead. There are many problems with this theory. First, hallucinations occur inside a person's mind. Hence, no two people (let alone the apostles or over 500 people at one time) can share the same hallucination. Yet, Jesus appeared to groups of people on numerous occassions. Second, people who have hallucinations are easily convinced by others that they are mistaken. They are certainly not willing to suffer and die for their hallucinations. Third, the hallucination theory does not explain the empty tomb. Since there is good evidence for the empty tomb, this also counts against the hallucination theory. Once again, few scholars

---

[543]Ibid., 99-103. For Habermas' statement concerning the *JAMA* article, see David Baggett, ed. *Did the Resurrection Happen? A Conversation with Gary Habermas and Antony Flew* (Downers Grove: Inter-Varsity Press, 2009), 25-26. Habermas notes that the three scholars who wrote the article on Jesus' death concluded that "Jesus died due to asphyxiation, complicated by shock and congestive heart failure." The journal article Habermas referred to is: William D. Edwards, Wesley J. Gabel, and Floyd Hosmer, "On the Physical Death of Jesus Christ," *Journal of the American Medical Association 255* (March 1986), pp. 1455-1463.

today entertain the hallucination theory.[544] Therefore, the most historically plausible explanation for the data in question is that Jesus of Nazareth did in fact bodily rise from the dead. Habermas' historical case for Jesus' bodliy resurrection is on solid epistemological ground.

CLASSIFYING HABERMAS' APOLOGETIC METHODOLOGY

Gary Habermas is willing to provide evidence for God's existence—he does so in the seminary classes he teaches as well as in some of his writings.[545] However, unlike the classical apologists, he does not believe that one must first present evidence for God's existence before presenting historical evidence for Christianity. In fact, Habermas believes that Jesus' resurrection is itself evidence for Jesus' theistic world view. In other words, Habermas believes Jesus' resurrection can be used as evidence for God.[546]

Hence, Habermas can not be classified as a classical apologist. Instead, he is an evidentialist; he can also be called a historical apologist. I use the terms interchangeably. His primary apologetic case for Christianity deals with historical evidences for Jesus' deity and resurrection. Habermas is not to be faulted for focusing almost exclusively on historical evidence for Jesus, for his dedication to researching the

---

[544]Gary R. Habermas, *The Resurrection of Jesus* (Lanham: University Press of America, 1984), 26-27. See also Habermas and Licona, 105-109.

[545]Terry L. Miethe and Gary R. Habermas, *Why Believe? God Exists!* (Joplin: College Press, 1993), 15-170.

[546]Habermas, *The Resurrection of Jesus*, 67-75.

evidence for Jesus' resurrection has done a great service for the cause of the Gospel in these "post-Christian" days.

Chapter 14

Gordon Clark's Dogmatic Presuppositionalism

Gordon Haddon Clark (1902-1985) was one of the greatest Christian thinkers of the twentieth century. He was the Chairman of the Philosophy Department at Butler University for 28 years.[547] He and Cornelius Van Til, although they disagreed on many points, were the two leading proponents of the presuppositional method of apologetics. In this chapter, Clark's apologetic methodology will be examined, and its strengths and weaknesses will be discussed.

CLARK'S REJECTION OF TRADITIONAL APOLOGETICS

Gordon Clark rejected the idea that unaided human reason could arrive at truths about God. Due to this fact, he rejected traditional apologetics. Clark stated that "The cosmological argument for the existence of God, most fully

---

[547]Gordon H. Clark, *Clark Speaks From the Grave* (Jefferson: The Trinity Foundation, 1986), 2.

developed by Thomas Aquinas, is a fallacy. It is not possible to begin with sensory experience and proceed by the formal laws of logic to God's existence as a conclusion."[548] After listing several reasons why he rejected the Thomistic arguments for God's existence, Clark added that even if the arguments were valid, they would only prove the existence of a lesser god, not the true God of the Bible.[549]

Clark not only despised the use of philosophical arguments to provide evidence for God's existence, but he also deplored the utilization of historical evidences in defense of Christianity. Clark reminded his readers that the facts of history do not come with their own built-in interpretation. He stated that "Significance, interpretation, evaluation is not given in any fact; it is an intellectual judgment based on some non-sensory criterion."[550]

Clark declared that while the conclusions of science constantly change, scriptural truth remains the same.[551] Therefore, believers should not rely on observable facts to prove Christianity. Instead, Christians must presuppose the truth of God's Word and allow revelation to interpret the facts of history for them.[552]

The reason behind Clark's distaste for traditional apologetics was his belief that unaided human reason could never discover any truth, religious or secular. This, Clark

---

[548]Gordon H. Clark, *Religion, Reason and Revelation* (Jefferson: The Trinity Foundation, 1986), 35.

[549]Ibid., 37.

[550]Clark, *Clark Speaks From the Grave*, 54.

[551]Ibid., 55.

[552]Ibid., 57.

believed, should convince a person of his need to presuppose the truth of the Christian revelation.[553] Without this presupposition, man cannot find truth. Clark emphasized this point at the conclusion of his textbook on the history of philosophy. He stated, "Does this mean that philosophers and cultural epochs are nothing but children who pay their fare to take another ride on the merry-go-round? Is this Nietzsche's eternal recurrence? Or, could it be that a choice must be made between skeptical futility and a word from God?"[554]

CLARK'S REJECTION OF EMPIRICISM

Empiricism is the attempt to find truth through the five senses. This school of thought believes "that all knowledge begins in sense experience."[555] According to Clark, Thomas Aquinas was an empiricist. Aquinas believed that "all knowledge must be abstracted out of our sensations."[556] Aquinas believed that each person begins life with his mind as a blank slate. He held that "everything that is in the mind was first in the senses, except the mind itself."[557] Although Aquinas believed that God created man's mind with the innate ability to know things and draw rational conclusions from

---

[553]Geisler, *Christian Apologetics*, 37.

[554]Gordon H. Clark, *Thales to Dewey* (Jefferson: The Trinity Foundation, 1989), 534.

[555]Norman L. Geisler and Paul D. Feinberg, *Introduction to Philosophy: A Christian Perspective* (Grand Rapids: Baker Book House, 1985), 431.

[556]Gordon H. Clark, *Three Types of Religious Philosophy* (Jefferson: The Trinity Foundation, 1989), 60-61.

[557]Geisler, *Thomas Aquinas*, 86.

sense data, Clark does not seem to do justice to this aspect of Aquinas' thought.[558] Instead, he merely attacks the idea that man could argue from sense data to the existence of God.

Clark turns next to William Paley. Paley argued from the evidence of design in the universe to the existence of an intelligent God as its Cause. Therefore, he, like Aquinas, began with sense experience and then argued to the existence of God. Clark agreed with the criticisms made by David Hume concerning the teleological argument (the argument for God's existence from design). Hume stated that experience cannot determine if there was one God or several gods who designed the world. Second, since the physical world is finite, nothing in man's experience tells him that its designer must be infinite. And third, since human experience includes such things as natural disasters, might not the world's designer be an evil being?[559]

Clark pointed out that Hume himself was an empiricist. But Hume was consistent in his thinking. Therefore, he realized that the principle of cause and effect, the existence of external bodies, and the reality of internal selves could not be proven through sense data alone. Therefore, Hume admitted that his empiricism inevitably led to skepticism.[560]

Clark emphasized the point that there is a wide gap between basic sense experience and the propositional conclusions made by empiricists.[561] Sense data (the facts of experience) do not come with their own built-in interpretation.

---

[558]Ibid.

[559]Clark, *Three Types of Religious Philosophy*, 64-70.

[560]Ibid., 71, 76-78.

[561]Ibid., 91.

Rational conclusions cannot come from sense experience alone. Empiricism, therefore, fails as a truth-finding method. Next, Gordon Clark turned his attention to rationalism.

CLARK'S REJECTION OF RATIONALISM

Rationalism is the attempt to find truth through reason alone. Though Clark admitted that Augustine was not a pure rationalist, he discussed his views of reason.[562] At a time when Greek philosophy was dominated by skepticism, which argued against the possibility of attaining knowledge, Augustine attempted to find a base for knowledge that could not be denied.[563] Augustine declared that "the skeptic must exist in order to doubt his own existence." Augustine therefore reasoned that even the skeptic should be certain of his existence. Augustine also showed that skeptics could not live like knowledge was impossible.[564]

Augustine also held that the laws of logic were universal, eternal, and unchanging truths. Since the human mind is limited and changing, it could not be the ultimate source of these eternal truths. Hence, there must be an eternal and unchanging Mind as their source. Obviously, this eternal Mind is God.[565]

Clark critiqued the views of Anselm. Anselm was even more rationalistic in his thought than Augustine. He believed that the existence of God could be proven through reason alone. Anselm referred to God as the greatest conceivable

---

[562]Ibid., 27.

[563]Ibid., 28-29.

[564]Ibid., 31.

[565]Ibid., 32.

Being. Therefore, if God does not exist, then one could conceive of a being greater than Him, a being that has the same attributes but does exist. But then this would be the greatest conceivable Being. Therefore, God (the greatest conceivable Being) must necessarily exist.[566] This is called the ontological argument for God's existence.

Clark wrote that Rene Descartes, also a rationalist, viewed sensation and experience as very deceptive. He attempted to find a single point of certainty by doubting everything until he found something he could not doubt. Through this process, he realized that the more he doubted, the more certain he became of the existence of himself, the doubter.[567]

Descartes borrowed Anselm's ontological argument for God's existence. Clark stated Descartes' version of this argument as follows: "God, by definition, is the being who possesses all perfections; existence is a perfection; therefore God exists."[568]

Clark related that Spinoza also used the ontological argument for God's existence. But Spinoza's version of the argument did not conclude with the God of the Bible. Instead he "proved" the existence of a god who is the universe (the god of pantheism).[569] However, this raised questions as to rationalism's claim to prove the existence of God with certainty, for Spinoza's god and Descartes' God cannot both exist. Spinoza was also more consistent in his rationalism than was Descartes. Spinoza realized that if all knowledge could be

---

[566]Ibid., 33-35.

[567]Clark, *Religion, Reason and Revelation*, 50-51.

[568]Clark, *Three Types of Religious Philosophy*, 35.

[569]Clark, *Thales to Dewey*, 332.

found through reason alone, then supernatural revelation is without value.[570]

Gordon Clark listed several problems with rationalism in his writings. He stated that rationalism has historically led to several contradictory conclusions (theism, pantheism, and atheism).[571] Also, Clark stated that "rationalism does not produce first principles out of something else: The first principles are innate . . . Every philosophy must have its first principles . . . Thus a presuppositionless description is impossible."[572] Although Clark made much use of reason in his own defense of the faith, he presupposed his first principles. He contended that without doing this, reason can never get off the ground.[573]

CLARK'S REJECTION OF IRRATIONALISM

In discussing the history of philosophy, Clark stated that "Hume had reduced empiricism to skepticism."[574] Immanuel Kant's views left man with a knowledge of "things-as-they-appear-to-us," but with no real knowledge of "things-in-themselves."[575] Clark emphasized this point with the following words: "In his view the uninformed sense data are entirely incoherent. Order is introduced into them by the mind

---

[570]Clark, *Religion, Reason and Revelation*, 53.

[571]Clark, *Three Types of Religious Philosophy*, 56.

[572]Ibid., 117-118.

[573]Ibid., 120.

[574]Ibid., 93.

[575]Clark, *Religion, Reason and Revelation*, 62.

alone, and what the real world might be like. . . remains unknowable. The whole Postkantian development from Jacobi to Hegel convicts Kant of skepticism."[576]

Clark added that though Hegel effectively critiqued Kant, Hegelianism also failed to justify knowledge.[577] In Hegel's theory of the unfolding of history, truth was seen as relative. What was true yesterday is not necessarily true today.[578] In short, the greatest minds the world has ever known have failed to escape skepticism. The philosophy of man cannot even prove that man can know anything. Empiricism and rationalism have both failed. This has caused some thinkers to accept irrationalism as the method of finding meaning to life. One such thinker was Soren Kierkegaard.

Kierkegaard denied the effectiveness of both reason and sense experience in finding truth. He believed that a man must stop reasoning. Only through a blind leap of faith can man find true meaning in life. An individual's subjective passion is of more importance than objective truth. Kierkegaard believed that the doctrines of Christianity were absurd and contradictory. Still, he chose to believe against all reason.[579]

Clark rejected the irrationalism of Kierkegaard even though it had become so widespread among modern thinkers, both secular and religious. Clark stated of Kierkegaard, "The fatal flaw is his rejection of logic. When once a man commits

---

[576]Gordon H. Clark, *A Christian View of Men and Things* (Jefferson: The Trinity Foundation, 1991), 315-316.

[577]Clark, *Religion, Reason and Revelation,* 63-68.

[578]Ibid., 98.

[579]Clark, *Three Types of Religious Philosophy*, 101-105.

himself to contradictions, his language, and therefore his recommendations to other people, become meaningless."[580]

As shown above, Gordon Clark rejected empiricism, rationalism, and irrationalism. He taught that they all eventually reduce to skepticism. Man has failed to find truth through these methodologies. Therefore, man, according to Clark, must make a choice between skepticism and a word from God.[581] Clark's method of finding truth is called presuppositionalism or dogmatism.

CLARK'S VIEW: DOGMATISM

When one finds that Clark saw all of secular philosophy as unable to justify knowledge, one might assume that Clark was himself a skeptic. But this was not the case. Skeptical futility is not the only option left. Clark referred to his view of finding truth as dogmatism. Clark argued that if all other philosophical systems cannot give meaning to life, then dogmatism is worth a try. Clark recommended that one dogmatically presuppose the truth of the teachings of Scripture.[582]

Clark's view may seem to some to be fideism. But this is not so (according to Clark). For everyone, no matter what their philosophical system may be, must presuppose something.[583] The rationalist must presuppose his first principles. Otherwise, he must look for reasons for everything.

---

[580]Ibid., 114.

[581]Clark, *Thales to Dewey*, 534.

[582]Clark, *Three Types of Religious Philosophy*, 116.

[583]Ibid., 118.

225

This would result in an infinite regress, and there would be no real base for knowledge.[584]

The empiricist must assume certain concepts which he cannot prove through sense experience. Such concepts as time, space, equality, causality, and motion are not derived from sense experience. They are brought into one's sense experience in the beginning to aid one in drawing conclusions from the sense data.[585] Logical Positivism is an extreme empirical view. One of its first principles is that truth can only be found through the five senses. However, this first principle refutes itself since it cannot itself be proven through the five senses.[586]

Clark argued that since rationalism and empiricism have failed to make life meaningful, Christian presuppositions should be utilized. For Christian presuppositions do give meaning to life.[587] Clark argued that "Christian Theism is self-consistent and that several other philosophies are inconsistent, skeptical, and therefore erroneous."[588] Clark added that Christianity "gives meaning to life and morality, and that it supports the existence of truth and the possibility of knowledge."[589]

One can see Clark's point more clearly by examining his critique of Kant. In Kant's thinking, there existed no order

---

[584]Ibid., 51-52.

[585]Ibid., 70-91.

[586]Ibid., 118-119.

[587]Clark, *A Christian View of Men and Things*, 324.

[588]Ibid.

[589]Ibid.

in sense data. Instead the mind introduces this order into the sense data. Therefore, Kant's view collapses into skepticism since one can only know things-as-they-appear-to-us and not things-as-they-are. One cannot know the real world. One can only know the world as it appears to him.[590]

Clark's response to Kant's dilemma is as follows. Clark presupposes the truth of the revelation found in Scripture. Therefore, Clark presupposes that "God has fashioned both the mind and the world so that they harmonize."[591] If one presupposes the truth of Christianity, then the order that the mind innately reads into the real world is the order which really exists in the real world.

Having discussed Clark's view of obtaining knowledge, one must now consider how Clark defended Christianity. Clark did this by convincing the nonbeliever that he is contradicting himself.[592] Clark was willing to use logic (the law of noncontradiction) to refute the belief systems of others. He did not feel that he was being inconsistent with his presuppositionalism or dogmatism, for Clark believed that God is Logic. In other words, logic is God-thinking. It flows naturally from God's Being.[593] In fact, Clark even translated

---

[590]Ibid., 315-316.

[591]Ibid., 316.

[592]Clark, *Three Types of Religious Philosophy*, 140-142.

[593]R. C. Sproul, John Gerstner, and Arthur Lindsley, *Classical Apologetics: A Rational Defense of the Christian Faith and a Critique of Presuppositional Apologetics* (Grand Rapids: Zondervan Books, 1984), 76.

John 1:1 as, "In the beginning was Logic, and Logic was with God, and Logic was God."[594]

The problem with rationalism is that it lacks sufficient first principles. But, according to Clark, once one presupposes the truth of the Bible, one can use reason to tear down the views of others. Clark spoke of reason in the following manner:

> Therefore I wish to suggest that we neither abandon reason nor use it unaided; but on pain of skepticism acknowledge a verbal, propositional revelation of fixed truth from God. Only by accepting rationally comprehensible information on God's authority can we hope to have a sound philosophy and a true religion.[595]

Clark not only defended the faith by tearing down other belief systems through use of the law of contradiction, but he (after presupposing the truth of Christianity) also was willing to confirm the truth of Christianity in two ways. First, Clark showed that it alone is self-consistent. And second, he appealed to its ability to provide man with meaning to life, moral values, and the genuine possibility of attaining true knowledge.[596] Since all other philosophies have failed to obtain knowledge, one must choose between skepticism and presupposing Christian revelation.[597]

---

[594]Ibid.

[595]Clark, *Religion, Reason and Revelation*, 87.

[596]Clark, *A Christian View of Men and Things*, 324.

[597]Clark, *Religion, Reason and Revelation*, 109-110.

Still, Clark seemed to revert back to fideism. This was due to his hyper-Calvinistic theology. He firmly believed that one really cannot convince another of the truth of Christianity, for God alone sovereignly bestows faith upon an individual.[598] When answering the question of why one person presupposes the Bible to be true and not the Muslim Koran, he simply replied that "God causes the one to believe."[599]

CLARK'S SOLUTION TO THE PROBLEM OF EVIL

In his writings, Gordon Clark attempted to answer the question, "How can the existence of God be harmonized with the existence of evil?"[600] If God is all-good, He would want to destroy evil. If God is all-powerful, He is able to destroy evil. But evil still exists. It seems that God cannot be both all-good and all-powerful. However, Christianity teaches that He is both. This is the problem of evil.[601]

Zoroastrianism attempts to resolve the problem by teaching that there are two gods. One is good while the other is evil. Neither of the two gods is infinite since they have both failed to destroy the opposing god. Plato's views also result in an unresolved dualism. In his thought, God is not the creator of all things. There exists eternal and chaotic space which the Demiurge cannot control.[602]

---

[598]Clark, *Three Types of Religious Philosophy*, 138.

[599]Ibid., 139.

[600]Clark, *Religion, Reason and Revelation*, 195.

[601]Ibid.

[602]Ibid., 195-196.

According to Clark, even Augustine's answer to the dilemma was inadequate. Clark stated that Augustine taught that evil is metaphysically unreal. It does not exist. Therefore, all that God created is good since evil is non-being.[603] (Whether or not Clark treated Augustine's view fairly will be discussed at a later point in this chapter.)

Clark pointed out that Augustine added to his response the doctrine of human free will. Though God is all-powerful, He has sovereignly chosen to give mankind free will. God allows man to make his own choices. Mankind has chosen evil. Therefore, all that God created is good. Evil can be blamed not on God, but on the abuse of free will by man.[604]

But Clark rejected this view of free will. Clark believed that the Bible does not teach that man is free to choose that which is right as opposed to that which is wrong. Clark stated that "free will is not only futile, but false. Certainly, if the Bible is the Word of God, free will is false; for the Bible consistently denies free will."[605]

Though Clark rejected the doctrine of free will, he believed man has free agency. "Free will means there is no determining factor operating on the will, not even God. Free will means that either of two incompatible actions are equally possible."[606] This Clark rejected. On the other hand, "Free agency goes with the view that all choices are inevitable. The liberty that the Westminster Confession ascribes to the will is a liberty from compulsion, coaction, or force of inanimate

---

[603]Ibid., 196.

[604]Ibid., 199.

[605]Ibid., 206.

[606]Ibid., 227.

objects; it is not a liberty from the power of God."[607] Clark argued that a man can still be responsible for his actions even without the freedom to do other than he has done. Clark stated that, "a man is responsible if he must answer for what he does . . . a person is responsible if he can be justly rewarded or punished for his deeds. This implies, of course, that he must be answerable to someone."[608]

Clark then asked the question, "Is it just then for God to punish a man for deeds that God Himself 'determined before to be done?'"[609] He answered in the affirmative. He stated that, "Whatever God does is just."[610] Man is responsible to God; but God is responsible to no one. Clark openly admitted that his view makes God the cause of sin. For, in his thinking, "God is the sole ultimate cause of everything."[611] But, while God is the ultimate cause of sin, He is not the author of sin. The author is the immediate cause of an action. Man is the immediate cause of his sin. But he was not free to do otherwise. For God is the ultimate cause of sin.[612]

Clark stated that, "God's causing a man to sin is not sin. There is no law, superior to God, which forbids him to decree sinful acts. Sin presupposes a law, for sin is lawlessness."[613] Clark explained that "God is above law"

---

[607]Ibid.

[608]Ibid., 231.

[609]Ibid.

[610]Ibid., 232-233.

[611]Ibid., 237-238.

[612]Ibid., 237-239.

because "the laws that God imposes on men do not apply to the divine nature."[614] Clark stated:

Man is responsible because God calls him to account; man is responsible because the supreme power can punish him for disobedience. God, on the contrary, cannot be responsible for the plain reason that there is no power superior to him; no greater being can hold him accountable; no one can punish him; there is no one to whom God is responsible; there are no laws which he could disobey. The sinner therefore, and not God, is responsible; the sinner alone is the author of sin. Man has no free will, for salvation is purely of grace; and God is sovereign.[615]

This was Clark's proposed solution to the problem of evil. God is in fact the ultimate cause of sin. But He is not evil, for He committed no sin. And He is not responsible for sin, for there is no one to whom He is responsible. God is just, for whatever He does is just. Therefore, the creature has no right to stand in judgment over his Creator.

STRENGTHS OF CLARK'S PRESUPPOSITIONALISM

Gordon Clark, as this study shows, was a very original thinker. Even if one disagrees with much of what he has written, he has made a tremendous contribution to Christian thought that should not be overlooked. There are several strengths which are evident in the thought of Gordon Clark.

His rejection of pure rationalism. Clark is absolutely correct when he points out the major deficiency of rationalism.

---

[613]Ibid., 239-240.

[614]Ibid., 240.

[615]Ibid., 241.

That is, rationalism cannot even get started until certain unproven assumptions are made. Reason cannot prove everything. This would result in an infinite regress, and nothing would be proven. First principles must be presupposed. They are not logically necessary (they cannot be proven with rational certainty).

His rejection of pure empiricism. Clark is right when he points out problems with extreme empiricism. Sense data and the facts of history do not come with their own built-in interpretations. They must be interpreted within the context of a person's world view. Empirical data alone cannot give us rational conclusions.

His rejection of irrationalism. Clark should be commended for his lack of patience for irrationalism. Once a person denies the law of contradiction, then the opposite of whatever that person teaches can be equally true with those teachings. But all human thought and communication comes to a halt if one allows such an absurd premise. A person who holds to irrationalism cannot even express his view without assuming the truth of the law of contradiction.

His knowledge of the history of philosophical thought. Rarely does one read the works of a Christian author who has the insights that Clark had. His knowledge of the thought of the great philosophical minds of the past should encourage all Christians to be more diligent in their own studies. Gordon Clark was a man who had something to say because he was a man who lived a disciplined life of study. Even if one disagrees with the thrust of Clark's thought, one must never dismiss the insights he shared with others concerning the history of philosophy.

His recognition of the fact that all people have hidden presuppositions. Too often Christians pretend that they have no biases whatsoever, but this is not the case. Every person, believer and nonbeliever alike, has presuppositions that are often hidden. Clark was right in his view that apologetics is more accurately the seeking of confirmation for our presuppositions than it is the unbiased search for truth.

His use of the law of noncontradiction. Clark was justified in his usage of the law of noncontradiction. If two opposite concepts can both be true at the same time and in the same sense, then all knowledge and communication become impossible. Any world view that either is a contradiction or generates contradictions is not worth believing.

He is very consistent in his Calvinism. Too often Christians claim to be Calvinists but actually deny or redefine several of the five main points of Calvinism. Clark is not only a strong defender of all five points, but he also consistently holds to the implications of these points. His rejection of human free will and his view of God as the ultimate cause of evil are unpopular concepts, even among Calvinists. Clark is to be credited with having the courage to believe that which is consistent with his system of thought.

He is right to seek confirmation for his Christian presuppositions. Many presuppositionalists are content in merely assuming the truth of Christianity. But Clark realizes that, after presupposing biblical truth, one must still seek justification for this assumption. Clark does this by showing that Christianity does what all secular philosophies have failed to do. They failed to give meaning to life, justify moral values, and find truth.

He is right that man must choose. Clark recognizes that since all secular philosophies have failed to justify their truth claims, man must make a choice. A person can choose to continue to live with contradictory views. Or a person can choose skepticism and suspend all judgment (except his judgment to be skeptical). Clark even remarks that, for some, suicide is their choice.[616] But Clark pleads with his readers to choose Christianity. If secular philosophies have failed to find truth and give meaning to life, then why not choose Christianity? Whatever the case, man must choose.

THE WEAKNESSES OF CLARK'S PRESUPPOSITIONALISM

His denial of the basic reliability of sense perception. Though Clark is correct when he states that concepts such as moral values, causality, time, and space cannot be derived from sense data alone, he goes too far when he speaks of the "futility of sensation."[617] With Clark's distrust for sense experience, how can he presuppose the truth of the Bible? For he must first use his sense of sight to read the Bible to find out what it is he is going to presuppose. In fact, the Bible itself seems to teach the basic reliability of sense perception. The Mosaic Law places great emphasis on eyewitness testimony, and the eyewitness accounts of Christ's post-resurrection appearances are presented as evidence for the truth of Christ's claims.

His denial of Thomistic first principles. While refuting rationalism, Clark stated that it needed first principles. For justification must stop somewhere. He pointed out that since first principles could not be proven through reason alone, rationalism fails to find truth without appealing to something other than reason. The first principles are not logically necessary. In this he is correct. However, Clark accepts the law of contradiction (what Thomists call the law of noncontradiction), though he says it is not logically necessary.

---

[616]Clark, *Thales to Dewey*, 534.

[617]Clark, *Three Types of Religious Philosophy*, 91.

235

He points out that if we do not accept this law, all knowledge and communication would cease. However, this is the same type of argument that Aquinas (and Aristotle long before him) used for his remaining first principles. Besides the principle of noncontradiction, Aquinas utilized the principles of identity, excluded middle, causality, and finality.[618] Aristotle and Aquinas argued that these principles "cannot actually be denied without absurdity."[619] In other words, they are actually undeniable (though not logically necessary). But this is very similar to what Clark claims for one of his first principles, the law of contradiction. If Clark is justified in using this principle, then the other Thomistic first principles of knowledge may likewise be justified. If one accepts the principle of causality (every effect has an adequate cause), then one can reason from the effect (the finite world) to its cause (the infinite Creator). This would deal Clark's entire system a lethal blow since it would justify the use of traditional arguments for God's existence. This would eliminate presuppositional apologetics as the only way for a Christian to defend his faith.

His downplaying of historical evidences for the Christian Faith. Clark rightly criticized deriving knowledge from sense data alone. Because of this, he minimized historical evidences. For facts of history, like sense data, do not come with their own built-in interpretations. However, if one accepts Thomistic first principles (because they are actually undeniable), then one can attempt to make sense of the facts of history. If a man claimed to be God and rose from the dead to prove His claim true, then one is not justified in explaining this resurrection in purely naturalistic terms. For

---

[618]Geisler, *Thomas Aquinas*, 72-74.

[619]Ibid., 78-79.

every event must have an adequate cause. And no naturalistic explanation has succeeded to account for the resurrection.[620] Only a supernatural cause is sufficient in this case.

He gives no credit to probability arguments. Clark points out that other systems of philosophy do not have a starting point based on certainty. They must presuppose their first principles. However, Clark's own first principles are also not based on certainty; they too must be presupposed. It seems that Clark is judging his own philosophical system in a more lenient fashion than he does other schools of thought. It is true that Clark finds confirmation for the Christian presupposition that is lacking in other presuppositions. Still, this is after the fact. And, as Clark admits, this confirmation itself only makes Christianity more probable than other views; it does not establish its certainty. It seems that more credit should be given to arguments for first principles based upon a high degree of probability. Why should an argument be rejected when its premises and conclusion are very probable, while opposing views are unlikely?

Other philosophers have settled for less than certainty but still have solid systems of thought. Some might argue from premises that they believe are "beyond all reasonable doubt." Norman Geisler, following in the tradition of Thomas Aquinas, uses the principle of "actual undeniability."[621] Some things cannot be denied without contradiction and therefore must be true. For instance, if I deny my existence I must first exist to make the denial. For nothing is nothing. Nothing cannot deny anything. Only an existent being can deny something. Therefore, it is actually undeniable that I exist.[622]

---

[620]Habermas, 26-33.

[621]Geisler, *Christian Apologetics*, 143.

[622]Ibid., 143-144.

Charles Hodge (1797-1878) based his philosophical arguments on what he believed were "self-evident truths." Though these truths could be denied by others, their denial is "forced and temporary." Once a philosopher finishes lecturing or debating, he returns to the real world and no longer denies self-evident truths such as his existence, the existence of others, and the reality of moral values.[623] He can deny moral values in the lecture hall, but once he is at home, he calls the police when he is robbed.

It seems then that Clark is mistaken. Christians can discover truths that are either "self-evident" or "actually undeniable." They can then dialogue with nonbelievers using these premises as common ground. Clark was wrong not to give proper due to first principles based upon a high degree of probability. This leaves the door open for traditional apologetics.

His attacks on traditional apologetics. Clark's attack on traditional apologetics is unfounded. This can be shown from his treatment of the Thomistic cosmological argument for God's existence. Aquinas argued that all existent beings which could possibly not exist need a cause or ground for their continuing in existence. In other words, all dependent existence must rely for its continued existence on a totally independent Being, a Being which is uncaused and self-existent.[624]

Clark comments that Aquinas has not ruled out the possibility of an infinite regress of dependent beings.[625]

---

[623]Charles Hodge, *Systematic Theology* (Grand Rapids: Eerdmans Publishing Company, 1989), vol. 1, 210.

[624]Thomas Aquinas, *Summa Theologiae*, 1a. 2,3.

[625]Clark, *Religion, Reason and Revelation*, 36-37.

However, Clark is mistaken. For Aquinas is not arguing indefinitely into the past. He is arguing for the current existence of a totally independent Being. Aquinas is arguing for the cause of the continued and present existence of dependent beings, not just the cause for the beginning of their existence.[626] Aquinas is pointing out that if one takes away the independent Being, then there is nothing to sustain the existence of all dependent beings. Every dependent being relies directly on the independent Being for preserving it in existence. The causality is simultaneous, just as a person's face simultaneously causes the existence of its reflection in a mirror. At the exact moment the person moves his face, the reflection is gone.

Clark raises another objection against the Thomistic cosmological argument. He states that even if the argument is valid, it would not prove the existence of the God of the Bible. Clark seems to imply that unless we prove every attribute of God, then it is not the identical God.[627] However, if Aquinas proves the existence of the Uncaused Cause of all else that exists, how could this possibly not be the God of the Bible? If Clark can refer to God as "Truth" and "Logic" and still be talking about the Triune God of the Bible, then Aquinas can identify God with the "Unmoved Mover."

Finally, Clark accuses Aquinas of using the word "exist" with two completely different meanings.[628] When Aquinas speaks of God, he speaks of God existing infinitely. But when he speaks of man, he speaks of man existing finitely.

---

[626]Craig, *Apologetics*, 63-65.

[627]Clark, *Religion, Reason and Revelation*, 37-38.

[628]Ibid., 38-39.

God is existence; man merely has existence. Though Clark's critique may seem valid, it is not. Aquinas would define existence as "that which is" whether it referred to God or man. True, Aquinas would apply the term "existence" to God infinitely, but to man only finitely. Still, the fact remains that whether Aquinas speaks of God or man, the meaning of existence remains the same.

Apparently, Clark misunderstands Aquinas' view of analogical language. Aquinas taught that we cannot have univocal (totally the same) knowledge of God. Still, our knowledge of God is not equivocal (totally different) since that would be no knowledge at all. Instead, according to Aquinas, our knowledge of God is analogical (similar). By this Aquinas did not mean that the concepts used of God and man have similar meanings. He meant that they have identical meanings, but that they must be applied only in a similar way. All limitations must be removed from a concept before it is applied to God. However, the concept itself continues to have the same meaning throughout.[629]

Not only did Clark express distaste for the cosmological argument for God's existence, he also disliked the teleological argument (the argument from design).[630] He accepted Hume's criticism of this argument. Hume concluded that it proved the existence only of a finite god or gods, and that this god or gods may be evil (due to the evil in the world). However, if one argues for the existence of one infinite God through the cosmological argument, and then finishes the argument with the teleological premises, the argument from design will add the attribute of intelligence to the Uncaused Cause. The problem of evil could also be dealt with as a

---

[629]Geisler, *Thomas Aquinas*, 40.

[630]Clark, *Three Types of Religious Philosophy*, 64-70.

separate issue. In short, Clark's attempt to destroy traditional apologetics has failed.

His failure to refute the Islamic Faith. After destroying secular philosophy through the use of the law of contradiction, Clark does not apply this law to Islam. Instead, he merely states that God causes some to accept the Bible when answering the question, "Why does one man accept the Koran and another the Bible?"[631] Apparently, after all is said and done, Clark's system relies on God alone to cause the person to believe. One wonders why Clark went to such trouble to refute secular philosophies. Could not the same response be given to them?

His misrepresentation of Augustine and Aquinas. While dealing with the problem of evil, Clark accused Augustine of denying the reality of evil. He stated that Augustine taught that "all existing things are good" and that "evil therefore does not exist—it is metaphysically unreal."[632] Clark represented Augustine as reasoning that since evil does not exist, God cannot be the cause of evil.[633] In this way, Clark makes it sound as if Augustine is in agreement with the Christian Science view of evil as an illusion. Clark is misrepresenting Augustine on this point.

Augustine did teach that God created everything that exists and that all that God created is good. However, evil is a perversion of that good brought about by the free choices of rational beings (fallen angels and men). Evil is a privation. It is a lack of a good that should be there.[634] An illustration of

---

[631]Ibid., 139.

[632]Clark, *Religion, Reason and Revelation*, 196.

[633]Ibid.

[634]Augustine, *The City of God*, 22.1.

this would be rust. God did not create rust. Still it exists, but only as a corruption of something that God created (metal). Therefore, evil is real, but it must exist in some good thing that God created. All that God created is good. God did not create evil. He created the possibility of evil (free will). Fallen rational beings actualized evil by abusing a good thing (free will) God gave them.

Clark also misrepresents Aquinas by downplaying Aquinas' emphasis on the active mind. It is true that Aquinas believed all knowledge comes through sense experience, but he also taught that God created man's mind with the innate ability to draw rational conclusions from sense data. Aquinas spoke of both the active mind (this innate ability to arrive at universals from particulars) and the receptive mind (the aspect of the mind which receives data from sense experience). Clark focuses on Aquinas' doctrine of the receptive mind, while de-emphasizing Aquinas' teaching about the active mind (also called the agent intellect).[635]

His proposed solution to the problem of evil. Clark's answer to the problem of evil is inadequate. He stated that God is not responsible for evil simply because there is no one above Him to whom He is responsible. Since Clark denied human free will (man could not choose to do otherwise), Clark made God the ultimate cause of evil.

The Augustinian approach, in the opinion of many Christian philosophers, is to be preferred. Augustine held that God gave man the freedom to disobey His commands. Therefore, God permitted sin; it was not part of His perfect will for man. A free will theodicy (attempting to propose a reason why God permitted evil) or a free will defense

---

[635]Geisler, *Thomas Aquinas*, 86.

(attempting to merely show that it is not impossible for an all-good and all-powerful God to coexist with evil) is a much more plausible solution to the problem of evil than the solution Clark proposed.[636] Of course, since Clark denied genuine free will, these options were not open to him.

He does not allow for the use of secular material during evangelism. Clark states, "in evangelistic work there can be no appeal to secular, non-Christian material."[637] However, this is exactly what the apostle Paul did on Mars Hill. When speaking to Stoic and Epicurean philosophers, he quoted from the writings of two ancient Greek poets to find common ground with his hearers (Acts 17:16-34). If one must choose between the evangelistic approach of Gordon Clark and that of the apostle Paul, then one should choose Paul.

No Christian can show that every non-Christian system of thought is inconsistent. Clark claims that since every non-Christian philosophy has failed, people should presuppose the truth of the Christian world view. However, it is impossible for Clark, or any other person, to thoroughly examine every non-Christian system of thought.[638] Even if it were possible for Clark to expose the contradictions in every non-Christian world view today, there is no guarantee that a totally consistent non-Christian world view will not be produced in the future.[639]

---

[636]Alvin C. Plantinga, *God, Freedom, and Evil* (Grand Rapids: Eerdmans Publishing Company, 1974), 28-31.

[637]Clark, *Three Types of Religious Philosophy*, 139.

[638]Gordon R. Lewis, *Testing Christianity's Truth Claims* (Lanham: University Press of America, 1990), 119.

[639]Ibid., 119-120.

POSTSCRIPT: TWO DISTINCT METHODOLOGIES?

Christian philosopher Ronald Nash has made an interesting observation concerning Gordon Clark's epistemology (theory of knowledge) and apologetic methodology. Nash believes that Gordon Clark's view of knowledge and his apologetic methodology had changed by the closing years of his ministry and life.[640] The early Clark was a proponet of *dogmatic presuppositionalism*. Clark believed that we must presuppose our first principles and then deduce all other truth from these starting points. Clark reasoned that the world view whose first principles explained the data without contradictions was the true world view. Clark dogmatically presupposed the existence of the Triune God who has revealed Himself in Scripture and the law of contradiction. According to Clark, this world view alone produced an internally consistent view of reality.

However, Nash contends that Clark's views changed later in his career. By the close of Clark's career, Clark promoted a view called *Scripturalism*. In this view, truth can only be deduced from the Bible and the Bible alone.[641] Only in the Bible can truth be found. Nash points out that this is a very weak view of knowledge since one cannot deduce one's own existence from the Scriptures.[642] Nash also pointed out that a person has to use their senses in order to know what the Bible says; yet, *Scripturalism* does not allow for any truth to be obtained through the senses. Truth can only be found in the Bible.

---

[640]Ronald H. Nash, ed. *The Philosophy of Gordon H. Clark* (Philadelphia: Prebyterian and Reformed, 1968), 173-174.

[641]Ibid., 173.

[642]Ibid., 174.

CONCLUSION

Assuming that Ronald Nash is correct in his assessment of Gordon Clark's shift in thought, Clark's later approach to apologetics (Scripturalism) fails. It is pure fideism—it accepts the Scriptures, and only what the Scriptures teach, by blind faith. Scripturalism fails to explain how we can even know what the Bible teaches since it rejects knowledge attained through sense perception. A scripturalist has no way to respond to a Muslim, someone who chooses to presuppose the Koran (a different "holy book").

Still, Clark's earlier presuppositional approach to apologetics (dogmatic presuppositionalism), with minor adaptions, is a worthy apologetic. Uncovering contradictions in non-Christian belief systems is a necessary component in one's defense of the faith. However, Clark's presuppositional approach is not the only method Christians can use when defending the faith. Although Clark successfully demolishes several secular philosophies, traditional apologetics survives his assault.

Chapter 15

Cornelius Van Til's Transcendental Presuppositionalism

Gordon Clark was not alone in his use of presuppositional apologetics. Another Calvinist scholar named Cornelius Van Til (1895-1987) also used this methodology. Despite the fact that both thinkers were presuppositionalists, they differed on many key points. Clark's presuppositionalism could be called dogmatic presuppositionalism,[643] whereas Van Til utilized what could be called transcendental presuppositionalism.[644] Still, their thought systems had much in common.

---

[643]Gordon H. Clark, *Three Types of Religious Philosophy*, 115-142.

[644]John M. Frame, *Apologetics to the Glory of God* (Phillipsburg: Presbyterian and Reformed Publishing, 1994), 69-75.

REJECTION OF TRADITIONAL APOLOGETICS

Like Clark, Van Til was opposed to traditional methods of apologetics. Van Til taught that because of man's Fall in the garden "every one of fallen man's functions operates wrongly."[645] Van Til stated that "on account of sin man is blind with respect to truth wherever truth appears."[646] Van Til taught that without the correct view about God, man cannot have the correct view of himself and the world.[647]

According to Van Til, the unsaved man is biased against God; he presupposes his own autonomy.[648] The unsaved man believes he can start with himself and find truth without aid from God. There is therefore no neutral ground between believers and nonbelievers.[649] The nonbeliever presupposes human autonomy; the believer presupposes the existence of God.

However, there is common ground: all mankind must live within God's universe.[650] All men live in the real world of reason and moral values. Because of this common ground, believers can reason with nonbelievers. Still, with the absence of neutral ground, traditional apologetics cannot even get

---

[645]Cornelius Van Til, *Christian Apologetics* (Phillipsburg: Presbyterian and Reformed Publishing Co., 1976), 43.

[646]Ibid., 42.

[647] Cornelius Van Til, *The Defense of the Faith* (Phillipsburg: Presbyterian and Reformed Publishing Co., 1967), 73.

[648]Ibid., 34.

[649]Ibid., 298.

[650]Ibid.

started. People are not unbiased observers who allow the facts to determine their world view. Instead, people interpret the facts by their preconceived world view (their presuppositions or biases).[651] Therefore, all apologetics must be by way of presupposition.[652]

Van Til disagrees with Roman Catholicism for declaring the autonomy of human reason. Roman Catholicism "ascribes ultimacy or self-sufficiency to the mind of man."[653] When Arminians, Evangelicals, and "less consistent" Calvinists defend the faith, they take the side of the Roman Church by assuming the mind of the unsaved man can of itself rise to a proper understanding of the Triune God.[654] Only a consistent Calvinistic position rightly denies the nonbeliever the ability to reason correctly (without faulty biases). Van Til adds that traditional apologetics would never prove the existence of the Triune God of the Bible. Instead, traditional apologetics only proves the existence of a finite god.[655] Van Til states that Roman Catholicism would never desire to prove the existence of an infinite God who controls whatever comes to pass. The Roman Church, according to Van Til, wants to protect man's self-sufficiency.[656]

---

[651]Gordon R. Lewis, 128.

[652]Van Til, *Defense of the Faith*, 34, 99-105, 179-180, 195, 197.

[653]Ibid., 90.

[654]Ibid., 78-79.

[655]Ibid., 77.

[656]Ibid., 78.

Van Til believed the root of the problem is found in the fact that all nonbelievers suppress their knowledge of the true God (Romans 1:18-22). Concerning the unsaved man, Van Til states that "deep down in his mind every man knows that he is a creature of God and responsible to God. Every man, at bottom, knows that he is a covenant-breaker. But every man acts as though this were not so."[657] By using traditional apologetics, believers mistakenly assume that the unsaved man honestly needs proof that the God of the Bible exists. Instead, Christians should directly confront the nonbeliever by proclaiming the gospel message from the start.[658]

According to Van Til, traditional arguments are also misguided in that they use inductive arguments for Christianity. Inductive arguments are probabilistic; they do not prove their conclusions with certainty. Therefore, traditional arguments give nonbelievers an excuse for rejecting the truth of Christianity, for if Christianity is only probably true, then it is also possibly false. Van Til believed that what was needed was not a probabilistic argument for Christianity, but an argument that proved the impossibility of the contrary. Van Til believed that his transcendental argument alone proved Christianity to be true with certainty.[659]

The traditional arguments for God's existence are therefore useless. The nonbeliever must be confronted with the gospel. Only in this direct approach will the believer find a point of contact with the nonbeliever. It should not be

---

[657]Ibid., 92, 94, 231.

[658]Ibid., 94.

[659]Ibid., 103.

assumed that the nonbeliever is an honest, neutral seeker of truth.[660]

REASONING BY PRESUPPOSITION

After rejecting traditional apologetics, Van Til unveils his own method of defending the faith. He states that "a truly Protestant apologetic must therefore make its beginning from the presupposition that the Triune God . . . speaks to him with absolute authority in Scripture."[661] Now that believers stand on Christian foundations, they can see "the futility of reasoning on non-Christian foundations . . ."[662] Thus, rather than argue to the existence of the Triune God who has spoken to man through His Word, apologists must presuppose His existence.

Van Til sees no middle ground at this point. Two opposing presuppositions are competing for a person's allegiance. The nonbeliever presupposes that he himself is the final or ultimate reference point in all human thought, but the believer rightly presupposes the final or ultimate reference point in human thought to be the Triune God who speaks to man through His infallible Word.[663] There is no neutral ground here. If humans were really products of chance as the nonbeliever assumes is the case, then there would be no possibility of knowing the world, ourselves, or anything else.[664] But human thought and knowledge is possible because

---

[660]Ibid., 94.

[661]Ibid., 99-105, 179-180, 195, 197.

[662]Ibid., 180.

[663]Ibid.

[664]Ibid.

251

man is who the Bible declares him to be, a being created by God.[665]

Van Til does engage in refuting the beliefs of others. For the sake of argument, believers may "place themselves with the unbeliever on his presupposition" in order to expose the contradictions which the nonbeliever holds.[666] However, even the law of noncontradiction is not presupposed by the Christian. It is only borrowed from the nonbeliever's system of thought and used by the Christian to show the internal inconsistencies of the anti-Christian thought.

In Van Til's apologetic system, only the "Triune God revealed in Scripture" is presupposed.[667] Not even nature or the laws of logic are presupposed. For man to start with himself rather than with God would be to deny his utter dependence on God. One cannot argue for Christianity. Instead, the validity of the gospel must be presupposed. However, Van Til will allow believers to utilize the presuppositions of nonbelievers in order to refute their views.

CIRCULAR REASONING

Cornelius Van Til stated that "all reasoning is, in the nature of the case, circular reasoning."[668] By this he meant that "the starting-point, the method, and the conclusion are always involved in one another."[669] In other words, when attempting

---

[665]Ibid.

[666]Ibid.

[667]Gordon R. Lewis, 131.

[668]Van Til, *Defense of the Faith*, 101.

[669]Ibid.

to prove something, a person must first assume the conclusion to be true before proving it to be true. Van Til was claiming that every argument contains its conclusion in its initial premise.

Philosophers refer to circular reasoning as "begging the question." It has long been considered an informal fallacy by logicians. To assume what you are attempting to prove has historically been considered to be an illegitimate form of argumentation. Most believers and nonbelievers agree on this point.

It is interesting that Van Til chooses to refer to "all reasoning" as circular. The point he is stressing is that we argue from our presuppositions, not to them.[670] Apart from regeneration by the Holy Spirit, a person will not presuppose the truth of Christianity.[671] Here, Van Til's Calvinism is evident.

PARADOX

Van Til does not believe that the law of contradiction can be found in God's being.[672] Whereas Gordon Clark viewed this law as an expression of God's very being, Van Til considers this law a human limitation that does not apply to God. He believed that Clark, and those who agree with him, make God subject to a human law. Van Til warns that the rational man will allow his reason to sit in judgment over God's Word. He will not allow the Bible to rule his life.[673]

---

[670]Ibid.

[671]Ibid., 299.

[672]Ibid., 298.

[673]Lewis, 133.

Van Til goes so far as to speak of God's Word as seemingly contradicting itself. Though he states that God does not actually contradict Himself, he adds that God's communication to man often appears contradictory to finite human minds.[674] But, Van Til cannot have it both ways. Either God cannot contradict Himself and the law of contradiction flows from His nature, or God can contradict Himself and the law is merely a human limitation.

If by paradox Van Til simply means an apparent contradiction, then even Clark would agree with his premise. Therefore, any criticism that Van Til made of Clark on this point would also apply to Van Til himself. However, if his usage of the term paradox does mean an actual contradiction, then nothing could be known of God. For God could both love mankind and not love mankind at the same time and in the same sense. It seems that Van Til should have withdrawn his criticism of Clark in this area and admitted that the law of contradiction flows naturally from God's being.

THE TRANSCENDENTAL ARGUMENT

Though Van Til rejected traditional apologetics, he was willing to do more than refute the nonbeliever's world view. Van Til was willing to use one argument for the truth of Christianity. He believed it to be the only valid argument for the true God. He called this argument the transcendental argument.

The transcendental argument attempts to uncover the hidden presuppositions of the nonbeliever. These hidden presuppositions are the necessary preconditions for human thought.[675] Van Til argued that all human thought and moral

---

[674]Ibid.

judgments would be impossible if the Christian God did not exist. Van Til claimed that if God did not exist, then man would know nothing. Even for man to be conscious of his own existence presupposes a consciousness of God's existence. When a nonbeliever argues against God's existence, he must first presuppose God's existence just to argue at all.[676]

For the sake of argument, a believer can place himself within the unbeliever's world view to show that the unbeliever has to presuppose the truth of Christianity just to raise an objection against Christianity.[677] Only Christianity justifies man's ability to reason. Only Christianity gives meaning to life. All other world views lead to irrationality and chaos.[678] In fact, scientific induction makes no sense in a universe without God, for only the Christian God guarantees the uniformity and order of nature necessary for scientists to argue from the particulars of nature to general conclusions about the world in which he lives.[679]

COMPARISON WITH GORDON CLARK

When comparing the thought of Cornelius Van Til with that of Gordon Clark, one finds several points of agreement as well as several areas of disagreement. First, some points of agreement between these two men will be examined.

---

[675]Van Til, *Defense of the Faith*, 60, 150, 180, 298.

[676]Frame, 69-75.

[677]Van Til, *Defense of the Faith*, 180.

[678]Ibid.

[679]Ibid.

Both were serious and consistent Calvinists. Because they both believed that no one could freely choose Christ apart from the Holy Spirit's regenerating work, direct attempts to persuade nonbelievers were thought to be counterproductive.

Both agreed that the gospel should be presupposed and not argued for. Van Til and Clark felt that to defend the truth of the gospel was to deny the Calvinist doctrine of the total depravity of man. They both believed that man's reason was damaged due to the Fall and that direct argumentation for the truth of Christianity would be useless. Still, both were willing to refute the beliefs of the nonbeliever and provide indirect confirmation for the truth of Christianity.

Both agreed that secular philosophy was a complete failure. Clark taught that all non-Christian philosophy eventually reduced to skepticism. Van Til believed that secular philosophy was futile since human reason was fallen. In his view, without presupposing the God of the Bible, no knowledge was attainable. However, Van Til believed that even nonbelievers presuppose God's existence (though they suppress this truth) in order to find truth.

Both agreed that traditional apologetics is unbiblical and useless. Throughout their writings, Clark and Van Til belittled the traditional method of defending the faith. They believed that there was no neutral battle ground between the believer and nonbeliever where Christianity could be defended. The gospel was to be presupposed rather than defended. They saw no use for the classical arguments for God's existence or for traditional usage of historical evidences for the Christian Faith.

Besides these points of agreement between Clark and Van Til, there were areas of disagreement. The following examples will illustrate this.

They disagreed about circular reasoning. Van Til believed that all reasoning is circular. The conclusion of one's

256

arguments can always be found in one's premises. However, Clark was more rationalistic in his thinking. He considered circular reasoning a logical fallacy. Because of this, Clark dogmatically presupposed his first principle (the existence of the God of the Bible) and then deduced his beliefs from this first principle.

They disagreed about the status and use of the law of contradiction. Clark believed that the law of contradiction flowed from God's nature. He taught that God is logic. Therefore, when he presupposed the Triune God who revealed Himself in the Bible, he also presupposed the law of contradiction. He would then use this law to destroy the belief systems of nonbelievers.

Van Til, however, believed this law to be a human limitation which Clark forced upon God. Van Til believed that Clark had subjected God to this law. Though Van Til would use this law to refute other belief systems, it was only because he chose to use the "enemy's own ammunition to defeat the enemy in battle." In fact, Clark's view of the law of noncontradiction is probably what caused the widest gap between the thought of these two men. Clark presupposed the law of noncontradiction when doing apologetics. Van Til refused to do so.

STRENGTHS OF VAN TIL'S SYSTEM

In the presuppositional apologetics of Cornelius Van Til there is much to be commended. The following examples will make this clear.

He stresses the sinfulness of man. Too often, defenders of the faith tend to de-emphasize the effects of the Fall on mankind. But this is not true of Van Til. If Van Til can be accused of any fault in this area, it would be overkill. For, due to his Calvinism, man is not free to accept Christ; regeneration precedes faith.

He stresses man's suppression of God's truth. Many apologists assume that the reason why nonbelievers do not come to Christ is merely an intellectual one. Van Til rightly shows that men willfully suppress whatever knowledge of the true God they have. Van Til is correct in his view that the problem is ultimately that of a moral choice rather than an intellectual one. God has proven his existence to all men through His visible creation (Romans 1:18-22). Therefore, man has no excuse for rejecting Him.

He stresses God's work in salvation. Even non-Calvinists should commend Van Til for his focus on God's work in salvation. Apart from God's grace, no man would be saved. Traditional apologists often imply that they can lead people to Christ through argumentation alone. More emphasis is needed on the inward persuasion of the Holy Spirit concerning those to whom apologists witness. God can use traditional argumentation. Still, it is God who does the saving. The apologist can remove intellectual stumbling blocks to the faith, but only God can persuade one to turn to Christ.

He stresses the importance of faith over reason. Van Til emphasizes that one must believe in Christ to be saved. Without Christ, even the wisest man in the world will be eternally lost. Though traditional apologists are right in that man can reason to the true faith (Van Til disagrees with this), once a person through reason finds the true faith, he must submit his reason to it.

He is willing to tear down the belief systems of those who oppose the gospel and use an indirect argument for Christianity. If it were not for this point, Van Til would probably be classified as a fideist. Though he rejects traditional apologetics (like the fideist), he is willing to refute non-Christian views and give one argument for his beliefs (unlike the fideist). Van Til's transcendental argument goes beyond refuting non-Christian world views; it presents positive evidence for the Christian faith. Still, it does so in an indirect manner, rather than in the direct fashion found in traditional apologetics.

WEAKNESSES OF VAN TIL'S SYSTEM

Despite the many good things that could be said about Van Til's apologetics, there are many weaknesses in his thought. A few of these weaknesses are mentioned below.

He denies that man has the ability to test revelation-claims. Given Van Til's system, there seems to be no way to decide whether the Bible or the Koran is the Word of God. Yet the Bible frequently commands us to test the spirits, the prophets, and the messages they proclaim (1 John 4:1; Deuteronomy 18:20-22; Matthew 7:15-23; Galatians 1:8-9).[680] Also, God provided ample evidence for His revelation-claims by performing miracles through His spokesmen and by raising Jesus from the dead (Jn 20:30-31; 1 Cor 15:3-8). It seems that God has given even fallen man the ability to test revelation-claims. Whether or not man uses this ability wisely is another question. Again, Van Til's Calvinism can be seen. For without regeneration by the Holy Spirit, no one will accept the Bible as God's Word.

His view that all reasoning is circular. It is true that much of Van Til's thought is circular. It is not true that all thought is circular. Even though all men have presuppositions, they can be tested just as scientific hypotheses are tested. One does not have to sneak one's presuppositions into the premises of one's arguments. Any argument that uses circular reasoning is fallacious, regardless of whether or not the conclusion is true.

---

[680]Gordon R. Lewis, 144.

His rejection of the law of noncontradiction being universally valid. Though Van Til claimed that he only used the law of noncontradiction for the sake of argument when he shared his faith with nonbelievers, he often criticized many of his colleagues for being inconsistent Calvinists.[681] Though Van Til implied that this law is a man-made principle (or, at least only applicable to man and not to God), he diligently labored to keep his system free from contradictions. Van Til should have realized that there could be no thought or communication whatsoever without the law of contradiction. Even God cannot contradict Himself. And, since God is not subject to anything outside Himself, Clark was right to view this law as naturally flowing from God's being.

Van Til's transcendental argument is not the only valid argument for Christianity. Even John Frame, a former student of Van Til, saw problems with Van Til's transcendental argument.[682] Although Frame recognized the worth of this argument for apologetics, he did not believe it was the only valid argument for Christianity.

First, Frame doubts that the transcendental argument could be persuasive without "the help of subsidiary arguments of a more traditional kind."[683] Second, Frame thinks Van Til was wrong in his assertion that the traditional arguments proved something less than the God of the Bible.[684] Third, Frame believes that some traditional arguments often work despite the fact that the traditional apologist might wrongly

---

[681]Ibid., 146.

[682]Frame, 69-75.

[683]Ibid., 71.

[684]Ibid.

assume that their arguments do not themselves presuppose a Christian world view.[685] Fourth, Frame doubts that the whole of the Christian faith can be established by a single argument which stands alone.[686] Fifth, if Van Til is right in his claim that the apologist must prove the whole biblical doctrine of God rather than just one or a few of His attributes, then the transcendental argument also fails. For the God of the Bible is more than the source of meaning, morality, and rationality. Even the transcendental argument must be supplemented by other arguments.[687] And, sixth, Frame believes that any argument (including the transcendental argument) can be rejected. Hence, further argumentation may be needed to defend the original argument.[688] Therefore, though the transcendental argument of Van Til may be a good argument for the God of the Bible, it is not the only good argument for the God of the Bible. The traditional arguments (cosmological, teleological, moral) for God's existence may also be used by the apologist.

His rejection of traditional apologetics. Finally, Van Til was wrong to reject traditional apologetics. The Bible commands believers to defend the faith (1 Peter 3:15; Colossians 4:5-6). The apostles used historical evidences to lead others to Christ (1 Corinthians 15:3-8). Even Van Til admits that man suppresses the truth that God has given him in nature (Romans 1:18-22). If this is the case, then why shouldn't apologists use traditional arguments to attempt to

---

[685]Ibid., 71-72.

[686]Ibid., 72.

[687]Ibid., 73.

[688]Ibid.

dislodge these truths from the nonbelievers' subconscious mind? As the last chapter showed, traditional apologetics is on much more solid ground than the presuppositional apologetics of either Van Til or Clark would admit.

Chapter 16

The Apologetic Methodology of John Frame

John Frame is one of Cornelius Van Til's most famous students. Frame is a graduate of Princeton, Westminster, and Yale. He was the professor of apologetics and systematic theology at Westminster Seminary in California. Though many people think of Frame as a Van Tillian presuppositionalist, this is not actually the case. Though Frame greatly respects his late mentor, he has significantly amended Van Til's strategy for defending the faith.

Frame refers to himself as a "presuppositionalist of the heart."[689] If he was a strict Van Tillian, he would just refer to himself as a presuppositionalist. Unlike Van Til (or Gordon Clark for that matter), Frame is willing to put his Christian presuppositions to the test. In other words, he uses his presupposition as a hypothesis or an explanation of reality. He is willing to test his hypothesis. By calling himself a presuppositionalist of the heart, Frame believes that

---

[689]John M. Frame, *Apologetics to the Glory of God*(Phillipsburg: P & R Publishing, 1994), 85-88.

presuppositionalism is more "an attitude of the heart, a spiritual condition."[690] He acknowledges that many apologists (even classical apologists and evidentialists) may be presuppositionalists of the heart, yet, they do not consider themselves Van Tillians. Strict Van Tillian pre-suppositionalists like the late Greg Bahsen would say that Frame's "presuppositionalism of the heart" is not really Van Tillian presuppositionalism at all.

As shown in the previous chapter, Frame admits that Van Til's one positive argument for God (the transcendental argument) actually fails to prove Christianity without support of other arguments.[691] Hence, Frame is willing to use traditional arguments for God (i.e., cosmological, teleological, moral, etc.) and historical evidences for Christianity.[692] This is totally outside the bounds of Van Tillian presuppositionalism.

Though he refers to himself as a "presuppositionalist of the heart, Frame is not really a presuppositionalist in the Van Tillian sense. He is actually a verificationalist and a cumulative case apologist. As a verificationalist, he treats Christianity as a hypothesis to be tested. He believes Christianity is the best explanation of reality, but exposes this explanation to verification and falsification. As a cumulative case apologist, Frame is willing to use several different arguments for God and Christianity—he does not build his case for Christianity on one argument.

Unlike Van Til, Frame is not opposed to using traditional arguments for God and historical evidences for

---

[690]Ibid., 87.

[691]Ibid., 69-75.

[692]Ibid., 89-147.

Christianity. However, like Van Til, he rejects the idea of neutral ground between Christianity and the world. While Frame, unlike Van Til, uses traditional arguments and historical arguments, he just believes that we do not make these arguments on neutral ground (between the church and the world). Instead, all ground is Christian ground. Hence, the apologist should acknowledge his Christian presuppositions before and while defending the faith.[693] Still, he is open to using classical arguments for God and historical evidences for Christianity, thus clearly placing himself outside the Cornelius Van Til or the Gordon Clark presuppositional camps. Also, his willingness to put his Christian presuppositions to the test goes against the Van Til and Clark schools of thought.

Frame, in his apologetic textbook, also responds to the problem of evil, the greatest objection to the existence of the Christian God.[694] He rejects Alvin Plantinga's "free will defense" since it assumes the libertarian view of human freedom—that humans are free to choose their actions.[695] Frame believes that the Bible does not teach that humans are genuinely free (in the libertarian sense of the word). Instead of the free will defense, Frame believes that the Bible tells us that only God knows why He allows evil and human suffering to occur. The Holy Spirit gives Christians new hearts so that we can trust God and believe He will work even the evil in the world for purposes of a greater good. Still, the Bible does not tell us what that greater good is; so we must trust God at His Word. Frame tells us that we know (from the Bible) that God

---

[693]Ibid., 9.

[694]Ibid., 149-190.

[695]Ibid., 159-163.

265

has a good reason for everything He foreordains. But, He is under no obligation to give us His reasons for allowing specific cases of evil. We are called to trust Him and know He is good.[696]

Frame closes his apologetic for Christianity by refuting non-Christian belief systems. He classifies non-Christian belief systems in two categories: atheism and idolatry, although he does argue that atheism itself is actually a form of idolatry. Frame argues that the natural result of atheism is the loss of values (i.e., moral and epistemological relativism). Frame commends the late Christian thinker Francis Schaeffer for vividly presenting "the implications and dangers of atheistic relativism."[697]

Frame defines idolatry as "giving one's ultimate allegiance to some being other than the God of Scripture." Frame argues that since atheists desperately need truth, morality, and meaning, even atheists engage in some sort of idolatry.[698]

To refute atheism, Frame asks atheists to explain how they can be certain that moral relativism is right, and how they can live consistently with their relativism. To refute idolatry, Frame asks the idolater what makes him think his god is absolute, and how does his god account for the origin of the world, the ground of logic, mathematics, ethics, and universal judgments in science. Basically, Frame's refutation of both atheism and idolatry uses Van Til's transcendental argument. These things only make sense if God exists. When the atheist or the idolater accept these things (i.e., the existence of the

---

[696]Ibid., 184-190.

[697]Ibid., 194-202.

[698]Ibid.

universe, truth, morality, meaning, the validity of science, etc.), he is living like Christianity is true—he is living on "borrowed capital" from the Christian world view.[699]

So, when everything is said and done, we see that Frame is not really a Van Tillian presuppositionalist. He allows the Christian presupposition to be put to the test. Hence, he is a verificationalist, not a presuppositionalist.

---

[699]Ibid., 197-202.

Chapter 17

The Verificational Apologetics of Francis Schaeffer

Francis Schaeffer (1912-1984) was one of the twentieth century's greatest defenders of the faith. Schaeffer was a Presbyterian minister who had studied under the teachings of Cornelius Van Til. Still, Schaeffer developed his own unique way to defend the faith. Though he greatly respected his old professor, he was not a Van Tillian presuppositionalist.

In 1955, Schaeffer and his wife Edith started L'Abri ("the Shelter") in Switzerland. L'Abri became a place where intellectual drop outs could come and find a loving community, and search for meaning in life. The Schaeffer's loved their visitors enough to listen to their questions and provided these people with Christian answers in terms that "modern man" could understand.

Though Schaeffer emphasized rationally defending the faith, he knew that the ultimate apologetic (the defense of the faith) was a loving, caring Christian community. Schaeffer took seriously the words of the Lord Jesus Christ: "By this all men will know that you are My disciples, if you love one another" (John 13:35). Schaeffer believed we must proclaim the truth, but he emphasized that we must "speak the truth in love" (Ephesians 4:15).

The Schaeffer's genuinely loved people—they opened up their lives and their home to them. They cared enough for people to spend time with them and to answer their difficult questions. Francis Schaeffer had the ability to rationally defend the Christian world view. But, he and his wife also created a genuine sense of Christian community at L'Abri. This caused many of their visitors to see the reality of God's love displayed in the lives of the Schaeffer's.

SCHAEFFER'S APOLOGETIC METHODOLOGY

The line of despair. Francis Schaeffer argued that contemporary man had fallen below what he called "the line of despair."[700] By this he meant that contemporary man has given up any hope of ever finding absolute truth, absolute morality, or meaning in life. Schaeffer identified three thinkers whose ideas led to this loss of absolutes: Immanuel Kant (1724-1804), Georg Wilhelm Friedrich Hegel (1770-1831), and Soren Kierkegaard (1813-1855).

Immanuel Kant argued that we can know reality as it appears to us (phenomena), not reality as it is (noumena).[701] Mind cannot bridge the gap between the two realms. The a priori categories of the mind read order into reality, not an order that is already there. Hence, according to Kant, man cannot know reality as it is. When one begins with unaided human reason, the phenomena and the noumena never meet. At this point, according to Schaeffer, secular philosophers gave up their attempt to find "a unified rationalistic circle that would contain all thought, and in which they could live."[702] In short, Kant's philosophical views led to modern man's skepticism in reference to knowing reality as it is.

---

[700]Francis A. Schaeffer, *The Complete Works of Francis A. Schaeffer*, vol. 1. (Westchester: Crossway Books, 1982), 8.

[701]Ibid., vol. 5, 177-178.

[702]Ibid., vol. 5, 178., vol. 1. 10.

The next thinker emphasized by Schaeffer was Hegel. Before him, philosophers for thousands of years had attempted to find truth based on antithesis. This meant that they held to the idea of absolute truth. Something could not be both true and not true at the same time and in the same sense. But Kant had shown that unaided human reason within the boundaries of antithesis led to skepticism about the real world. Hegel therefore concluded that man must try a new method. He recommended abandoning absolutes. His dialectical approach allowed for the synthesizing of contradictory statements.[703] Hegel defined truth as the unfolding world process. History unfolds in the form of a thesis which is opposed by its contrary—the antithesis. The thesis and antithesis are eventually synthesized to produce a new truth.[704] Before Hegel, the thesis was viewed as true, while the antithesis was considered false. Now, due to Hegel's influence, many believe that two contradictory statements can be synthesized. Hence, the law of non-contradiction (A cannot equal non-A at the same time and in the same way) is denied. This shift in the concept of truth from antithesis (absolute truth) to synthesis (truth is relative) resulted, according to Schaeffer, in modern man's new way of viewing reality.[705] At this point, modern man faced great despair. For there is no longer any hope of man finding truth or genuine meaning in life. There are no absolutes—truth is relative.

Schaeffer then discussed the thought of Soren Kierkegaard. With the rejection of absolutes, modern man was left without truth or meaning in life. Despair seemed to be the only alternative. But this is where Kierkegaard enters the

---

[703]Ibid., vol. 1, 232-233.

[704]Ibid., vol. 1, 13-14.

[705]Ibid., 10.

scene. Schaeffer states that Kierkegaard realized that "Man has no meaning, no purpose, no significance" in the rational realm. There is only pessimism concerning man as man." But if man takes a leap of blind faith into the non-rational realm, says Kierkegaard, this non-reasonable faith gives man optimism.[706]

Kierkegaard emphasized the subjective nature of truth and de-emphasized the objective nature of truth. He believed that meaning, truth, and values cannot be found in the realm of reason. Hence, to find meaning, truth, and values we must take a leap of blind faith into the nonrational realm. Kierkegaard argued that truth is found by a passionate act of the will, and not through reason.[707]

The modern disciples of Kierkegaard are often called "existentialists." Atheistic existentialists (as opposed to religious existentialists like Kierkegaard) believe that life is absurd, and that, if man is to have meaning, he must create meaning for his life. The French philosopher Jean-Paul Sartre was an example of this form of atheistic existentialism. But, Schaeffer understood that not all modern men would be able to take this non-rational leap to create meaning for themselves. The result for many modern people is nihilism—the view that everything is meaningless and chaotic; life is absurd. Nihilism results in despair. And, the inevitable result of nihilistic despair is suicide. Schaeffer believed the Christian must show the optimistic existentialists that their optimism is unfounded—at least the nihilist courageously faces the consequence of a world without God. The nihilist understands that if there is no God, then man has no meaning. Life is absurd. But, we must not leave modern man in his misery and

---

[706]Ibid., 238.

[707]Ibid., 14-16.

despair; we must show modern man that Christianity has the answers that give life meaning.[708]

According to Schaeffer, the influence of these three thinkers (Kant, Hegel, and Kierkegaard) has caused contemporary man to either deny the reality of absolute truths or at least give up the search for absolute truths. The places man below "the line of despair." The only option for modern man, if he desires to move above the line of despair, is through a Kierkegaardian non-rational leap in order to find truth, morality, and meaning. If Schaeffer is correct in his assessment of contemporary man, then the Christian must defend the concept of absolute truth before proclaiming the gospel, for the gospel is "true truth," (i.e., true in the traditional sense; absolutely true; true for all people, at all times, in all places). The gospel is not merely true in a subjective sense (i.e., true for me, but not true for you).

Schaeffer believed the denial of meaning and absolute truth has moved from philosophy into the arts (i.e., art, music, film, etc.). From the arts, this rejection of truth and meaning has spread to the general public. Once embraced by the culture, theology then becomes infected. Schaeffer lamented that theologians did not lead culture; instead, theologians often follow cultural trends rather than provide society with the real answers—Christian answers.[709]

Schaeffer pointed out that some non-Christian thinkers (i.e., Aldous Huxley and Timothy Leary) believed they needed to artificially induce their existential leaps through the use of hallucinigenic drugs such as LSD. These thinkers influenced an entire generation of young people by producing the counter culture in America. Many young people turned to

---

[708]Ibid., 57-59, 140-141.

[709]Ibid., 54.

drugs as they searched for meaning in the non-rational realm.[710] Schaeffer made his point: ideas have consequences. And, the consequences of bad ideas have the potential to destroy a culture.

Schaeffer's critique also seems to apply to postmodern thinkers. Postmodernism denies absolute truth and absolute morality. In fact, man is dead in postmodern thought, for the individual is swallowed up in his community and defined by his community's narrative. With reason and truth discarded, all that is left are stories. Each community gathers around its narrative. The narrative functions as if it were true, but it is only "true" to the community. In fact, Schaeffer's critique of secular thought may directly apply to postmodernism. If one replaces the existentialist's leap of faith with a postmodern community's narrative, then Schaeffer's assessment is on target.

Whatever the case, Schaeffer sees modern man (or what we might today call postmodern man) as facing a choice between despair and a non-rational, false hope. Schaeffer's method of evangelizing modern man is to show him that he must reason with absolutes; for the only way to deny absolutes is to assume there are absolutes.[711] The Kierkegaardian leap into the non-rational realm is therefore not an option. If modern man refuses to turn to the God of the Bible, he is damned to a meaningless life of despair (that is, if he has enough courage to refrain from a non-rational leap). According to Schaeffer, only when a person accepts the existence of the God of the Bible can life have true meaning. Without God, life is absurd. Without God, the reasonable man

---

[710]Ibid., 22-23.

[711]Ibid., 229.

will wallow in despair. Hope for deliverance can only be found in the God of the Bible.

Man's dilemma. Francis Schaeffer states that "Anyone with sensitivity and concern for the world can see that man is in a great dilemma. Man is able both to rise to great heights and to sink to great depths of cruelty and tragedy."[712] Schaeffer speaks of the *nobility of man* as well the *cruelty of man.* Schaeffer declares, "So man stands with all his wonder and nobility, and yet also with his horrible cruelty that runs throughout the warp and woof of man's history."[713]

Schaeffer, in his attempt to explain the fact of man's nobility and cruelty, suggests that the only answer to the dilemma is the Christian answer. Man was created perfect and in God's image. But man has fallen into sin. Schaeffer states:

> In the area of morals, we have nothing of these answers except on the basis of a true, space-time, historic Fall. There was a time before the Fall, and then man turned from his proper integration point by choice; and in so doing, there was a moral discontinuity—man became abnormal.[714]

In the tradition of Pascal, Schaeffer sees Christianity as the only solution to the dilemma of man. Without the doctrines of Creation and the Fall, there would be no explanation for the greatness and wretchedness of man.

The mannishness of man. Schaeffer argued that man is unique in the universe. His personality and ability to verbalize places man above the animal kingdom. Schaeffer argued that

---

[712]Ibid., 109.

[713]Ibid., 293.

[714]Ibid., 304.

since we are created in God's image, God can communicate propositionally to us. Schaeffer reasoned that only a personal God could produce personal man. If we deny the existence of the personal God then we must also deny man's nobility, or else we must take a leap of blind faith to retain some value to human life.[715]

What is the purpose of man? Schaeffer believed that modern man has no answer to this question. Christianity does provide mankind was the answer: our purpose is to fellowship with the "God who is there." Only through Christ can our personal relationship with the personal God be restored.

Schaeffer also concluded that moral values (our knowledge of right and wrong) make no sense in a world without absolutes; and, absolutes only make sense in a theistic world. Apart from Christian presuppositions, man fails to distinguish reality from unreality, man from animal, and right from wrong.

According to Schaeffer, finite, fallen man cannot find certain knowledge if he autonomously begins with himself. Only in Scripture can finite man find certain, though not exhaustive, knowledge. Without God's revelation in the Bible, we have no final answers in regard to truth, morality, and epistemology (knowledge). Only Christianity offers an adequate explanation of the universe and man. The atheist may deny God's existence. Still, he must live in God's world. The atheist cannot live consistently with his world view. As Francis Schaeffer's former teacher Cornelius Van Til has said, the non-believer must live on "borrowed capital" from the Christian world view.[716]

Tests for truth. Schaeffer utilized three tests for truth in his apologetic for the Christian faith. First, for something to

---

[715]Ibid., 119-122.
[716]Ibid., 323-344.

be true it must be non-contradictory. Second, the view must explain the phenomena in question. And third, a person must be able to live consistently with his theory. Schaeffer believed only the Christian world view passed all three of these tests.[717]

Schaeffer applied these three tests for truth to the possible answers for existence. The possible explanations are as follows: 1) everything came from nothing without a cause, 2) everything had an impersonal start, 3) everything is an illusion, and 4) everything had a personal start. Schaeffer argued that the first explanation is absurd for it is not possible to get something from nothing without a cause. But the second option (everything had an impersonal start) is also a faulty explanation since "the impersonal plus time plus chance" could not produce personal man—this goes against all experience. The third option is ruled out since man cannot live consistently with the assertion that everything is an illusion. Only the fourth option—that everything had a personal start— makes sense and adequately explains the mannishness of man—human personality. This fourth option is non-contradictory, it explains the data in question, and it is livable. Only the Christian answer makes sense—everything had a personal start. The infinite/personal/rational God exists and He is the cause of all else that exists.[718]

Schaeffer's method of evangelism. Francis Schaeffer developed his own method of evangelizing others. He recognized the importance of pre-evangelism when witnessing to modern man. No longer could a person be expected to come to Christ merely because of what the Bible says. The culture had become "post-Christian." To reach modern man we must dialogue with him to find out what his

---

[717]Ibid., 121.

[718]Ibid., 280-287.

world view is. We must start where the nonbeliever is and bring his thought to its logical conclusion. This will leave the person with a decision: wallow in despair because life is without meaning or be open to the Christian world view. Some will choose to take the non-rational leap. Schaeffer would then show them the folly of their leap and then ask them to face despair as the logical outcome of their world view. Schaeffer called this "taking the roof off" of the person's world view.[719] Schaeffer did not believe we should allow people to feel comfortable in their unbelief. He believed we should show them that their leap is irrational and their despair is unbearable. Only embracing the Christian world view will free a person from despair or irrationalism. Only Jesus can provide true meaning in life.

Schaeffer gave two memorable examples of the inconsistency of trying to live consistently with a non-Christian world view. The first example was existentialist musician John Cage. The second was a Hindu college student.

John Cage attempted to apply his chance view of the universe to his composing of songs. He would flip a coin to determine the next note of his composition. When the orchestra would play his songs, the audience would boo loudly at the chance compositions. Cage's ultimate creation was his song entitled "four minutes and thirty-three seconds." When "playing" this song, Cage would merely sit at his piano and watch a stop watch tick away four minutes and thirty-three seconds. He would then stand and bow before the booing crowd. In Cage's world view, there is no distinction between music and non-music—everything is the product of chance and completely without meaning. Schaeffer points out that Cage was often bothered by the fact that he could not live consistently with his chance view of the universe when

---

[719]Ibid., 140-142.

engaging in his favorite hobby—the eating of mushrooms. For, Cage understood that he had to ignore his chance view of reality in order to differentiate between poisonous and non-poisonous mushrooms before eating them. If Cage applied his chance view of reality to his eating of mushrooms, then Cage would no longer be alive! Even John Cage had to live as if the world is not a product of chance; even John Cage had to live as if Christianity is true.[720]

Schaeffer also wrote about a Hindu college student who was unable to live consistently with his Eastern religious view of reality. Schaeffer was lecturing to college students in a dorm when he stated that there is absolute right and wrong. The Hindu student disagreed. He stated that there is no distinction between cruelty and non-cruelty. Just then another student heard the tea pot whistling. The student grabbed the pot of boiling water and held it over the head of the Hindu student. The Hindu student asked what the other student was doing. The other student replied, "There's no difference between cruelty and non-cruelty." At that point, rather than admit that he could not live consistently with his Eastern world view, the Hindu student walked out into the night.[721]

The final apologetic. Though Schaeffer was willing to reason with people to show them the contradictions and non-livability of their false world views, He realized that the ultimate defense of the faith was not to be found in the realm of reason. Instead, it could only be found in the realm of love. Jesus said, "The World will know that you are my disciples when you have love for one another" (John 13:35). The final apologetic is a loving, Christian community.[722] Modern man

---

[720]Ibid., vol. 1, 77-79; vol. 5, 202-203.

[721]Ibid., vol. 1, 110.
[722]Ibid., 187.

longs for a loving community. At L'Abri, that loving, Christian community could be found.

SCHAEFFER'S MISUNDERSTANDING OF KEY THINKERS

Though Francis Schaeffer's apologetic methodology is an effective way to defend the faith, trained philosophers have identified several thinkers whose thought Schaeffer misrepresented. Although Schaeffer did not fully understand the beliefs of these key thinkers, he was still very perceptive about identifying trends in the thought of "modern man." Still, we must clear up the confusion Schaeffer caused by misunderstanding the key ideas of important thinkers. *Schaeffer mistakenly blamed Aquinas for the rise of secular thought.* Schaeffer acted as if Thomas Aquinas was the cause of modernistic/humanistic thought.[723] Modern man thinks he does not need a word from God; divine revelation is not needed. But, this arrogance is nowhere to be found in Thomistic thought. However, the opposite is more likely to be true. Aquinas provided Christian thinkers with a thorough defense of the faith that is able to withstand the modernistic assault on Christianity, even though Aquinas predated modernism by several centuries. Also, Aquinas did not promote the idea that man could find all truth and solve all his problems through unaided human reason. This autonomous view of man finds its source in the thought of Rene Descartes, not Aquinas. Descartes' epistemological starting point "I think therefore I am" is the starting point of modern thought. On the other hand, Aquinas drew a clear distinction between truths of reason and truths of faith. Truths of reason could be

---

[723]Ibid., 209-211, 240.

proved by unaided human reason. However, truths of faith could only be attained through trust in the authority of God's Word. In short, Aquinas did not believe we could find all truth through reason alone—his philosophy placed great trust in God. Therefore, contrary to what Schaeffer taught, Aquinas cannot be blamed for the rise of autonomous, modern thought.[724] In fact, Schaeffer's argument for God from personality is somewhat similar to the way Aquinas argued for God. It appears that Schaeffer learned his mistaken and inaccurate ideas about Aquinas from his old professor Cornelius Van Til.

He misunderstood the Hegelian dialectic. Schaeffer was too quick to blame Hegel for the epistemological relativism (i.e., denial of absolute truth) we see in much of contemporary thought. Though Hegel's views were incompatible with traditional Christianity, he did not deny absolute truth altogether (as Schaeffer implies). Hegel's idealism denied the contemporary view that all truth is relative to the observer. Instead, Hegel believed that all beliefs fall short of absolute truth, and that history is an unfolding process which will produce absolute truth. Today's epistemological relativists are of a much different sort than Hegel.[725] Schaeffer oversimplifies the history of philosophy by arguing for a direct connection when there is none.

He misrepresented Kierkegaard's views. Many Christian scholars, (i.e., Clark Pinnock, C. Stephen Evans, and Ronald W. Ruegsegger, etc.) believe Schaeffer misrepresents

---

[724]Ronald W. Ruegsegger, ed. *Reflections on Francis Schaeffer* (Grand Rapids: Zondervan Publishing House, 1986), 112-115, 185-186. See also Norman L. Geisler, *Thomas Aquinas: An Evangelical Appraisal* (Grand Rapids: Baker Book House, 1991), 12, 57-62.

[725]Ruegsegger, 115-118.

the thought of Kierkegaard.[726] Though Kierkegaard did emphasize the volitional and existential aspects of true faith, he was not an irrationalist. Many contemporary Christian thinkers do not believe that Kierkegaard was a theological liberal or an irrationalist. They understand Kierkegaard to be emphasizing the fact that true saving faith involves an act of the will, not merely intellectual assent to correct doctrines. Though Kierkegaard was not a traditional apologist (he did not rationally provide evidences for Christianity), he was not anti-reason, nor should he be understood as denying the central truths of the Christian Faith. He was merely putting a much needed focus on the place of the will in the Christian walk. Later existentialists who threw out propositional truth altogether should not be considered the direct descendants of Kierkegaardian thought.

Schaeffer's apologetic methodology, despite these misunderstandings, has lasting value. Even though Schaeffer misunderstood many of the thinkers he discussed, his apologetic method does not lose any force. Though he may have misdiagnosed the causes of certain aspects of modern thought, he rightly understood what modern, post-Christian thought espouses. And, he presented a strong case for the truth of the Christian world view as well as an excellent refutation of modern thought. Though we should not follow Schaeffer in his misreading of the ideas of these great thinkers, we should not discard the general outline of Schaeffer's apologetic methodology. It is a defense of the faith that can be used effectively in our day. Francis Schaeffer was definitely not a trained historian of philosophical thought. Still, he understood the way contemporary man thinks, and he communicated and defended the gospel in such a way that many contemporary

---

[726]Ibid., 118-120, 187.

thinkers found attractive. We should not dispose of Schaeffer's unique and effective apologetic approach merely because of his lack of philosophical sophistication.

SCHAEFFER'S CULTURAL APOLOGETICS

Francis Schaeffer proclaimed that Western culture is now in a "post-Christian era." By this he meant the same thing Nietzsche meant when he declared "God is dead." Schaeffer was saying that the Christian world view was no longer the dominant presupposition of Western culture. Now, a secular humanistic view of reality permeates the thought of the West.[727] Due to this change in world view, modern man has fallen below what Schaeffer called "the line of despair."[728] Schaeffer meant that, by throwing the God of the Bible out of the equation, modern man, left to himself and without divine revelation, could not find absolute truth and eventually gave up his search for it. According to Schaeffer, modern man no longer thinks in terms of antithesis (i.e., the law of non-contradiction); he now views truth as relative. And, since he believes there are no absolutes, modern man has rejected universal moral laws and has embraced moral relativism.

Schaeffer wrote concerning America, "our society now functions with no fixed ethics," and "a small group of people decide arbitrarily what, from their viewpoint, is for the good of society at that precise moment and they make it law."[729] Schaeffer compares this present climate of arbitrary lawmaking to the fall of the Roman Empire. The finite gods

---

[727]Francis Schaeffer, *A Christian Manifesto* (Westchester: Crossway Books, 1981), 17-18.

[728]Francis Schaeffer, *Complete Works*, vol. 1, 8-11.

[729]Schaeffer, *A Christian Manifesto*, 48.

of Rome where not sufficient to give a base in law for moral absolutes; therefore, the Roman laws were lax and promoted self-interest rather than social harmony. This eventually led to a state of social anarchy as violence and promiscuity spread throughout the empire. To keep order, the Roman Empire had to become increasingly more authoritative. Due to Rome's oppressive control over its people, few Romans believed their culture was worth saving when the barbarian invasions began.[730] Schaeffer saw that America, like ancient Rome, had turned to arbitrary laws which have led to an increase in crime and promiscuity, which in turn has led to ever-increasing government control. Schaeffer stated this principle as follows:

> The humanists push for "freedom," but having no Christian consensus to contain it, that "freedom" leads to chaos or to slavery under the state (or under an elite). Humanism, with its lack of any final base for values or law, always leads to chaos. It then naturally leads to some form of authoritarianism to control the chaos. Having produced the sickness, humanism gives more of the same kind of medicine for the cure. With its mistaken concept of final reality, it has no intrinsic reason to be interested in the individual, the human being.[731]

Schaeffer also noted that most American leaders no longer consider themselves subject to God's laws. They often view themselves as answerable to no one. They do not acknowledge "inalienable rights" given to each individual by God. Instead, American leaders play God by distributing "rights" to individuals and by making their own arbitrary laws.

---

[730]Schaeffer, *Complete Works*, vol. 5, 85-89.

[731]Schaeffer, *A Christian Manifesto*, 29-30.

Schaeffer quotes William Penn who said, "If we are not governed by God, then we will be ruled by tyrants."[732]

Schaeffer saw the 1973 legalization of abortion as a by-product of man playing God by legislating arbitrary laws and by the few forcing their will on the many.[733] But, according to Schaeffer, this is just the beginning, for once human life has been devalued at one stage (i.e., the pre-birth stage), then no stage of human life is safe. Abortion will lead to infanticide (the murdering of babies already born) and euthanasia (so called "mercy-killing").[734] Christianity teaches that human life is sacred because man was created in God's image, but now that modern man has rejected the Christian world view (the death of God), the death of man will follow (unless modern man repents) and man will be treated as non-man.

Schaeffer documents the erosion of respect for human life in the statements of Nobel Prize winners Watson and Crick. These two scientists, after winning the Nobel Prize for cracking the genetic code, publicly recommended that we should terminate the lives of infants, three days old and younger, if they do not meet our expectations.[735]

In his response to behavioral scientist B. F. Skinner's book *Beyond Freedom and Dignity*, Schaeffer argued that Western culture's rejection of God, truth, and God's moral laws will lead to the death of man. Written in 1971, Skinner's book proposed a "utopian" society ruled by a small group of intellectual elitists who control the environment and genetic

---

[732]Ibid., 32-34.

[733]Ibid., 49.

[734] Schaeffer, *Complete Works*, vol. 5, 317. see also vol. 4, 374.

[735]Ibid., vol. 5, 319-320.

makeup of the masses. Schaeffer stated, "We are on the verge of the largest revolution the world has ever known—the control and shaping of men through the abuse of genetic knowledge, and chemical and psychological conditioning."[736] Schaeffer referred to Skinner's utopian proposals as "the death of man,"[737] and wrote concerning Skinner's low view of C. S. Lewis:

> Twice Skinner specifically attacked C. S. Lewis. Why? Because he is a Christian and writes in the tradition of the literatures of freedom and dignity. You will notice that he does not attack the evangelical church, probably because he doesn't think it's a threat to him. Unhappily, he is largely right about this. Many of us are too sleepy to be a threat in the battle of tomorrow. But he understands that a man like C. S. Lewis, who writes literature which stirs men, is indeed a threat.[738]

Schaeffer understood not only the failure of secular humanism, but he also realized that Eastern pantheism offered no escape from the death of man. Only a return to the Christian world view could save the West from the death of man. He stated:

> Society can have no stability on this Eastern world-view or its present Western counterpart. It just does not work. And so one finds a gravitation toward some form of authoritarian government, an individual tyrant or group of tyrants who takes the

---

[736]Ibid., vol. 1, 381.

[737]Ibid., 383.

[738]Ibid., 382-383.

reins of power and rule. And the freedoms, the sorts of freedoms we have enjoyed in the West, are lost. We are, then, brought back to our starting point. The inhumanities and the growing loss of freedoms in the West are the result of a world-view which has no place for "people." Modern humanistic materialism is an impersonal system. The East is no different. Both begin and end with impersonality.[739]

Schaeffer called upon evangelicals to sound the alarm, warning the church and society to repent, for the death of man is approaching:

> Learning from the mistakes of the past, let us raise a testimony that may still turn both the churches and society around—for the salvation of souls, the building of God's people, and at least the slowing down of the slide toward a totally humanistic society and an authoritarian suppressive state.[740]

CLASSIFYING SCHAEFFER'S METHOD OF APOLOGETICS

Francis Schaeffer was neither a presuppositionalist nor a classical apologist. It would probably be best to classify him as a verificationalist. Schaeffer was not a presuppositionalist in that his "presupposition" of the existence of the Christian God functioned more like a hypothesis—it could be verified or falsified. Whereas presuppositionalists like Cornelius Van Til and Gordon Clark started with the Triune God and argued from Him to everything else, Schaeffer was willing to test his

---

[739]Ibid., vol. 5, 381.

[740]Ibid., vol. 4, 364.

287

God hypothesis. Van Til and Clark never allowed their presupposition to be tested.

Schaeffer was also not a classical apologist. He never used traditional arguments for God. He refused to argue from something to God. Instead, he started with the hypothesis of the Triune God who revealed Himself in Scripture and then put this hypothesis to the test. Schaeffer was willing to have his so-called presupposition tested or verified. Still, he did not argue from created things to God (although his argument for God from personality does seem to go against the main flow of Schaeffer's thought). Rather, he argued that the Christian explanation or hypothesis is the only explanation that explains the data in question and gives meaning to life.

Hence, Schaeffer is neither a presuppositionalist nor a classical apologist. Instead, he is a verificational apologist. Verificationalism is something akin to a half-way house between presuppositionalism and classical apologetics.

It should also be added that Schaeffer not only used his verificational approach in his defense the faith, but he was also willing to utilize cultural apologetics to argue for the truth of Christianity. As a cultural apologist, Schaeffer argued that Western civilization's rejection of the Christian world view has led to a destructive influence in our societies. And, reasoned Schaeffer, only a return to the Christian world view can reverse this dangerous trend.

Schaeffer's unique method of defending the faith should not be ignored. Despite the oversimplifications and misunderstandings in his thought, there is much apologetic ammunition to be found in the thought of Francis Schaeffer. His apologetic method can be used today with great success.

Chapter 18

The Apologetic Methodology of Edward J. Carnell

Edward J. Carnell (1919-1967) wrote extensively on apologetic issues. He was very eclectic in his approach to defending the faith. At Westminster Tehological Seminary he studied under Cornelius Van Til. From Van Til, Carnell got the starting point for his apologetic system—the Triune God of the Bible. He learned to use the test of non-contradiction while studying under Gordon Clark at Wheaton College. During his years of Ph.D. study at Boston University he borrowed the test of empirical fit from professor Edgar Brightman. And finally while doing Th.D. research at Harvard, he studied the thought of Soren Kierkegaard and Reinhold Niebuhr and learned to appreciate the importance of world views to one's personal or existential experience. Carnell combined the insights of these great thinkers to produce his unique (and hard to classify) apologetic methodology.[741]

---

[741]Gordon R. Lewis, *Testing Christianity's Truth Claims* (Lanham, MD: University Press of America, 1990), 176.

Hypothesis Testing and the Facts of Experience

The starting point for Carnell's apologetic method was the existence of the Triune God who has revealed Himself in Scripture. But, unlike Cornelius Van Til and Gordon Clark, this starting point was not for Carnell an unquestioned presupposition; instead, it was a hypothesis that was to be tested.[742] Carnell believed that hypothetical reasoning was more characteristic of the way contemporary man attempts to find truth in everyday life, as well as in science and philosophy. Like Van Til, Carnell believed that the Triune God is the Christian answer to the unity and diversity we experience in the world; for, the God of the Bible is Himself both one and many.[743]

Carnell believed that a proposed hypothesis must be non-contradictory, for reality cannot be contradictory. But, the hypothesis must also adequately explain the experiential data in question. A true hypothesis must be non-contradictory, but it must also fit the facts of human experience, both the internal facts and the external facts.[744]

Though Carnell agreed with Gordon Clark that all non-Christian belief systems ultimately result in skepticism, he disagreed with Clark on the issue of common ground. Whereas Gordon Clark had argued that there was no common ground between believers and non-believers, Carnell insisted that there was.[745] For Carnell, common ground between

---

[742] Edward John Carnell, *An Introduction to Christian Apologetics* (Grand Rapids: Eerdmans, 1948), 124.

[743] Ibid.

[744] Gordon Lewis, *Testing Christianity's Truth Claims*, 178-179.

Christians and non-Christians consists in the innate and changeless truths found in the human mind. Carnell disagreed with Thomas Aquinas who taught that man starts life with his mind as a blank slate. Aquinas believed that man comes into the world with no innate ideas. Contrary to Aquinas, Carnell believed that humans are born with innate ideas of truth, goodness, and beauty. These innate ideas are common to all humans since man was created in God's image. Even though man is now fallen, he still bears enough of God's image to have innate ideas of logic, ethics, and beauty. This common ground establishes a point of contact between the church and culture—between believers and non-believers. Without this common ground, no real communication of the Gospel would be possible.[746]

Carnell believed that the non-contradictory hypothesis which best fits all the relevant facts of experience (both empirical and psychological) with the least amount of difficulties is the most systematically consistent world view. As the most systematically consistent world view, it should be embraced as the true world view.[747] Carnell believed the Christian world view to be more probable than any rival hypothesis.

Carnell believed that the reality of Christian experience also pointed to the truth of the Christian world view. Throughout history, the Gospel has transformed the lives of many people from many different cultures. The best

---

[745]Ibid., 181-184.

[746]Carnell, *An Introduction to Christian Apologetics*, 158-168.

[747]Ibid., 60. See also, Gordon Lewis, *Testing Christianity's Truth Claims*, 184-187.

explanation for these transformed lives is that Christianity is true.[748]

Carnell considered the existence of science to be best explained by Christian assumptions.[749] For, if Christianity is true, man should expect there to be an actual correlation between the human mind and the world it observes. The Christian world view teaches that God created man and the world in such a way that the human mind could actually find truth about the world. But Carnell noted that the fact that man is finite (i.e., limited in knowledge) and fallen (i.e., sinful and prone to deception and error) explains why much of the universe remains a mystery to man. Still, God created the human mind with the ability to learn about nature. God also created nature in such a way that it operates in regular patterns that could be discerned as natural laws. Still, the Creator is able to suspend these natural laws by performing miracles when He wills to do so.

Evidence for the Bible

Carnell believed that the best explanation for human history was found in the Bible. Without the biblical perspective, human history appears to be void of meaning. Carnell saw evidence for the divine inspiration of Scripture in its realism, its unity, and its relevance to human needs. The realism of the Bible is shown in the way is deals with the real issues of life. Also, the characters of the Bible are real people; they are not the products of fiction. The unity of Scripture can be seen in the fact that though it is comprised of sixty-six

---

[748]Lewis, *Testing Christianity's Truth Claims*, 196.

[749]Carnell, *An Introduction to Christian Apologetics*, 230-233.

books written by different authors in different imes and places, it is unified in theme and purpose. This is a clue to the Bible's divine authorship. And though the Bible was written long ago, it is still relevant to human needs thousands of years later. The insights transcend time.[750]

Evidence for Jesus

Carnell finds excellent evidence that Jesus is in fact God incarnate. Jesus actually did claim to be God. This is confirmed by independent witnesses: the four Gospels, Paul's writings, and other New Testament books. Jesus confirmed His claim to be God to be true by fulfilling numerous Old Testament prophecies, performing miracles, and rising from the dead. Carnell points to the ancient creed quoted by Paul in 1 Corinthians 15:3-7 as evidence that Christ's resurrection was verified by several sincere eyewitnesses. In fact, argues Carnell, the reason why the early church grew so rapidly in Jerusalem was that the resurrection could not be disproved by the enemies of Christianity.[751]

Christianity and Man's Psychological Needs

Carnell believed that only Christianity meets man's psychological needs, for only the Christian world view can rescue us from boredom, despair, anxiety, and guilt. The world can only offer man with despair or diversions (i.e., things that distract us from our real problems). Only in Christianity can man's greatest psychological needs be met. Man needs to be eternally significant and man needs to be eternally loved. Only in Christ can we have an adequate ground for hope—hope beyond the grave. Man desparately

---

[750]Ibid., 110-111, 207-209.

[751]Lewis, *Testing Christianity's Truth Claims*, 195-196.

293

needs real forgiveness to remove his guilt and real hope to obliterate his despair. Carnell argues that without Christ's atonement, there is no real forgiveness. Without Christ's resurrection, there is no real hope. Only in Christ can man's deepest psychological needs be met.[752]

Christianity and Man's Moral Experience

Carnell believed that only Christianity makes sense of our moral experience. Humans make universal moral value judgments. This makes no sense if there is no universal moral standard. Man's moral experience makes no sense, argues Carnell, unless there exists an omnipresent Administrator of justice. This is because man is not accountable to things, but to persons. Hence, the Administrator must be personal.[753]

Classifying Carnell's Apologetic Methodology

Like Clark and Van Til, Carnell presupposed the existence of the Triune God who has revealed Himself in Scripture. But, unlike Clark and Van Til, Carnell was willing to submit his starting point to testing. Hence, he was not a presuppositionalist; he was a verificationalist since he used his starting point as a hypothesis to be tested. But, not only was Carnell a verificationalist, he was also very ecclectic in his defense of the faith. He was willing to use philosophical, ethical, historical, and psychological evidence for the truth claims of Christianity. Hence, some believe it is best to

---

[752]Ibid., 231-245. See also Edward J. Carnell, *The Kingdom of Love and the Pride of Life* (Grand Rapids: Eerdmans, 1960), 7, 19, 91, 105.

[753]Edward John Carnell, *Christian Commitment: An Apologetic* (New York: Macmillian, 1957), 54, 56, 103, 108.

classify Edward J. Carnell as a verificational apologist who was willing to use other approaches based on evidences for Christianity found in many fields of study.

Others call Carnell's methodology "combinationalism" since he was willing to combine several apologetic methodologies in order to defend the Christian faith. Cumulative case apologetics combines different arguments for Christianity. However, combinationalism combines different apologetic methodologies (i.e.., different ways to defend the faith). Hence, it seems best to classify Edward J. Carnell as a combinationalist and a verificationalist.

Chapter 19

The Apologetic Methodology of Alvin Plantinga:

God as a Properly Basic Belief

Former Notre Dame professor Alvin Plantinga, one of the world's leading philosophers, has proposed a very unique apologetic methodology. His way to defend the faith is called *reformed epistemology*. He argues that belief in God is a basic belief—it does not need to be defended. Plantinga leads a group of contemporary philosophers who reject evidentialism—the idea that there must be good evidence for a particular belief to be justified. Instead, Plantinga argues that a person's religious beliefs can be fully justified even if there is no evidence supporting those beliefs. Leading philosophers Nicholas Wolterstorff and William P. Alston also hold to Plantinga's view. One of the leading apologists who adhere to Plantinga's reformed epistemology is Kelly James Clark.

God, Freedom, and Evil

Before dealing with Plantinga's reformed approach to defending the faith, it is important to deal with one of Plantinga's earlier apologetic works entitled *God, Freedom, and Evil*.[754] This work was originally publsihed in 1974. This work, while defending the Christian faith in some respects, shows Plantinga's dissatisfaction with traditional apologetics (i.e., classical apologetics and evidentialism). *God, Freedom, and Evil*, in some respects laid the foundation for Plantinga's "reformed epistemology."

First, Plantinga deals with the problem of evil. Enemies of Christianity have claimed that it is impossible for an all-powerful, all-good God to co-exist with evil and human suffering. In response to the problem of evil and contrary to most traditional apologists, Plantinga rejects formulating a theodicy. A theodicy attempts to explain the *actual* reason or reasons why God allows evil. Plantinga finds it unnecessary to build a theodicy. Instead, he attempts to construct a free will defense.[755] A defense (rather than a theodicy) merely argues for a *possible* reason as to why God allows evil. In other words, Plantinga builds a case that shows is it possible (i.e., not contradictory) for God and evil to co-exist without attempting to explain why God actually allows evil to exist. By merely showing a possible resolution to the problem of evil (i.e., a defense), the apologist has succeeded in refuting the attempted disproof of God from evil.

Of all the logically possible worlds God could have actualized, Plantinga suggests that God has a good reason for

---

[754]Alvin C. Plantinga, *God, Freedom, and Evil* (Grand Rapids: Eerdmans Publishing Company, 1974).

[755]Ibid., 28.

actualizing this particular world (i.e., the world He created).[756] A logically possible world (i.e., a conceivable world) that has all the good that is found in the actual world, but has no evil, may not actually be possible. In other words, a logically possible world is not automatically an actually possible world.[757] Plantinga reasons that there may be no possible world, that God could have actualized, that contains a better balance of moral good to moral evil than the world He did actualize (i.e., the real world).[758] Hence, the free will defense of Alvin Plantinga shows that the existence of God is compatible with the existence of evil found in the world.

Plantinga also deals with natural evil such as natural disasters. He follows the thought of Saint Augustine by arguing that it is possible that all natural evil can be reduced to moral evil (i.e., free choices of moral beings). Augustine suggested that natural evil is due to the free activity of non-human persons (i.e., Satan and his demons).[759] Plantinga finds Augustine's explanantion of natural evil to be coherent.

Plantinga shows that other arguments against belief in God fail. First, verificationalism argues that only that which is empirically verifiable is coherent (i.e., makes sense).[760] Hence, since God cannot be verfied by the five senses, His existence is incoherent. To say that God exists is to utter a meaningless statement. Plantinga responds that the verification principle fails it's own test for coherence—it

---

[756]Ibid., 31.

[757]Ibid., 44, 54.

[758]Ibid., 63.

[759]Ibid., 58.

[760]Ibid., 64-65.

cannot be verified by the five senses. Hence, verificationalism is incoherent. Also, the principle is rather arbitrary; hence, the theist can simply respond to it by rejecting it.

Second, Plantinga responds to the atheist claim that God's omniscience is not compatible with human free will. Plantinga responds by stating that God, since He is all-knowing, knows what would happen in every possible world. If the free choice of a person was different (i.e., if the actual world were a different possible world), than God's foreknowledge of that choice would have different.[761] Hence, God's omniscience and human free will are not incompatible.

Plantinga also adresses the traditional arguments for God (i.e., cosmological. teleological, and ontological). He does not believe the cosmological argument (arguing to God as the Creator of the universe) is successful. He believes Thomas Aquinas failed to show that all contingent (i.e., finite, changing, dependent) beings need a Necessary Being to ground their existence. Plantinga argues that it is at least possible that everything that exists is contingent and that no Necessary Being is needed to ground contingent existence.[762]

Plantinga rejects the teleological argument (the argument for God from design). He agrees with David Hume's critique of the argument. Plantinga believes the teleological argument does not rule out the possibility of polytheism (many gods or designers). Also, since every intelligent person that we experience has a body, than maybe the Designer has a body? Maybe the "stuff" of the universe is eternal? In that case, even if the teleological argument proves the existence of an intelligent designer, maybe the designer is different from

---

[761]Ibid., 66-73.

[762]Ibid., 77-80.

the Creator?[763] For these reasons, Plantinga thinks the teleological argument fails to prove God's existence. It should be noted that Plantinga never addresses the possibility of combining the cosmological, teleological, and moral arguments to show that the uncaused Cause of the universe must be both intelligent and moral. It seems that he considers these arguments failures whether used in isolation are combined.

Finally, Plantinga does find one traditional argument for God that he believes is successful—the ontological argument. Still, he thinks this argument needs to be reformulated and updated. The ontological argument argues to the actual existence of God from the mere idea or concept of God. As he did in his response to the problem of evil, Plantinga turns to his philosophy of logic, which deals with the idea of possible worlds, in his attempt to reconstruct the ontological argument.[764]

Traditional theists often referred to God as the greatest possible Being. Rather than deal with the greatest possible *Being*, Plantinga chooses to deal with *the property of maximal greatness*. A being which has this property is a possible being. However, a being having this property, by definition, must exist in every possible world as the greatest being in each of these possible worlds. The actual world is not an impossible world; it is by definition not possible for an impossible world to be actualized. Since the actual world is a possible world, a being that has the property of maximal greatness must exist in the actual world (since this being exists in all possible worlds). Hence, God necessarily exists.[765]

---

[763]Ibid., 81-84.

[764]Ibid., 85-112.

It is clear that Plantinga is not a classical apologist or an evidentialist. Eventually, he spelled out his own apologetic methodology which he called "reformed epistemology." This title can be misleading since many reformed apologists do not embrace Plantinga's apologetic methodology. Reformed scholars can be classical apologists (i.e., R. C. Sproul, John Gerstner, Arthur Lindsley, etc.), cumulative case apologists (i.e., Paul Feinberg), presuppositionalists (i.e., Cornelius Van Til, Greg Bahsen, Gordon Clark, etc.), verificationalists (Francis Schaeffer) and combinationalists (Edward J. Carnell). Whatever the case, Plantinga developed his rather unique apologetic methodology and he called it "reformed epistemology."

Reformed Epistemology: God as a Properly Basic Belief

Plantinga rejects strong foundationalism, a view that finds its fullest expression in the thought of French philosopher and mathematican Rene Descartes. Strong foundationalism is the view that all our beliefs should be based upon the foundation of self-evident truths. These foundational truths should be undeniable or logically inescapable. All other beliefs should be deduced from these self-evident foundational truths.[766]

Plantinga disagrees. He believes that strong foundationalism sets the bar far too high for the justification of knowledge. He argues that our knowledge of the existence of other minds and the reality of a physical world existing outside our minds is not logically inescapable knowledge. Yet, most people (even most philosophers) acknowledge these

---

[765]Ibid., 111-112.

[766]Alvin Plantinga, *Warranted Christian Belief* (New York: Oxford University Press, 2000), 83-84.

basic beliefs. In the real world (i.e., outside of philosophy lecture halls), humans regularly accept things as being true without any evidence for them being true. Hence, argues Plantinga, we should be moderate foundationalists. In other words, we are justified in embracing basic beliefs that are not rationally necessary or self-evident. Man is justified in believing some things without evidence.[767]

When Plantinga applies his epistemology (i.e., his theory of knowledge) to theology, the result is interesting. He reasons that belief in God can be properly basic even if we do not have evidence for this belief. Hence, a theist is fully justified in holding the view that belief in God is properly basic even if others disagree with him. When the atheist claims that a person needs evidence before believing in God, the Christian can respond by saying, "We humans believe many things to be true without evidence, and we are justified in doing so. I believe that belief in God is one of those basic beliefs." Plantinga sees no reason why belief in God cannot be one of those properly basic beliefs.[768]

Though Plantinga does not believe the theist needs any evidence to justify his belief in God, the theist may choose to use rational arguments to confirm his belief in God, or to prepare the way for faith for others. Still, rational arguments are not necessary for a person's belief in God to be justified. Traditional arguments for God can be appealed to as clues pointing to God's existence. In fact, a beautiful sunset, feelings of guilt, and feelings of God's forgiveness may gently point a person in the direction of belief in God.[769] Under these

---

[767]Ibid., 97-99.

[768]Ibid., 99-102.

circumstance (and others) a person may experience God's presence. This experience may be more existential than rational. Yet, belief in God, like other basic beliefs, is justified. A person might be reading his Bible and have the experience that God is speaking to him. Plantinga does not believe this person is unjustified in his belief that God exists.

Classifying Plantinga's Apologetic Methodology

Though many apologists might agree with Plantinga that a person could be justified in holding a belief without being able to rationally prove that belief, that does not mean that the belief in question lacks proof. A person may accept a belief without being able to rationally defend the belief; but, if the belief is justified, there should be good reasons for believing it (even if the person is unable to articulate these reasons). Since Palntinga disagrees, his reformed epistemology (or God as a basic belief) collapses into a mild form of *fideism*. Fideism is the view that religious beliefs cannot be defended—they are believed without evidence. Plantinga is not a strict fideist in that he allows for a believer to defend his belief in God. Plantinga's fideism is a mild form of fideism since, although a person can believe in God totally without evidence, he is allowed to defend his faith if he chooses to do so.

Hence, a major problem for Planinga's apologetic methodology is this: if the atheist, Muslim, or Hindu considers his world view as a basic belief then we are at a stalemate. The atheist could claim his lack of belief in God is properly basic. The Muslim can say his belief in Allah is properly basic. The Hindu can state that his belief in Brahman is properly basic. It

---

[769]Alvin Plantinga, "Reason and Belief in God," in Alvin Plantinga and Nicholas Wolterstorff, eds. *Faith and Rationality: Reason and Belief in God* (Notre Dame, IN:University of Notre Dame, 1983), 80.

seems that at this point, Planinga is left with a choice to make. Either he can throw up his arms and say "you just have to believe in the God of the Bible." But, then this is pure fideism and Plantinga's apologetic methodology becomes the antithesis of apologetics (for no defense is not a defense). Or, Plantinga can choose to use traditional arguments for God as clues to the existence of God, but then he begins to sound as if he is a mild sort of evidentialism. Plantinga cannot have it both ways. Either belief in God cannot be defended (i.e., fideism), or belief in God can be defended (some type of evidentialism).

Though Plantinga's belief in God as a basic belief can help the apologist refrain from the ultra-rationalism of Rene Descartes, it seems that Plantinga's reformed epistemology goes too far. If Plantinga emphasizes God as a basic belief, the result is fideism and the death of apologetics. But, since Plantinga leaves the door open for clues or arguments for God, at least some mild form of evidentialism comes into play.

It should also be noted that some philosophers believe that we do have good, though not rationally inescapable, reasons for believing in our basic beliefs. For example, why reject the basic belief that other minds exist when we cannot live consistently with the rejection of that belief? Also, why should someone deny the basic belief that a real world exists outside his mind when he cannot live consistently with that denial? If Plantinga says that rejection of the basic belief that God exists is not livable, then he seems to be arguing like an evidentialist.

In short, apologetics involves giving evidence for one' faith. If Plantinga is opposed to presenting evidence for Christianity, then he is a fideist and not an apologist at all. If, on the other hand, he is willing to provide evidence for his belief in God, then he is some sort of evidentialist, though a mild evidentialist at that. Whatever the case, Plantinga considers his apologetic methodology to be coherent. Therefore, whether one agrees that Plantinga's way of defending the faith is coherent or not, Plantinga has developed his own apologetic methodology: "reformed epistemology" (God as a basic belief).

Chapter 20

The Apologetic Methodology of Blaise Pascal

Blaise Pascal (1623-1662) was a French mathematician and scientist who is famous for his work dealing with the pressure of liquids and the theory of probability. He also designed a calculating machine, and, at the age of sixteen, wrote a book on Geometry which caught the attention of the great mathematician, Rene Descartes.[770]

Pascal was a devout Roman Catholic who had a vibrant faith in Jesus Christ.[771] Towards the end of his life, Pascal began to write and gather notes for a book on Christian apologetics. Unfortunately, Pascal died before he completed the project. A few years after his death the notes were

---

[770]*The World Book Encyclopedia* (Chicago: World Book, Inc., 1985), vol. 15, "Blaise Pascal," by Phillip S. Jones, 167.

[771]Thomas V. Morris, *Making Sense of It All* (Grand Rapids: William B. Eerdmans Publishing Company, 1992), 8.

published in a book entitled Pensees, which means "thoughts."[772]

Since Pascal did not himself complete his task on the *Pensees*, readers must study Pascal's ideas and attempt to organize them in as coherent a fashion as possible. Notable advancements have been made in this area by Tom Morris[773] (formerly of Notre Dame) and Peter Kreeft[774] of Boston College. In this chapter, I will attempt to construct a basic outline of the apologetic methodology of Blaise Pascal. I will also attempt to show the contemporary relevance of the Pascalian method.

PASCAL'S VIEW OF REASON

Pascal was opposed to the use of traditional proofs for God's existence. He wrote:

> The metaphysical proofs for the existence of God are so remote from human reasoning and so involved that they make little impact, and, even if they did help some people, it would only be for the moment during which they watched the demonstration, because an hour later they would be afraid they had made a mistake.[775]

---

[772]Ibid., 10.

[773]Ibid., entire book.

[774]Peter Kreeft, *Christianity for Modern Pagans* (San Francisco: Ignatius Press, 1993), entire book.

[775]Blaise Pascal, *Pensees*, trans. A. J. Krailsheimer, (London: Penguin Books, 1966), 190. (In this chapter, the number following any quote from the *Pensees* is the number of the Pensee, not the page number.)

And this is why I shall not undertake here to prove by reasons from nature either the existence of God, or the Trinity or the immortality of the soul, or anything of that kind: not just because I should not feel competent to find in nature arguments which would convince hardened atheists, but also because such knowledge, without Christ, is useless and sterile. Even if someone were convinced that the proportions between numbers are immaterial, eternal truths, depending on a first truth in which they subsist, called God, I should not consider that he made much progress towards his salvation.The Christian's God does not consist merely of a God who is the author of mathematical truths and the order of the elements. That is the portion of the heathen and Epicureans.[776]

Pascal believed that even if these arguments for God's existence were valid, few would reason well enough to be persuaded by them. And, even if the arguments persuaded someone, that person would still not be saved. Pascal was concerned with leading people to Christ, not merely to monotheism (the belief in the existence of one God). Therefore, he believed the traditional arguments for God's existence were counterproductive.

Pascal was also opposed to the pure rationalism of Descartes. Pascal realized that there were more ways to find truth than through reason alone. Man could also find truth through his heart. By the heart, Pascal meant what we intuitively know as opposed to what we know through deductive reasoning.[777] We perceive and believe in God with

---

[776]Ibid., 449.

our hearts. We will with our hearts.[778] We know first principles through the heart. Pascal not only recognized other ways of knowing besides reason, but he saw that man's reason is often influenced by other factors. Man is not always true to his reason. Pascal's view of reason can be seen in the following quotes:

> We know the truth not only through our reason but also through our heart. It is through the latter that we know first principles, and reason, which has nothing to do with it, tries in vain to refute them. The skeptics have no other object than that, and they work at it to no purpose. We know that we are not dreaming, but, however unable we may be to prove it rationally, our inability proves nothing but the weakness of our reason, and not the uncertainty of all our knowledge, as they maintain. For knowledge of first principles, like space, time, motion, number, is as solid as any derived through reason, and it is on such knowledge, coming from the heart and instinct, that reason has to depend and base all its argument. . . It is just as pointless and absurd for reason to demand proof of first   principles from the heart before agreeing to accept them as it would be absurd for the heart to demand an intuition of all the propositions demonstrated by reason before agreeing to accept them. Our inability must therefore serve only to humble reason, which would like to be judge of everything, but not to confute our certainty. As if reason were the only way we could learn![779]

---

[777]Kreeft, 228. See also Frederick Copleston, *A History of Philosophy* vol. IV (New York: Image Books, 1960), 166-167.

[778]Kreeft, 228.

[779]*Pensees*, 110.

The mind of this supreme judge of the world. . . Do not be surprised if his reasoning is not too sound at the moment, there is a fly buzzing round his ears; this is enough to render him incapable of giving good advice.[780]

Would you not say that this magistrate, whose venerable age commands universal respect, is ruled by pure, sublime reason, and judges things as they really are, without paying heed to the trivial circumstances which offend only the imagination of the weaker men? See him go to hear a sermon . . . If, when the preacher appears, it turns out that nature has given him a hoarse voice and an odd sort of face, that his barber has shaved him badly and he happens not to be too clean either, then, whatever great truths he may announce, I wager that our senator will not be able to keep a straight face. . . Anyone who chose to follow reason alone would have proved himself a fool . . . Reason never wholly overcomes imagination, while the contrary is quite common.[781]

Be humble, impotent reason! Be silent, feeble nature! Learn that man infinitely transcends man, hear from your master your true condition, which is unknown to you. Listen to God.[782]

---

[780]Ibid., 48.

[781]Ibid., 44.

[782]Ibid., 131.

Descartes. . . we do not think that the whole of philosophy would be worth an hour's effort.[783]

The heart has its reasons of which reason knows nothing.[784]

It is the heart which perceives God and not the reason. That is what faith is: God perceived by the heart, not by the reason.[785]

It is important to note that Pascal is not an irrationalist. He recognizes that reason has its place; still, he reminds us that there are other ways of finding truth besides reason:

Two excesses: to exclude reason, to admit nothing but reason.[786]

Reason's last step is the recognition that there are an infinite number of things beyond it.   It is merely feeble if it does not go as far as to realize that. If natural things are beyond it, what are we to say about supernatural things?[787]

If we submit everything to reason our religion will be left with nothing mysterious or supernatural.[788]

---

[783]Ibid., 84.

[784]Ibid., 423.

[785]Ibid., 424.

[786]Ibid., 183.

[787]Ibid., 188.

[788]Ibid., 173.

It is apparent that Pascal is not a fideist. He believed there was a place for reason in religious discussions. Still, he was not a pure rationalist. He differed from Descartes in that he did not believe that man could find all truth through reason alone; he did not believe man could deduce everything from from one point of rational certainty. Pascal respected the role of reason in knowing truth; but, he also recognized that reason has its limits.[789]

Pascal was willing, as we shall see, to use reason to defend the Christian Faith. Still, he recognized man to be more than a thinking machine. Man comes complete with prejudices, emotions, a will, and a vivid imagination. The whole man must be evangelized, not just his mind. According to Peter Kreeft, "Like Augustine, Pascal knows that the heart is deeper than the head, but like Augustine he does not cut off his own head, or so soften it up with relativism and subjectivism and 'open-mindedness' that his brains fall out."[790]

Before reason can get started certain things must be presupposed. However, unlike modern presuppositionalists, Pascal held that these first principles could be known with certainty through the intuition of the heart. The Cartesian attempt to prove everything by reason alone was totally futile from Pascal's perspective. First principles are self-evident truths recognized intuitively by the heart. They cannot be proven by reason; they must be assumed in order for a person to even begin to reason.

---

[789]Morris, 183.

[790]Kreeft, 235.

Pascal was a man before his time. He saw where Descartes' rationalism would lead man. When pure rationalism (which characterized much of modern philosophy) failed to produce the answers expected of it, it eventually collapsed into skepticism and irrationalism (post-modernism). This was due to the failure to recognize the limits of reason.

The time is now ripe for Pascalian apologetics. When pure rationalism is scorned (even if it should not be), Christian apologists must learn to speak to the hearts, as well as the minds, of men. And we can learn this art if we sit at the feet of Blaise Pascal.

PASCAL'S WAGER

In my estimation, the next step in the Pascalian apologetic is known as Pascal's wager. Some believe that Pascal's wager is the climax of Pascal's case for Christianity; but I believe this is mistaken. Pascal first tells his readers that we do not use our reason in an unbiased way. Then he uses his wager argument to show that the wise man will be biased for God's existence *before* looking at the evidence. After showing that humans do not use their reason in an unbiased manner, Pascal pleads with his readers to wager their lives on God:

> . . . let us say: 'Either God is or he is not.' But to which view shall we be inclined? Reason cannot decide this question. Infinite chaos separates us. At the far end of this infinite distance a coin is being spun which will come down heads or tails. How will you wager? Reason cannot make you choose either, reason cannot prove either wrong. . . Yes, but you must wager. There is no choice, you are already committed. Which will you choose then? . . . Let us weigh up the gain

and the loss involved in calling heads that God exists. Let us assess the two cases: if you win you win everything, if you lose you lose nothing. Do not hesitate then; wager that he does exist. . . . And thus, since you are obliged to play, you must be renouncing reason if you hoard your life rather than risk it for an infinite gain, just as likely to occur as a loss amounting to nothing. . . . Thus our argument carries infinite weight, when the stakes are finite in a game where there are even chances of winning and losing and an infinite prize to be won.[791]

Pascal tells his readers that we must wager our lives on either God existing or God not existing. Reason, due to its limitations, cannot make the decision for us. We cannot avoid choosing sides; for, to not wager is equivalent with wagering against God. If you wager on God, there are only two possible outcomes. If He exists, you win eternal life. If He does not exist, you lose nothing.

However, if you wager against God existing, there are also only two possible consequences. If He does not exist, you win nothing. But, if He does exist, you lose everything. Therefore, since you have nothing to lose and everything to gain, the wise man will wager that God exists. Pascal is not trying to rationally prove God's existence with this argument. Instead, he is attempting to persuade the unbeliever that it wise to live as if God exists, while it is unwise to live as if God does not exist. Pascal believed that everyone who sincerely seeks God will find Him (Jeremiah 29:13).

Pascal attempts to show his readers that the wise man will be biased for God, not aginst God. He knew that human reason is limited and fallible, and that we do not use our reason

---

[791]*Pensees*, 418.

in an unbiased manner. Through his wager argument, Pascal tries to convince his readers that, since we will use our reason in a biased manner, there are good reasons to be biased in favor of theism, and no reason to be biased for atheism.

The wager argument is Pascal's attempt to convince the nonbeliever to seek God. Pascal wrote:

> . . . there are only two classes of persons who can be called reasonable: those who serve God with all their heart because they know him and those who seek him with all their heart because they do not know him.[792]

Richard Creel illustrates the strength of Pascal's wager with the following words:

> It would not be irrational for me to continue to search a lake and its environs for a child that I concede, along with everyone else, has almost certainly drowned. If you ask me if I believe that the child has drowned, then I will say "yes"—but I will add that I hope that my belief is false and that I think that my continued efforts to find the child alive are justified by the great good that would obtain were I to succeed. . . . In conclusion, when God is thought of as infinitely perfect goodness, it seems consummately rational to hope that there is a God and to live as though there is, as long as there is no conclusive proof that there is not.[793]

---

[792]Ibid., 427.

[793]24. Richard E. Creel, "Agatheism: A Justification of the Rationality of Devotion to God," *Faith and Philosophy*, vol. 10 (January 1993): 40, 45.

Once we recognize that we need to wager our lives on God, we are ready to examine the evidence for Christianity. It is at this point that Pascal discusses existential (i.e., psychological) and historical evidence for Christianity.

THE PARADOX OF MAN

Pascal believed that only the Christian religion rightly explained man's nature. Man is both wretched and great. Many religions recognize man's greatness, but fail to see man's wretchedness. The New Age movement is an example; man is God and sin is an illusion. Other religions accept man's wretchedness but ignore his greatness. Secular Humanists consider man to be an animal; Behaviorists view man as a machine. Only Christianity sees man for what he really is— man is both wretched and great.

Pascal concludes that the Christian doctrines of Creation and the Fall alone adequately explain the paradox of man. Pascal believed that man's greatness could be explained in the fact that man was created in God's image. And he argues that man would not understand his wretchedness unless he had some remembrance of a former greatness from which he had fallen. Pascal wrote:

> Man is only a reed, the weakest in nature, but he is a thinking reed. There is no need for the whole universe to take up arms to crush him: a vapour, a drop of water is enough to kill him. But even if the universe were to crush him, man would still be nobler than his slayer, because he knows that he is dying and the advantage

the universe has over him. The universe knows none of this. Thus all our dignity consists in thought.[794]

Man's greatness comes from knowing he is wretched: a tree does not know it is wretched. Thus it is wretched to know one is wretched, but there is a greatness in knowing one is wretched.[795]

All these examples of wretchedness prove his greatness. It is the wretchedness of a great lord, the wretchedness of a dispossessed king.[796]

Man's greatness and wretchedness are so evident that the true religion must necessarily teach us that there is in man some great principle of greatness and some great principle of wretchedness.[797]

Man is neither angel nor beast. . .[798]

There are in faith two equally constant truths. One is that man in the state of his creation, or in the state of grace, is exalted above the whole of nature, made like unto God and sharing in His divinity. The other is that in the state of corruption and sin he has fallen from that first state and has become like the beasts. . .[799]

---

[794]*Pensees*, 200.

[795]Ibid., 114.

[796]Ibid., 116.

[797]Ibid., 149.

[798]Ibid., 678.

[799]Ibid., 131.

For a religion to be true it must have known our nature; it must have known its greatness and smallness, and the reason for both. What other religion but Christianity has known this?[800]

The dilemma of man, that he is both great and wretched, is easy to document. The gap between animals and man is too great for evolution to adequately explain. No animal species will ever produce a Plato or Aristotle. Yet, the cruelty of man waged against man is unheard of in the animal kingdom. No animal species will ever produce a Hitler or Stalin.

Only Christianity with its doctrine of Creation and the Fall can adequately explain both aspects of man. Twentieth-century Christian apologists such as Francis Schaeffer[801] and Ravi Zacharias[802] continued the Pascalian tradition by using man's greatness and wretchedness as evidence for Christianity.

THE HUMAN CONDITION

Pascal sees the human condition as ultimately a one-way road to death. Death is a fact from which all men try to hide; nonetheless, it is a fact. We will all eventually die. . . and we know it. However, we live as if we will never die. The words of Pascal are haunting:

---

[800]Ibid., 215.

[801]Francis A. Schaeffer, *Trilogy* (Wheaton: Crossway Books, 1990), 109-114.

[802]Ravi Zacharias, *Can Man Live Without God?* (Dallas: Word Publishing, 1994), 133-145.

Imagine a number of men in chains, all under sentence of death, some of whom are each day butchered in the sight of the others; those remaining see their own condition in that of their fellows, and looking at each other with grief and despair await their turn. This is an image of the human condition.[803]

It is absurd of us to rely on the company of our fellows, as wretched and helpless as we are; they will not help us; we shall die alone.[804]

The last act is bloody, however fine the rest of the play. They throw earth over your head and it is finished forever.[805]

Let us ponder these things, and then say whether it is not beyond doubt that the only good thing in this life is the hope of another life. . .[806]

We desire truth and find in ourselves nothing but uncertainty. We seek happiness and find only wretchedness and death.[807]

God alone is man's true good. . .[808]

---

[803] *Pensees*, 434.

[804] Ibid., 151.

[805] Ibid, 165.

[806] Ibid., 427.

[807] Ibid., 401.

[808] Ibid., 148.

All men will die, and they know they will die. Yet, they do not all live lives of despair. Pascal explains how man copes despite his hopeless condition.

MAN'S RESPONSE TO HIS HOPELESS CONDITION

Pascal states that man responds to his hopeless condition in three ways: diversion, indifference, and self-deception. Rather than admit human wretchedness and death and look for a cure, we would rather ignore the human condition and lie to ourselves. Pascal wrote concerning diversion:

> Diversion. Being unable to cure death, wretchedness and ignorance, men have decided, in order to be happy, not to think about such things.[809]

> If our condition were truly happy we should not need to divert ourselves from thinking about it.[810]

> We run heedlessly into the abyss after putting something in front of us to stop us seeing it.[811]

> I can quite see that it makes a man happy to be diverted from contemplating his private miseries by making him care about nothing else but dancing well. . .[812]

---

[809]Ibid., 133.

[810]Ibid., 70.

[811]Ibid., 166.

[812]Ibid., 137.

Contemporary society has multitudes of diversions. Television, radio, computers, video games, the theater, sports events, and our careers are just a few of the many ways we can occupy ourselves so as to keep our focus off of our wretchedness and inevitable death. If the NFL went on strike this football season, would church attendance increase? We need to remind our fellow man that eternal matters are of more importance than the temporary pleasures of this life.

Recently, I saw a truck with a bumper sticker which read, "Everyone needs something to believe in. . . I believe I'll have another beer." Pascal was right; man diverts his attention through temporary pleasures to hide the truths he wishes to ignore.

Indifference is another way in which man avoids dealing with his coming death:

> The immortality of the soul is something of such vital importance to us, affecting us so deeply, that one must have lost all feeling not to care about knowing the facts of the matter. . . Thus the fact that there exist men who are indifferent to the loss of their being and the peril of an eternity of wretchedness is against nature. With everything else they are quite different; they fear the most trifling things, foresee and feel them; and the same man who spends so many days and nights in fury and despair at losing some office or at some imaginary affront to his honour is the very one who knows that he is going to lose everything through death but feels neither anxiety nor emotion. It is a monstrous thing to see one and the same heart at once so sensitive to minor things and so strangely insensitive to the greatest.[813]

---

[813]Ibid., 427.

The roar of a crowd at the Super Bowl is deafening, but place that same crowd into a church, and there will be only silence. They are passionate about the outcome of a football game, but indifferent concerning the eternal things of God.

The unsaved man not only ignores the horror of his wretchedness and impending death through diversion and indifference. He also chooses to deceive himself and others in an attempt to hide from the truth:

> Self-love. The nature of self-love and of this human self is to love only self and consider only self. . . it takes every care to hide its faults both from itself and others, and cannot bear to have them pointed out or noticed. . . For is it not true that we hate the truth and those who tell it to us, and we like them to be deceived to our advantage, and want to be esteemed by them as other than we actually are? . . . people are more wary of offending those whose friendship is most useful and enmity most dangerous. A prince can be the laughingstock of Europe and the only one to know nothing about it.[814]

Blaise Pascal saw that the use of reason alone would lead few, if any, to Christ. Pascal realized man is ruled more by his passions than by his reason. Therefore, his apologetic methodology focused on shaking men out of their indifference and removing their diversions. His apologetic reminds men that eternal issues are of far greater worth than mere temporary ones. Pascal did not try to reason men into the kingdom; he attempted to sway men to desire Christianity to be true. He

---

[814]Ibid., 978.

encouraged men to earnestly seek the God of the Bible. Modern society is based more on pleasures and desire than on reason. Therefore, Pascal's method of defending the faith has great potential in our day.

Pascal believed that abstract argumentation is not appealing to most people; he recognized that man would rather discuss the concrete things of everyday life. Therefore, Pascal started his apologetic where most people would feel comfortable—with the person himself. Then Pascal would attempt to take the person out of their comfort zone by revealing the hidden, unattractive truths (such as wretchedness, death, and self-deception) about the person. All this was done to reveal to the person the shallowness of this life and the need for the eternal things of God.

HISTORICAL EVIDENCES FOR THE CHRISTIAN FAITH

Pascal is not a classical apologist, for he rejects the traditional arguments for God's existence.[815] But, he is also

---

[815]Classical apologists such as Anselm, Aquinas, Bonaventure, Paley, Norman Geisler, William Lane Craig,and J. P. Moreland are willing to use philosophical and scientific arguments to provide evidence for God's existence. Pascal, on the other hand, considered traditional arguments for God's existence to be a waste of time. His wager argument is not technically an argument for God's existence; rather, it is an argument that a person ought to hope that God exists and live as if God exists. Boa and Bowman state, ". . . classical apologists maintain that at least one, and perhaps several, of the traditional arguments [for God's existence] are sound." See Kenneth D. Boa and Robert M. Bowman Jr., *Faith Has Its Reasons—An Integrative Approach to Defending Christianity* (Waynesboro, GA: Paternoster, 2005), 133. The distinguished apologist Norman Geisler states "Classical apologetics stresses rational arguments for the existence of God

not a fideist or a presuppositionalist,[816] for no fideist or true presuppositionalist would provide historical evidences for the Christian faith:

> Prophecies. If a single man had written a book foretelling the time and manner of Jesus' coming and Jesus had come in conformity with these prophecies, this would carry infinite weight. But there is much more here. There is a succession of men over a period of 4,000 years, coming consistently and invariably

---

and historical evidence supporting the truth of Christianity. . . Classical apologetics is characterized by two basic steps. Its first step is to establish valid theistic arguments for the truth of theism apart from (but with appeal to) special revelation in Scripture. Its second step is to compile historical evidence to establish such basic truths of Christianity as the deity of Christ and the inspiration of the Bible." See Norman L. Geisler, *Baker Encyclopedia of Christian Apologetics* (Grand Rapids: Baker Book House, 1999), 154, 41-42. Pascal was disinterested in the first step of the classical apologetic methodology—he did not consider using traditional arguments for God's existence as a worthwhile endeavor. After pointing out the limitations of human reason, he pragmatically argues that we should wager our lives on God (i.e., desire that God exists and be open to evidence for Christianity in history). He then combines psychological apologetics with historical evidences (often called evidentialism) to make his case for Christianity. Though Pascal can be considered an evidentialist or a historical apologist (for he is willing to use historical evidences for Christianity), his apologetic methodology is so unique that it is probably best to refer to his methodology as "Pascalian." For descriptions of different types of apologetic methodologies see Boa and Bowman, 33-36, and Geisler, 41-44.

[816]Fideists do not believe in providing any evidence for Christianity. Presuppositionalists do not argue to the God of the Bible; rather they presuppose His existence and then argue from Him to certain aspects of human experience. Both fideists and presuppositionalists would not use historical evidences to argue for the truth claims of Christianity.

one after the other, to foretell the same coming; there is an entire people proclaiming it, existing for 4,000 years to testify in a body to the certainty they feel about it, from which they cannot be deflected by whatever threats and persecutions they may suffer. This is of a quite different order of importance.[817]

Advantages of the Jewish people. . . This people is not only of remarkable antiquity but has also lasted for a singularly long time, extending continuously from its origin to the present day. For whereas the peoples of Greece and Italy, of Sparta, Athens, Rome, and others who came so much later have perished so long ago, these still exist, despite the efforts of so many powerful kings who have tried a hundred times to wipe them out. . . They have always been preserved however, and their preservation was foretold. . .[818]

. . . Thus instead of concluding that there are no true miracles because there are so many false ones, we must on the contrary say that there certainly are true miracles since there   are so many false ones, and that the false ones are only there because true ones exist.[819]

Proofs of Jesus Christ. The hypothesis that the Apostles were knaves is quite absurd. Follow it out to the end and imagine these twelve men meeting after Jesus' death and conspiring to say that he had risen from the dead. This means attacking all the powers

---

[817]*Pensees*, 332.

[818]Ibid., 451.

[819]Ibid., 734.

that be. The human heart is singularly susceptible to fickleness, to change, to promises, to bribery. One of them had only to deny his story under these inducements, or still more because of possible imprisonment, tortures and death, and they would all have been lost. Follow that out.[820]

The Apostles were either deceived or deceivers. Either supposition is difficult, for it is not possible to imagine that a man has risen from the dead. While Jesus was with them he could sustain them, but afterwards, if he did not appear to them, who did make them act?[821]

Pascal was willing to use historical evidences as proof for the Christian faith. He viewed the prophecies that Jesus had fulfilled and the preservation of the Jewish people despite centuries of persecution as strong evidence for Christianity. Pascal considered miracles, especially Christ's resurrection from the dead, to be valuable ammunition for the arsenal of the apologist. Pascal did not tell unbelievers to "just believe." He gave them evidence for the truth of Christianity. Still, he refused to use reason alone; his apologetic attempted to reach the whole man, not just his mind. Since Pascal used historical evidences for Christianity's truth claims, he can be classified as an evidentialist (also called a "historical apologist"). However, the unique aspects of his apologetic system (i.e., his emphasis on the limitations of human reason, his wager argument, and his focus on the psychological makeup of man) merit the title of "Pascalian Apologetics" for his approach to defending the Christian faith.

---

[820]Ibid., 310.

[821]Ibid., 322.

CONCLUSION

Blaise Pascal had a unique apologetic methodology. He was not a classical apologist, for he denied that the traditional theistic proofs were sound or useful in the apologetic project.[822] He was not a fideist, for he defended the faith.[823] And, he was not a pure presuppositionalist, for he used pyschological and historical evidences to prove the truth of Christianity.[824] At best, Pascal's methodology could be classified as a unique combination of psychological

---

[822]Classical apologists utilize theistic proofs (i.e., arguments for God's existence). They first provide evidence for God's existence and then argue for the historical truth claims of Christianity. Classical apologists believe that the Holy Spirit will often use theistic arguments to chip away at the hardened hearts of nonbelievers, causing them to consider the reality of God's existence. In a second step, the classical apologist will usally turn to historical evidences for the truth claims of Christianity. See Geisler, 154, 41-42, and Boa and Bowman, 133. Contrary to classical apologists, Pascal did not believe arguing for the existence of God was a worthwhile usage of time.

[823]Fideists do not defend their faith; they believe that religious beliefs are to be accepted by faith, totally apart from rational evidences.

[824]Presuppositionalists are not fideists—they are willing to defend the faith. Presuppositionalists are also not traditional apologists because they refuse to argue from something other than God to the existence of God. Presuppositionalists start with God—they presuppose the existence of the Triune God of the Bible—and then argue to common aspects of human experience (i.e., our moral experience, meaning in life, reason, etc.). The two greatest presuppositionalists of the twentieth century were Cornelius Van Til and Gordon Clark. An overview of their apologetic methodologies can be found in this work.

apologetics and historical apologetics.[825] He was a psychological apologist, for he attempted to speak to the entire man, not just his intellect. But, he was also a historical apologist since he was willing to use historical data to provide evidence for Christianity.

Though I appreciate and utilize traditional arguments for God's existence, I believe that the apologetic methodology of Blaise Pascal should not be ignored. Pascal has much to offer the contemporary Christian apologist. Every apologist can benefit from examining Pascal's insight into man's fallen nature, his identification of the limitations of human reason, and his desire to convert people to Christianity, not merely monotheism. Studying Pascal's apologetic methodology, and incorporating aspects of it into our own apologetic ministry, can make our defense of the faith more effective.

Today, unfortunately, many people are not concerned about finding rational truth.[826] But, they are very concerned about their existential experience. Many people seek meaning

---

[825]Gordon R. Lewis, *Testing Christianity's Truth Claims* (Lanham: University Press of America, 1990), 231-253. Lewis classifies Pascal's method as "psychological." Still, we must not overlook the stress Pascal also puts on historical evidences.

[826]In the West, world views such as existentialism and postmodernism have led many people to deny the existence of absolute truth or man's ability to find truth through his reason. Eastern religions (i.e., Hinduism, Buddhism, etc.) de-emphasize or outright deny absolute truth. Many Americans have been influenced by these Western world views and/or Eastern religions and consequently de-emphasize truth and reason, choosing to focus on the will, emotions, intuition, desires. Obviously, these people are greatly mistaken and they cannot live consistently with their world views. But, Pascal's psychological approach has great potential for aiding the Christian apologist in his attempt to reach people who are no longer interested in reason or truth.

in life; they also want their deepest desires to be satisfied. At the same time, many people are reluctant to admit their faults. Therefore, the Pascalian apologetic methodology has great potential for contemporary society, for Pascal forces us to look at ourselves in the mirror. He forces us to see ourselves as we are: wretched, miserable people who will all eventually die. Pascal then tugs at our hearts and declares to us that only in Jesus can life have meaning. Only in Jesus can we find satisfaction and forgiveness. Only in Jesus can death, our greatest enemy, be defeated. Pascal beseeches contemporary man to wager his life on the God of the Bible. He calls us to seek God with all our being, for Pascal knows that if we seek Him with all our being, we will find Him. And if we find Him, we win eternity.

Chapter 21

The Dialogical Apologetics of David Clark

Christian philosopher David Clark has developed his own method of defending the faith called "Dialogical Apologetics." Clark is professor of theology at Bethel Seminary. He unveiled his unique apologetic methodology in his 1993 book *Dialogical Apologetics: A Person-Centered Approach to Christian Defense.*[827]

There are several aspects of Clark's apologetic methodology that should be noted. First, dialogical apologetics is person-centered. This means that since each non-believer is a unique person, we may have to use a different approach and different arguments when we witness to different people. In other words, the apologist should not restrict himself to the same argument or arguments when dealing with different people.[828] An argument that one non-

---

[827]David. K. Clark, *Dialogical Apologetics: A Person-Centered Approach to Christian Defense* (Grand Rapids: Baker Book House, 1993.

[828]Ibid., 112-113.

331

believer finds unconvincing might be persuasive to another non-believer. We should care enough about the person with whom we are dialoguing to get to know them and the way they think. This will increase the effectiveness of our communicating and defending the gospel.

Second, dialogical apologetics does not attempt to defend the faith with any single argument, nor does it try to prove God's existence or Jesus' resurrection with logical necessity. Instead, a cumulative case is constructed for the truth claims of Christinaity.[829] Several different arguments, clues, or evidences are presented. These arguments have a certain degree of probability, but the evidence for Christinaity begins to build as the sum effect of these arguments are added. The non-believer may find some of the arguments unconvincing; but, just a few of these arguments or clues might get through to the non-believer. According to dialogical apologetics, the defender of the faith should not "put all his eggs in one basket." Nor should the apologist try to conclusively prove Christianity with one or two arguments. A cumulative case is most effective.

Third, dialogical apologetics, as mentioned above, does not seek to prove the case for Christianity with logical necessity. Instead of hard rationalism (which attempts to prove Christinaity with rational certainty), the dialogical apologist settles for a lesser degree of certainty—he settles for probability. Humans do not normally think in terms of rational certainty (except when doing math). In the real world, most of our choices and decisions are made in terms of probability. Clark believes probabalistic arguments should be used in our apologetic endeavors. The dialogical apologist does not throw away reason; he merely uses reason in a more humble fashion.

---

[829]Ibid., 87-90, 100-101.

He prefers soft rationalism rather than hard or extreme rationalism.[830]

Fourth, the dialogical apologist takes an eclectic approach to defending the faith. This means that the dialogical apologist is not only willing to use several different arguments for God's existence and the truth claims of Christianity, but he is also willing to utilize several different apologetic methods.[831] At times the dialogical apologist may argue like a classical apologist or an evidentialist. At other times the dialogical apologist may sound like a presuppositionalist or a verificationalist. Just as the Apostle Paul told us, we are to "become all things to all men" so that we might lead some to Christ (1 Cor. 9:19-23). The dialogical apologist does not restrict himself to one apologetic methodology—he is willing to be eclectic in his defense of the faith.

Fifth, while adhereing to the general rules of evidence, the dialogical apologist treats theism (the belief in a personal God) or Christianity as a hypothesis or total explanation of reality. The dialogical apologist attempts to show that Christian theism is more plausible than any of its rival world views—Christianity provides man with the best explanation of reality. It explains the data in question more adequately than any other world view.[832]

Sixth, the dialogical apologist shows the non-believer the logical consistency of the Christian world view.[833] Biblical Christianity is not incoherent; it is internally consistent. No self-contradictory belief system can be true; contradictions

---

[830]Ibid., 48-51, 90-95, 100-101, 113.

[831]Ibid., 108-112.

[832]Ibid., 57-60, 89-90.

[833]Ibid., 85-86.

must be false. Hence, the dialogical apologist must be willing to show the non-believer that the Christian world not only explains the data of reality, but it is also internally consistent.

In conclusion, David Clark has done a great service to the study of Christian apologetics. He has provided a new unique way to defend the faith. He has developed a humble and ecclectic way to defend the faith once for all delivered to the saints. Rather than arguing that apologists can only use one method to defend the faith, Clark encourages us to be willing to use different approaches. He encourages apologists to formulate our arguments for Christianity in such a way that we appeal to the individual with whom we are dialoguing.

Chapter 22

Testimonial Apologetics

Even many Christians who claim to be opposed to apologetics (i.e., fideists), without realizing they are doing apologetics, actually defend the faith by sharing their testimonies. Also, many Christians who do defend their faith using evidences for Christianity will often share their testimonies as further evidence for the truth of Christianity. Testimonial apologetics is a type of pragmatic argument for the Christian Faith. It provides evidence to show that Christianity works; it changes lives.

Alone, the testimony of transformed lives does not provide an adequate defense of the gospel, for there are those who claim that another religion has changed their lives for the better. Therefore, it is better to argue for Christianity through other means first, and then use testimonial apologetics to strengthen one's case.

Still, there are people who do not need intellectual arguments to come to Christ. Instead, they are more likely to come to Christ through hearing how Jesus has changed another person's life for the better. They long to have their lives changed as well, and they find through another person's testimony that Christ can do this for them. In this chapter, the evidence of how Jesus Christ changes lives will be examined. If Jesus is truly alive today, then He is still in the business of changing lives.

When using evidence from changed lives, three things should be noted. First, there must be *thorough transformation.* The changes in the life of the person using testimonial apologetics must be so thorough that it could not have been produced through human will power alone. If a person quit smoking cigarettes due to accepting Christ, this is not enough. Many non-Christians have given up smoking without conversion. Evidence from other areas of the Christian's life must be shared as well.

Second, there must be *genuine transformation.* Often, a person's testimony is later discovered to be filled with lies and exaggerations. This can only push people further away from Christ. When a Christian shares his testimony, he must not exaggerate or fabricate portions of his conversion story.

Third, there must be *permanent transformation.* Too often new converts are called upon to publicly share their testimonies. Then, a short time later, these supposed converts are once again practicing their old lifestyles. Sometimes the "new Convert" changes their mind and no longer professes faith in Jesus. A sufficient amount of time is needed to assure others that the changes are of a permanent nature.

Biblical Support

The Bible supports the practice of testimonial apologetics. First, it teaches that Jesus changes the lifestyles of those He saves. James tells us that "faith without works is dead" (James 2:26). Thus, true saving faith will produce good works in the life of a believer. After listing many sins of the unrighteous, the apostle Paul states, "And such were some of you; but you were washed, but you were sanctified, but you were justified in the name of the Lord Jesus Christ, and in the Spirit of our God" (1 Corinthians 6:11). Paul also taught that "we are His workmanship, created in Christ Jesus for good works" (Ephesians 2:10). Jesus declared that "not everyone who says to Me, 'Lord, Lord,' will enter the Kingdom of heaven; but he who does the will of My Father who is in heaven" (Matthew 7:21).

Second, the Bible records the apostle Paul sharing his testimony on two separate occasions to provide evidence for the truth of Christianity (Acts 22:1-21; 26:1-23). Therefore, testimonial apologetics should not be ignored when discussing ways to defend the faith. Still, it must be remembered that it is not the only way to provide evidence for the faith.

The remainder of this chapter will provide several brief examples of lives that had been transformed by Jesus Christ. First, the lives of three apostles will be discussed. Then the lives of other Christians will also be examined.

The Apostle Peter

This Jewish fisherman had sat under the teachings of Jesus for over three years. Still, when Christ was arrested, he became fearful and three times denied knowing Christ (Matthew 26:69-75).

After Jesus rose from the dead, Peter confessed his love for Jesus three times (John 21:15-17). Just before He ascended to heaven, Jesus promised to send the Holy Spirit to empower Peter and the other apostles (Acts 1:8-9). The Holy Spirit came upon Peter, the apostles, and the rest of the church ten days later (Acts 2:1-4). Filled with the power of the indwelling Holy Spirit, Peter boldly proclaimed Christ's salvation message despite opposition from the Jewish religious leaders. No longer was he overcome with fear. Three thousand people accepted Christ as their Savior due to Peter's first message (Acts 2:14-42).

The courage that Peter had on that day, due to the transforming work of Christ, continued to be evident throughout his life. This apostle suffered great persecution for the Christian faith (Acts 4:1-3; 5:40-42). Eventually, Peter was martyred for preaching the gospel. He was crucified (possibly upside down).[834]

The Apostle Paul

Paul was schooled in the Old Testament from his youth. At a young age he became a Pharisee, a Jewish religious leader specializing in teaching the Old Testament (Philippians 3:4-6). His greatest desire was to serve the God of Israel. However, he mistook Jesus of Nazareth for an impostor and a false messiah. Therefore, he dedicated his energies to persecuting the church which he thought to be heretical.

When Paul was on the road to Damascus (attempting to persecute more Christians), he encountered the risen Christ. Falling to the ground and blinded by the light of Christ's glory, he realized that Jesus was who He claimed to be . . . the Jewish Messiah and Savior of the world. Christ then commissioned Paul to be the apostle to the gentiles (Acts 9:1-22; 22:3-16; 26:9-18).

From that day forth, Paul, who had previously led the persecution against the church, became the greatest missionary of the early church. Despite the horrible

---

[834]Carsten P. Thiede, *Simon Peter* (Grand Rapids: Zondervan Publishing House, 1988), 190.

persecution he was to suffer, he managed to spread the gospel of Jesus Christ throughout the Roman Empire. He was stoned, scourged, shipwrecked, beaten, and mocked (2 Corinthians 11:24-33). But nothing could deter him from his mission. His life was totally devoted to the one he had met on the road to Damascus.

This persecutor of the church had been transformed into one of the church's greatest assets. He loved his Messiah and faithfully served Him until death. Eventually, he was beheaded for sharing the gospel sometime after 65AD.[835]

The Apostle James

James was the half-brother of Jesus (Matthew 12:46-50; 13:55-56). He and his brothers mocked Jesus during Jesus' earthly ministry (John 7:1-5). They did not believe Jesus was the Jewish Messiah.

However, shortly after Jesus' death and resurrection, James and his brothers are listed with the original apostles and the leaders of the early church in the Book of Acts (Acts 1:12-14). In fact, he became one of the three "pillars" (along with Peter and John) of the Jerusalem church (Galatians 1:18-2:10). Eventually, when Peter had to flee Jerusalem, James became the Bishop of the Jerusalem church (Acts 12:16-19; 15:1-21). James became so committed to the cause of the Gospel that he was brutally martyred for his faith in 62 AD when he was thrown off the temple and stoned to death by the Jewish religious leaders.[836]

---

[835]F. F. Bruce, *Paul Apostle of the Heart Set Free* (Grand Rapids: William B. Eerdmans Publishing Company, 1977), 450.

[836]Josephus, *The Works of Josephus: Complete and Unabridged.* Translated by William Whiston. (Reabody:
339

Saint Augustine

Saint Augustine (354-430AD) spent his early life seeking to find fulfillment in sexual immorality. Finding no true joy there, he accepted the Manichean teaching (matter is evil and co-eternal with God), but later found this inadequate.[837] He then began to despair. How could evil exist if all that God created is good? He doubted that he would ever find ultimate truth. All during this time, his Christian mother prayed for his salvation.[838]

Eventually, he was exposed to the philosophy of Plotinus and the teachings of Ambrose, a Christian philosopher. Ambrose, in a fashion similar to Plotinus, taught that evil exists only as a corruption or perversion of God's perfect creation.[839] This and other teachings of Ambrose answered much of the philosophical doubt that Augustine had in regards to the Christian Faith. In 386AD, while in a garden meditating on his spiritual thirst for God, Augustine heard a neighbor's voice stating, "Take up and read." Augustine, taking this to be a sign from God, opened his Bible to Romans 13:13-14 and began to read. This passage commands one to depart from sexual immorality and to appropriate the work of Jesus Christ to one's life. Augustine immediately broke off his

---

Hendrickson Publishers, 1987), 538. See also Eusebius, *The History of the Church*. Translated by a G. A. Williams. (London: Penguin Books, 1965), 58-61.

[837]Vernon J. Bourke, *Augustine's Quest of Wisdom: His Life, Thought, and Works* (Albany: Magi Books, 1993), 17-18.

[838]Ibid., 41.

[839]Ibid., 58.

immoral relationship with a woman and became a Christian.[840]

Augustine became one of the greatest scholars of church history. His many writings are still widely read by Catholics and Protestants alike. This great thinker's quest for truth led him to accept Jesus Christ as his Savior. His life of sexual immorality was replaced by a life of holiness.

John Newton

John Newton (1725-1807) sought lustful pleasures throughout his early life. He was also a man of extreme violence and was a ruthless slave-trader. However, this man who victimized men and women himself became a victim. His life collapsed as he himself was sold into slavery. In the midst of his despair he called out to Jesus for salvation. Once saved, his life was totally transformed. After his conversion, he was ordained to the ministry and fought slavery for the remaining years of his life.

Today, we do not remember John Newton as one of the vilest men who ever lived. Instead, we remember him as the man who penned the words, "Amazing grace, how sweet the sound that saved a wretch like me. I once was lost, but now am found; was blind, but now I see."[841]

Nicky Cruz

Nicky Cruz grew up on the streets of New York. He was the leader of a gang called the Mau Maus. His life was

---

[840]Ibid., 51-52, 65.

[841]Earle E. Cairns, *Christianity Through the Centuries* (Grand Rapids: Zondervan, 1981), 396.

filled with violence. He trusted in his own strength to solve his problems. But when a persistent preacher proclaimed the gospel message in his presence, the heart of this street warrior began to melt. He accepted Christ as his Savior, and his life has never been the same.

Now he speaks publicly throughout America, leading many city youths to faith in Christ. Because of Cruz's testimony, hundreds of youths have been directed off the path of destruction that he once traveled.[842]

Chuck Colson

Chuck Colson was one of the most powerful men in America. He was one of the top political figures in the country. He worked directly under the leadership of President Richard Nixon. But the Watergate Scandal brought down the kingdom Chuck Colson had built. Soon, he was just another inmate in just another prison. However, this man was set free from the spiritual imprisonment of his soul. As he read a book written by the Christian apologist C. S. Lewis, he came to know Jesus Christ as his Savior.

Chuck Colson no longer sought power over other men. For the rest of his life, he not only preached the gospel to large crowds and wrote books in defense of Christianity, but he also led the fight for prison reform throughout the world.[843]

---

[842]Nicky Cruz, *Run Baby Run* (Plainfield: Logos Books, 1968).

[843]Shirl Short, "Exclusive Interview with Chuck Colson." *Moody Monthly* (Chicago: Moody Bible Institute, Feb., 1976).

Frank Morison

Frank Morison was a journalist who set out to disprove Christ's resurrection. He proceeded to research the historical evidence in great detail. But, having examined the evidence, the skeptic was alarmed with his own conclusion: Christ had actually risen from the dead! Though reluctant at first, he decided to accept the evidence. He accepted Christ as his Savior and is now a defender of the gospel he once tried to destroy.[844]

Josh McDowell

When Josh McDowell attended college as a young man he lived a hedonistic lifestyle. Hosting and attending parties became his normal practice. But, Josh knew that true meaning and purpose in life eluded him. It was then that he noticed eight students and two teachers who seemed different—they seemed confident in their beliefs and content with life. Josh was drawn to them; he noticed they had a joy that did not depend on their circumstances. He desired that kind of joy. He befriended these people and asked them why they were different. But, when they responded that their faith in Christ made the difference, Josh ridiculed them for their beliefs. He thought that Christians were emotionally and intellectually weak people.[845]

Time and time again, his Christian friends challenged him to examine the evidence for Christianity. Finally, he took

---

[844]Frank Morison, *Who Moved the Stone?* (London: Faber and Faber, 1958).

[845]Josh McDowell, *Evidence that Demands a Verdict* (San Bernardino: Here's Life Publishers, 1979), 363-364.

up their challenge, thinking he would easily refute Christianity. But, Josh was surprised to find a tremendous amount of evidence for Christianity. During his second year of college, Josh trusted in Jesus for salvation.[846] He then dedicated the next thirteen years of his life compiling much of the evidence he had found for Christianity. This led to the writing of two of his books: *More Than a Carpenter*[847] and *Evidence that Demands a Verdict*.[848] Jesus began to change Josh's life for the better and he became one of Christianity's leading defenders.

Michael Brown

Michael Brown grew up in a Jewish home on Long Island. But, he did not practice his Jewish faith. He abused heroin, committed burglaries, and played drummer for a rock and roll band. He and some band members began attending a local church due to their attraction to some of the Christian girls who were members of the church. In the months that followed, Michael sensed the guilt and shame of his sinful lifestyle. In the early 1970's he turned to Jesus for salvation.[849]

Michael's father appreciated the moral reforms that Christianity brought to his son's life. But, he did not like the fact that his son had become a Christian. He took his son to

---

[846]Ibid., 364-367.

[847]Josh McDowell, *More Than a Carpenter* (Wheaton: Tyndale House Publishers, 1977).

[848]McDowell, *Evidence that Demands a Verdict.*

[849]See Lee Strobel's interview of Michael Brown in Lee Strobel, *The Case for the Real Jesus* (Grand Rapids: Zondervan Publishing, 2007), 193-194.

the local rabbis to discuss his conversion. These rabbis could not convince Michael to abandon his new-found faith. But, the discussions did convince Michael of his need to study the Hebrew language and culture. So, he completed doctoral studies at New York University. For the past three decades, Michael Brown has publicly debated rabbis, proving Jesus is the Jewish Messiah by showing that Jesus has fulfilled numerous Old Testament prophecies concerning the Messiah.[850]

Barry Leventhal

Barry Leventhal was born on May 7, 1943 in Los Angeles, California. He was the grandson of Jewish immigrants from Russia and Hungary. He grew up in a typical Jewish home. In the 1960's he was one of the team captains for the UCLA football squad. On January 1, 1966, he played in the Rose Bowl. UCLA won that game, and Barry believed life could not get any better.[851]

But, about this time, his friend Kent had become a born-gain Christian and began witnessing to Barry. He introduced Barry to a Campus Crusade for Christ leader named Hal. This Campus Crusade leader tried to prove to Barry that Jesus was the Jewish Messiah. He showed Barry numerous Old Testament predictions of the Messiah that were fulfilled by Jesus hundreds of years later.[852] But, Barry was

---

[850]Ibid., 194-195.

[851]Barry R. Leventhal, "Why I Believe Jesus is the Promised Messiah," Norman L. Geisler and Paul K. Hoffman, eds. *Why I Am a Christian* (Grand Rapids: Baker Book House, 2006), 235-236.

[852]Ibid., 236.

not impressed. He believed that Gentile Christians were using a "trick Bible" that changed the Old Testament to make it look like Jesus was the Messiah. But, Hal insisted that Barry check out the numerous Old Testament prophecies in his English translation of the Hebrew Old Testament called the Tanach. Several days later, Barry opened up his Tanach and was startled to find the Old Testament prophecies saying the same thing as Hal's "trick Bible."[853] When even his own rabbi (who was not a Christian) admitted that Isaiah 53 actually sounded like it was talking about Jesus, Barry admitted that Jesus was in fact the Jewish Messiah.[854]

After Hal gave Barry a copy of the Gospel of John to read, Barry trusted in Jesus for salvation. He never looked back. After graduating from Dallas Theological Seminary and teaching there for several years, Barry Leventhal is now the academic dean and a professor at Southern Evangelical Seminary in North Carolina.[855]

Louis S. Lapides

Louis Lapides grew up in the rough city of Newark, New Jersey. He was raised in a Jewish home. His family was not observant of the Sabbath, nor did they eat only kosher foods. Still, they did attend an Orthodox synagogue on the main Jewish feast days. A few years after making his bar

---

[853]Norman L. Geisler and Frank Turek, *I Don't Have Enough Faith to be an Atheist* (Wheaton: Crossway Books, 2004), 329.

[854]Ibid., 332.

[855]Ibid., 337-338.

mitzvah, Louis became disenchanted with his faith when his parents divorced. He became very skeptical in his beliefs.[856]

In 1967, he was drafted and saw battle in Vietnam. Looking for some meaning in all the chaos, he began to experiment with Eastern religious thought. When he returned to the United States, Louis also experimented with LSD. He also looked into Buddhism, Scientology, and Hinduism. The only thing that seemed to make sense to him was the reality of his own sinfulness. Eventually, a Christian pastor convinced Louis that Jesus had proven Himself to be the Jewish Messiah and the Savior of the world. As Louis studied the Old Testament, he became convinced that Jesus was in fact the Jewish Messiah. Louis gave his life to Jesus and trusted Him for salvation. Now, Louis pastors a church whose members are both Jewish and Gentile.[857]

Michael Franzese

Michael Franzese was born in 1971 in Brooklyn, New York. He was the son of an Italian mafia underboss for the Colombo crime family. As a young man, Michael himself rose in the ranks of the Colombo crime family. He used his intelligence to find innovative ways to, both legally and illegally, accumulate wealth—at one point raising over five-million dollars per week. But, everything changed for Michael when he met and fell in love with his future wife Cammy Garcia. Cammy was a born-gain Christian. She fell in love with Michael but convinced him to plead guilty to charges

---

[856]See Lee Strobel's interview with Louis Lapides in Lee Strobel, *The Case for Christ* (Grand Rapids: Zondervan Publishing, 1998), 172-175.

[857]Ibid., 175-181.

filed against him. She led Michael to faith in Christ. While spending several years in prison, he studied the Bible and grew in his faith. Once released from prison, he was reunited with his wife and they began to serve the Lord and build their family. Michael is the only known mafia leader to quit the mafia (without entering the witness protection program) and live. He now speaks to college and pro athletes about the dangers of illegal gambling on sports. He has written several books about his conversion and transformation in Christ.[858]

Nabeel Qureshi

Nabeel Qureshi was raised in a loving Muslim home. His family was originally from Pakistan, but moved to the united Staes where he was raised. As a youngster, Nabeel himself was a very devout Muslim, following in the footsteps of his parents. He read the Koran daily and would pray and fast regularly.[859]

Nabeel studied at universities in the United States, eventually earning a medical doctoral degree. But, while in college, he had several Christian friends who loved him even though he was a Muslim. They also shared the Christian faith with Nabeel. One such friend was the brilliant David Wood

---

[858]Michael Franzese and Dary Matera, *Quitting the Mob: How the "Yuppie Don" Left the Mafia and Lived to Tell His Story* (New York: Haper Collins Publishers, 1992). Michael Franzese, *Blood Covenant: He Quit the Mob and Lived* (New Kensington, PA: Whitaker House, 2003). Michael Franzese, *The Good The Bad and the Forgiven* (Colorado Springs: Outreach, Inc., 2009).

[859]Nabeel Qureshi, *Seeking Allah, Finding Jesus: A Devout Muslim Encounters Christianity* (Grand Rapids: Zondervan Publishing, 2014), 21-51.

(who would later become a Christian scholar and apologist).[860]

David would share with Nabeel evidence for the historical reliability of the New Testament, and evidence for the deity and bodily resurrection of Jesus. David also enlisted the help of two of his friends: Michael Licona and Gary Habermas, two of the world's leading experts on the evidence for Jesus' bodily resurrection. Mike and Gary also became good friends of Nabeel. Nabeel even attended a debate about Jesus' resurrection between Mike and Shabir Ally, one of Islam's leading apologists. Nabeel admitted that Mike won the debate.[861]

Little by little, as Nabeel examined the evidence, he began to accept the historicity of the New Testament portrait of Jesus. Eventually, Nabeel was persuaded that Jesus did in fact die on the cross and rise from the dead, even though this is contrary to what Islam teaches. Eventually, he acknowledged that Jesus died for His sins, and that Jesus was God the Son become a man.[862] Though, as a Muslim, Nabeel had major problems with the Christian doctrine of the Trinity (i.e., the one true God is three equal Persons), he eventually embraced this doctrine as truth.[863]

In Nabeel's autobiography, he traces the steps that God took to bring him to salvation. Even after intellectually accepting the truth of many Christian doctrines, it was still necessary for God to show him the darker side of Muhammad's life and teachings (the founder of Islam), as

---

[860]Ibid., 120-123.

[861]Ibid., 147-151, 162-168.

[862]Ibid., 174-205.

[863]Ibid., 190-196.

well as problems with the Koran (the Muslim holy book). In fact, God even spoke to Nabeel in three dreams. Finally, Nabeel trusted in Jesus for salvation, much to the dismay of his family.[864] Today, Nabeel is a great defender of the Christian faith who publicly speaks and debates in defense of Christianity.

Rabi R. Maharaj

Rabi R. Maharaj grew up in India. He was descended from a long line of Brahman priests and gurus. He, like his father (who had died when Rabi was only a child) before him, was very advanced at Yoga and was disciplined enough to meditate many hours each day. Rabi was worshiped as a god by many Hindus even though he was only a child. Yet, deep inside his soul, he knew he was not God.[865]

In deep meditative states he would visit an unseen world of spirits and Ascended Masters, many of whom appeared to be evil entities who wished to do him harm. He continued his daily hours of meditation; but, still he felt no genuine peace. As he became more and more disillusioned with the traditions of his heritage and with the Hindu faith, he began to search for peace and meaning.[866]

Though there were very few Christians in his community, he heard enough about Jesus to be curious about Him. But, fellow Hindus told Rabi that Jesus was just one of many manifestations of God, and that all religions lead to

---

[864]Ibid., 208-273.

[865]Rabi R. Maharaj, *Death of a Guru* (Eugene, OR: Harvest House Publishers, 1977, 1984), 13-16.

[866]Ibid., 15-16, 56-57, 66-76.

enlightenment. Still, as a teenager, he began to dialogue with Christians and read the Bible. He saw that Jesus claimed to be not one of many ways to God, but the only way to be saved (John 14:6). In fact, Jesus claimed that he died for the sins of mankind—Jesus died for Rabi's sin—He came to give Rabi peace and forgiveness.[867]

After several of his close Hindu friends converted to Christianity, they invited Rabi to a small Christian church. Eventually he visited the church. He heard the songs of praise to Jesus, and he saw the joy in the hearts of the believers. He wanted the peace they had. Rabi knew deep down inside that he was not god—he knew he was a sinner. He knew he needed the peace, salvation, and eternal life that only Jesus could give. Rabi trusted in Jesus alone for salvation that day. Finally, the peace and contentment he had longed for came into his life.[868]

As a new believer, Rabi faced much verbal persecution from his relatives. In their eyes, he had not only abandoned Hinduism, but he had also betrayed the traditions of his family. His own mother pleaded with him to return to Hinduism. But, young Rabi would not waver in his faith. In fact, he began to engage in public speaking and preaching of the Gospel with Youth for Christ. Truly, this was the *death of a guru*—Rabi had been born again into the Kingdom of the true God.[869]

---

[867]Ibid., 118-147.

[868]Ibid., 122-130.

[869]Ibid, 135-147.

Tal Brooke

During the late 1960's, an American named Tal Brooke flew to India on a religious pilgrimage, attempting to find truth. He quickly became the leading Western disciple of an Indian guru and miracle worker named Sai Baba. This guru claimed to be a manifestation of God. Sai Baba took Tal into a world that seemed to shatter reality as understood by the Western mind. In an attempt to achieve godhood and enlightenment, Tal Brooke found himself plunged deep into the demonic realm. After two years of following Sai Baba, Tal began to see the spiritual evil behind the occultic power of his guru. He also discovered the immorality of his Indian mentor. Finally, Tal turned to the Bible to discover the true identity of Sai Baba. Tal randomly opened the Bible and read, "And there shall come false prophets and false Christs working great signs to deceive, if it were possible, even God's very elect" (Matthew 24:14). At that moment he knew that Sai Baba was a deceiver.[870] As time went on, Tal gained the courage he needed to leave Sai Baba's cult and expose the false teachings of his guru. Tal embraced Jesus as his Savior and pleaded with his friends to trust in Jesus as well.[871] Since his conversion, Tal has become a leading defender of the Christian faith. He is now the president of the Spiritual Counterfeits Project in northern California.

---

[870]Tal Brooke, *Avatar of Night* (Berkeley: End Run Publishing, 1999), 338-341.

[871]Ibid., 363-389.

Dennis Jernigan

Dennis Jernigan, in his autobiography, tells about how he had a confused childhood. He never felt accepted by his peers. He never felt like he was masculine enough, and he was often bullied by other boys. In his autobiography, Dennis chronicles events and hurts in his early life that led him into the homosexual lifestyle. He fell into homosexual sins for several years. Eventually, after bouts of depressions and suicidal thoughts, Dennis was led to salvation in Jesus. God began to heal Dennis of his homosexual desires. Dennis began to devote his life to prayer and devotional study of God's Word. He used his musical talent to write songs of worship to his God.[872]

Dennis is now happily married to his wife Melinda. Together, they have nine children. Dennis is now a Christian singer and musician. He also speaks publicly about Jesus delivering him from homosexuality. Dennis believes that, despite our hurts, homosexuality is a sinful choice, and that Jesus can set homosexuals free from their sin.

Conclusion

These are just a few examples of how Jesus Christ has transformed lives throughout history. Many others could be given. These testimonies speak loudly of Christ's ability to make good come out of the worst of situations. Jesus is alive, He saves, and He is still in the business of changing lives.

Paul E. Little speaks of the transforming power of Christ:

---

[872]Dennis Jernigan, *Sing Over Me: An Autobiography* (Innovo Publishing, 2014).

The late Harry Ironside was preaching, some years ago, when a heckler shouted, "Atheism has done more for the world than Christianity!" "Very well," said Ironside, "tomorrow night you bring a hundred men whose lives have been changed for the better by atheism, and I'll bring a hundred who have been transformed by Christ." Needless to say, his heckler friend did not appear the next night.[873]

Although many people claim that only ignorant people become Christians, this is not the case. People from different walks of life have become Christians. They have had different levels of education. Some have been poor; some have been rich. Some were successful; others were failures. Some Christian apologists have even suggested that there is more evidence for atheists fitting into a tightly defined group than there is for Christians.[874] Many leading atheists throughout history have had either absent or passive fathers.[875] It can be argued that atheists deny God's existence because of their desire to kill the father image.[876]

It seems that a merely psychological explanation for a conversion to Christianity is unacceptable. The transformed lives of Christians who have come from many different backgrounds provide strong confirmation for the life-changing power of Jesus Christ.

---

[873] Paul E. Little, *Know Why You Believe* (Wheaton: Victor Books, 1967), 145-146.

[874] Moreland, *Scaling the Secular City*, 229.

[875] Ibid.

[876] Ibid.

Chapter 23

Scientific Apologetics

Scientific apologetics involves using scientific evidences to argue for the biblical God as creator of the universe. Norman Geisler and J. Kerby Anderson's scientific apologetic approach has already been discussed in this work in the chapter on Geisler's apologetic methodology. Geisler and Anderson are old-earth creationists—they believe that God created the universe thirteen to eighteen billion years ago, and that God did not utilize evolution to bring about His creation. Other Christian apologists believe that God used evolution (i.e., theistic-evolutionists), while many defenders of the faith believe that God created the universe in six literal days around six thousand years ago (i.e., young earth creationists).

Other Old Earth Creation Scientists

Besides Norman Geisler and J. Kerby Anderson, other leading old earth creationists include Philip Johnson, Hugh Ross, William Dembski, Jonathan Wells, and Michael Behe. Like Geisler and Anderson, these apologists accept big bang cosmology and the results of evolutionary dating methods. But, also like Geisler and Anderson, they reject evolution and argue for creation by an intelligent Designer.

Attorney Philip Johnson, author of *Darwin on Trial*,[877] is considered by many to be the founder of the "Intelligent Design Movement." This movement argues that scientific evidence does not support atheistic evolution. Instead, the scientific data shows the universe to be a product of intelligent design. Adherents of this movement do not claim to be religious. They claim to only go as far as the scientific evidence will take them. However, they believe the scientific evidence clearly indicates that the universe reveals itself to be a product of intelligent design.

Hugh Ross, author of *The Creator and the Cosmos*,[878] is an astrophysicist who believes the big bang model proves the beginning of the universe and the existence of God (the Creator). Ross sees the anthropic principle and the fine-tuning of the universe for intelligent life as strong evidence for God as the intelligent Designer of the universe. Ross provides strong scientific arguments for God as both the Creator and the designer of the universe. Ross relates that the anthropic (from the Greek word *anthropos* for man) principle shows that the universe appears as if it was fine-tuned to support human life on the planet earth. He lists twenty-five narrowly defined parameters in the universe for life to exist on planet earth.[879] If any of these twenty-five factors were changed just slightly, there would be no life on the planet earth. Ross also lists thirty-two narrowly defined parameters necessary for life on earth found in our galaxy and solar system.[880] Again, slight

---

[877]Phillip E. Johnson, *Darwin on Trial* (Downers Grove: IL, 1991).

[878]Hugh Ross, *The Creator and the Cosmos* (Colorado Springs: NavPress, 1993).

[879]Ibid., 111-114.

changes in these factors would make life on earth impossible. It seems that the universe and our galaxy were fine-tuned (or designed) for the purpose of enabling the planet earth to support life, even human life.

Mathematician and philosopher William Dembski, author of *Intelligent Design*,[881] points to the specified complexity found in single-celled animals as evidence for intelligent design. The highly complex information found in even the most basic unit of life (i.e., the cell) demands the intelligent design explanation. Only intelligence produces the highly complex information known as specified complexity. The laws of nature, time, and chance can never produce specified complexity. Intelligence is the only known cause for specified complexity.

Dembski spells out the precise formula to detect products of intelligent design. A product of intelligent design, as opposed to a product of mere chance, must be contingent (not necessary), complex (not simple), and specified (i.e., it must contain meaningful information).[882]

In another work entitled *Understanding Intelligent Design*, co-authored with Sean McDowell, Dembski points out a major problem for evolutionary theory and the origin of life dealing with DNA, protein, and RNA. Dembski and McDowell stated: "DNA depends on protein for proper functioning, yet protein relies on DNA for correct sequencing. Protein cannot arise apart from DNA, yet DNA needs protein to function. So which came first? How did two separate systems arise simultaneously that rely on one another for

---

[880]Ibid., 129-132.

[881]William A. Dembski, *Intelligent Design* (Downers Grove, IL: Intervarsity Press, 1999).

[882]Dembski, 127-139.

survival and function."[883] They also point out that RNA could not have formed on primitive earth without living cells (which contain DNA).[884] DNA, RNA, and proteins are interdependent—they cannot exist and function without each other. It is highly unlikely (if not impossible) that one evolved into existence, then another, and then finally the third developed. It is much more likely that RNA, DNA, and proteins were created at the same time.

Jonathan Wells shows in his work *Icons of Evolution*[885] that much of what is taught in high school and college science textbooks has been rejected by evolutionary scientists themselves. Yet, these teachings still show up in textbooks. There seems to be no sense of urgency to remove these false teachings.

These "icons" include: 1) the mistaken idea that the Miller-Urey experiment proved life evolved from non-life, 2) that the history of living things resemble Darwin's tree of life, 3) that similarities in vertebrate limbs prove common ancestry, 4) that drawings of Haeckel's embryos really do represent the development of human embryos, 5) that Archaeopteryx really is the missing link between reptiles and birds, 6) that photos of peppered moths on tree trunks somehow prove evolutionary theory, 7) that Darwin's finches are strong evidence for evolution, 8) that the production of four-winged fruit flies in the lab proves evolution, 9) that there is agreement among evolutionists about the family tree of

---

[883]William Dembski and Sean McDowell, *Understanding Intelligent Design* (Eugene: OR: Harvest House Publishers, 2008), 129.

[884]Ibid., 130.

[885]Jonathan Wells, *Icons of Evolution: Science or Myth?* (Washington, DC: Regenery Publishing, 2000).

modern horses, and 10) that there is widespread agreement concerning the supposed missing links between apes and humans.[886] The vast majority of the world's leading evolutionary scientists reject all ten of these "icons." The fact that these ten discredited ideas are still in textbooks is probably due to the fact that without them the evolutionary model shows itself to be unsupported by the evidence.

Michael Behe, author of *Darwin's Black Box*,[887] is an associate professor of biochemistry at Lehigh University. His work has shown that, on the sub-molecular level, entities exist that are as complex as space ships or computers. Yet, these entities are irreducibly complex. In other words, though they are as complex as space ships or computers, they could not function or survive if they were any less complex. If one part were removed, they would cease to exist. In other words, they could not have evolved into their present state—they had to have been created in their fully functional and complex state.[888] Evolution fails to explain the origin of these irreducibly complex entities. Behe points to the bacterial flagellum as an example of a sub-molecular entity that is irreducibly complex. The flagellum is a propeller that is rotated by a motor. This allows many bacteria to "swim." In order to perform this task, the flagellum is very complex. Many distinct parts must be in place to have a functioning flagellum. Yet, it cannot function unless it exists with all its parts—it is irreducibly complex.[889]

---

[886]Ibid., 9-228.

[887]Michael J. Behe, *Darwin's Black Box* (New York: Free Press: 1996).

[888]Ibid., 39, 46-48.

[889]Ibid., 69-73.

The Theistic-Evolutionary Views of Francis Collins

Francis Collins is the author of *The Language of God*.[890] He is one of the world's leading geneticists, having been selected to head the "Human Genome Project." Collins believes young earth creationism, old earth creationism, and the intelligent design movement are all pseudo-science. Collins apparently believes that science must restrict itself to natural causes—a scientist must never be open to the possibility that a supernatural cause might be the only adequate explanation for a natural effect.[891] Since Collins has arbitrarily limited science to the search for natural causes, any scientific evidence for God is automatically ruled out a priori (before the evidence is examined). Apparently, Collins does not see that his rejection of creationism and the intelligent design movement is totally arbitrary.

Still, despite his opposition to nature pointing to the supernatural, Collins converted to Christianity as an adult and a scientist. It was not because he found God in science. No, it is because he found that science could only explain the physical world. But, reality is much more than the physical world. Though Collins accepts evolution, he acknowledges that science cannot explain man's moral experience. Collins was convinced by C. S. Lewis' moral argument for God that natural causes cannot account for man's moral experience. Due to Lewis' moral argument for God and science's inability to adequately explain the reality of morality, Collins

---

[890]Francis S. Collins, *The Language of God: A Scientist Presents Evidence for Belief* (New York: Free Press, 2006).

[891]Ibid., 171-195.

converted to Christianity.[892] Hence, though Collins argues for God, he is a theistic evolutionist.[893]

In fact, though he is a scientist, his arguments for God are more philosophical than scientific. Although he does think the Big Bang Model allows for a theistic explanation, his primary argument for God is philosophical (the moral argument), not scientific.

The theistic-evolutionary approach of Collins views the first few chapters of Genesis as Divinely-inspired mythology. This approach does not consider the Genesis account of creation to be literal. But, this raises numerous problems. First, Jesus Himself did take the Genesis account of creation (and the fall and flood) literally. Second, if one rejects the literal creation account of Genesis, this seems to do damage to the Genesis account of the fall of mankind. But, if the first humans did not literally fall into sin in the Garden, then what need is there for a Savior? It would appear that a better approach for Bible-believing Christians is to take the Genesis account of the creation and the fall literally. Theistic-evolution should not be a viable option for anyone who takes the Bible seriously and believes it is the inerrant Word of God.

The Young Earth Creationism of Henry Morris and Duane Gish

Henry Morris and Duane Gish of the Institute of Creation Research were the twentieth-century's leading young earth creationists. The work of Morris and Gish is being continued by a new generation of young earth creation scientists such as: Jonathan Sarfati, John Morris, Steve Austin,

---

[892]Ibid., 11-31.

[893]Ibid., 197-211.

Russell Humphries, Jason Lisle, Paul Nelson, John Mark Reynolds, and Kurt Wise. Unlike old earth creationists, young earth creationists reject the evolutionary dating methods; they do not believe the universe is billions of years old. Instead, these scientists believe the universe is only several thousands of years old.

Young earth creationists do not believe the fossil record unveils the history of life on planet earth. Rather, they interpret the fossil record primarily to be evidence for the global flood spoken of in the Book of Genesis. Young earth creationists often point out the unproven assumptions of evolutionists, as well as other problems with evolution. Young earth creationists literally interpret the Biblical account of creation as spelled out in the first few chapters of Genesis. They believe that there was no death in the animal kingdom before mankind fell into sin. Young earth creation scientists reject big bang cosmology and deny the existence of any authentic missing links or transitional forms.

THERMODYNAMICS

Thermodynamics deals with the relationship between heat, energy, and work.[894] The first and second laws of thermodynamics pose serious problems for evolution. The first law of thermodynamics is called energy conservation. It states that the amount of energy in the universe remains constant; no energy is now being created or destroyed.[895] This

---

[894]Tom M. Graham, *Biology, the Essential Principles* (Philadelphia: Saunders College Publishing, 1982), 75.

[895]Ibid.

means that if the universe had a beginning, whatever process or act that brought the universe into existence is no longer in operation today. In other words, the "creation process" is no longer operating today. Therefore, either the universe is eternal or the universe was created in the past; no continuing creative process is occurring.

The second law of thermodynamics is called entropy. Though the amount of energy in the universe remains constant, it changes form. The second law states that when energy changes form it becomes less usable.[896] Therefore, the amount of usable energy in the universe is running out. This means that the day will come when all the energy in the universe will have been used up. This will be the death of the universe. There must have been a time when all the energy of the universe was usable; this would be the beginning of the universe. In other words, since the universe is going to have an end, it is not eternal. If it is not eternal, then it must have had a beginning. The big bang model (which is rejected by young earth creationists) and the expansion of the universe also confirm the beginning of the universe.[897]

The evolutionist faces a dilemma. The first and second laws of thermodynamics together declare that the universe had a beginning. The evolutionists cannot deny these laws, for they are considered to be the most firmly established laws of modern science.[898] But, evolution runs counter to these two laws. When a scientific model contradicts a scientific law, the model should be abandoned. Since the first and second laws

---

[896]Ibid.

[897]Hugh Ross, *The Fingerprint of God* (Orange: Promise Publishing Company, 1991), 53-105.

[898]Henry M. Morris, *Science and the Bible* (Chicago: Moody Press, 1986), 17.

of thermodynamics teach that the universe had a beginning, then something outside the universe must have caused the universe to come into existence. For, from nothing, nothing comes. Therefore, the universe could not have evolved into existence out of nothing.

EVOLUTIONARY DATING METHODS

The evolutionary dating methods are inconsistent and unreliable. All evolutionary dating methods are based upon uniformitarianism.[899] Uniformitarianism assumes that there were no world-wide catastrophes; therefore, the rate of decay has remained constant. Uniformitarianism assumes that today's processes have continued at the same rate throughout all time. However, if there were a world-wide flood and a special creation by God, then this uniformitarian assumption would be unwarranted.[900]

Evolutionary dating methods have been shown to be unreliable. Rocks known to have been only a few hundred years old have been dated to be hundreds of millions of years old.[901] Henry Morris has stated that there are many different ways to date the earth's age, but evolutionists only use those methods which give astronomically old dates since evolution needs millions of years to seem even slightly possible.[902] Two examples of dating methods which point to a young earth are

---

[899]Ibid., 66.

[900]Ibid.

[901]Morris, *Many Infallible Proofs* (El Cajon: Master Books, 1974), 292-293.

[902]Ibid., 294.

364

population statistics and the earth's magnetic field.[903] If one assumes the principle of uniformitarianism, then due to the present rate at which the population of mankind increases, the start of the present population would take one back 4,300 years to the traditional date for the flood.[904] Concerning the strength of the earth's magnetic field, if one assumes that the present rate of decay remains the same going back indefinitely into the past, then about 7,000 years ago it would have been too strong to sustain life.[905]

The most convincing argument for an old earth is probably that of the speed of light.[906] The speed of light is assumed by scientists to be constant. The light of distant stars and galaxies can be seen on earth. Since it would have taken billions of years for the light of some of these celestial bodies to reach earth (assuming the speed of light has remained the same throughout all time), the universe must be billions of years old.[907] However, Barry Setterfield of Australia studied every measurement of the speed of light and found that the speed of light has not been constant throughout all time; it had been faster in the past.[908] Setterfield's research, if reliable, reveals the age of the universe to be only 6,000 years old.[909]

---

[903]Ibid., 295-296.

[904]Ibid., 296.

[905]Ibid., 295.

[906]Paul D. Ackerman, *It's A Young World After All* (Grand Rapids: Baker Book House, 1986), 72.

[907]Ibid., 73.

[908]Ibid., 74.

[909]Ibid., 75.

Young earth physicist Russell Humphreys also proposes a cosmology with the universe being only several thousand years old. His model of the universe utilizes Einstein's General Law of Relativity, gravitational time dilation, and white hole cosmology.[910] However, his model does not argue that the speed of light is slowing down.

Even if the universe is old, this would not refute the creation model. Many creationists believe in an old universe.[911] However, if the universe is young, the evolution model is destroyed. One thing is clear: the principle of uniformitarianism is an assumption that appears to go against the evidence. If uniformitarianism is true, then all the dating methods would reveal the same approximate dates. These dates would be old or young; they would not be old and young. Since some dating methods point to an old earth and others point to a young earth, the evolutionary dating methods are unreliable. Since uniformitarianism is not a given, the date of the universe is an open question.

THE FOSSIL RECORD

The fossil record is assumed to prove evolution, but, this is not the case. The fossil record shows no evidence of transitional forms (missing links). New life forms appear suddenly and fully developed.[912] There are no animals with half-fins or half-wings in the fossil record. If there were

----

[910]D. Russell Humphreys, *Starlight and Time* (El Cajon: Master Books, 1994), 9-29.

[911]See Hugh Ross, *Creation and Time* (Colorado Springs: NavPress, 1994).

[912]Geisler and Anderson, *Origin Science*, 150-153.

transitional forms, why have none been found? This is a serious problem for evolutionists. Harvard paleontologists Stephen Jay Gould and Louis Agassiz have admitted this lack of evidence for evolution in the fossil record.[913] Aggassiz, a nineteenth-century creationist, stated:

> Species appear suddenly and disappear suddenly in the progressive strata.... the supposed intermediate forms between the species of different geological periods are imaginary beings, called up merely in support of a fanciful theory.[914]

Gould, a twentieth century evolutionist, stated:

> In any local area, a species does not arise gradually by the steady transformation of its ancestors; it appears all at once and "fully formed."[915]

It is interesting to note that the first geologists believed that the fossil record was evidence for the world-wide flood recorded in the Bible.[916] This view is strengthened by the fact that fossilization is extremely rare today. Even if the earth existed for millions of years, that would not be enough time for the present fossil record to have been produced without

---

[913]Ibid., 150-152.

[914]Louis Agassiz, "Contribution to the Natural History of the United States," *American Journal of Science*, (1860): 144-145.

[915]Stephen Jay Gould, "Evolution's Erratic Pace," *Natural History*, (May 1977): 14.

[916]Morris, *Science and the Bible*, 67.
367

any world-wide catastrophes.[917] Fossilization is world-wide and caused by the rapid burial of animals, which is something a world-wide flood would do.[918]

Another problem for evolution concerning the fossil record is polystrate fossils. These are fossils that extend through two or more layers of sedimentary rock.[919] These fossils are usually trees. In order for a standing tree to be fossilized, it would have to be quickly buried before it decayed. However, in these polystrate fossils, the several layers of earth through which the tree extends supposedly took millions of years to form.[920] This reveals that evolutionists are mistaken when they assume that layers of sedimentary rock must take millions of years to form and therefore indicate large quantities of time. No tree can live for millions of years. Therefore, these layers of sedimentary rock are not evidence for an old earth. They had to have been formed rapidly.[921]

Another problem for evolution is the fact that the fossil record often appears out of sequence.[922] Sometimes "old" fossils appear resting on rock layers containing "younger" fossils.[923] The geologic column is "an imagined chronological arrangement of rock units in columnar form with the

---

[917]Scott M. Huse, *The Collapse of Evolution* (Grand rapids: baker Book House, 1983), 46.

[918]Ackerman, 83.

[919]Ibid., 84.

[920]Ibid.

[921]Ibid.

[922]Morris, *Science and the Bible*, 68-69.

[923]Ibid.

presumed oldest units at the bottom and presumed youngest at the top."[924] However, the world is full of strata appearing in the wrong order.[925] If these layers took millions of years to be formed as evolutionists say, then this would not be the case.

If one assumes the possibility that the fossil record was formed rapidly, the world-wide flood offers a better explanation. The flood would tend to bury fossils in this order. First, deep oceans creatures would be fossilized. After that, creatures in shallower water would be buried, followed by amphibians and land-bordering creatures. Next would be swamp, marsh, and low river-flat creatures (especially reptiles). After that, higher mammals that retreated to higher ground in their attempt to escape the flood would be fossilized. Finally, humans would be overtaken.[926] This would be the "standard" order; still, there would be many exceptions due to upheavals in the earth's crust during and after the world-wide flood.[927] A world-wide catastrophe such as the flood offers a much more plausible explanation for these exceptions than evolution does.[928]

Other interesting aspects of flood geology are the canopy theory and the global ice age. The canopy theory refers to Genesis 1:6-8.[929] In that passage, the Bible teaches that God surrounded the earth's atmosphere with a huge canopy of water. This would have worked liked the ozone layer does

[924]Huse, 147.

[925]Morris, *Science and the Bible*, 70.

[926]Ibid., 73.

[927]Ibid., 74.

[928]Ibid., 75.

[929]Ibid., 82-85.

today. It would have filtered out poisonous rays from the sun, thus increasing longevity. This may explain why the Bible records pre-flood men living more than nine-hundred years (Genesis 5). After the flood, man's life-span would drastically decrease. The water contained in the canopy descended in the great flood (Genesis 6:11-12) and covered the entire earth (Genesis 7:19). This would explain why three-fourths of the earth's surface is covered with water. In fact, if the earth were a completely smooth sphere, it would be covered by water 1.5 miles in depth.[930] After the flood, tremendous upheavals in the earth's crust due to the catastrophe would cause valleys to sink and mountains to rise (Psalm 104:5-9). The mountains that rose would become the dry land man now inhabits. The upheavals in the earth's crust could also explain much of the continental shifts that scientists have shown to have occurred.

A global flood would cause a global ice age.[931] Today, evolutionists accept the global ice age, but they reject a universal flood which could have caused it. Because of this, glacial geologists have failed to determine what caused the ice age. Also, the lack of vegetation due to the ice age would have killed off most of the dinosaurs (though some recent dinosaur sightings are well-documented).[932]

---

[930]Ibid., 83.

[931]Ibid., 81.

[932]Henry M. Morris, *The Biblical Basis for Modern Science* (Grand Rapids: Baker Book House, 1984), 350-359. Some of the recent dinosaur sightings noted by Morris include: smaller brontosaurus in the rain forests of the Congo, living plesiosaurs in the Loch Ness and numerous other waterways, and what appears to be a freshly decayed plesiosaur captured and photographed by Japanese fishermen off the coast of New Zealand.

LACK OF TRANSITIONAL FORMS

A devastating problem for the evolution model is the lack of transitional forms. No one possesses an undisputed missing link. All the supposed missing links between apes and men have been dismissed. Neanderthal Man and Cro-Magnon Man both have the features of modern man.[933] Colorado Man turned out to be a member of the horse family.[934] Java Man (also known as Pithecanthropus) was shown to be the remains of a large gibbon.[935] Heidelberg Man consisted of only a lower jaw.[936] Obviously, a lower jaw is insufficient evidence for a missing link. One can only speculate as to the makeup of the rest of the skull and skeleton. The Piltdown Man was revealed to be a clever hoax.[937] The Peking Man is now thought to be a large monkey or baboon.[938] The Southern Ape (also called Australopithecus), Dryopithecus, and Ramapithecus were extinct apes.[939] The East African Man (Zinjanthropus) was shown to be an ape.[940] Finally, the Nebraska Man, which consisted of only one tooth, was proven to be the tooth of an

---

[933]*Morris, Science and the Bible*, 58.

[934]Huse, 98.

[935]Morris, *Science and the Bible*, 56.

[936]Marvin Lubenow, *Bones of Contention* (Grand Rapids: Baker Book House, 1992), 79.

[937]Morris, *Science and the Bible*, 56.

[938]Ibid.

[939]Ibid., 57-58.

[940]Lubenow, 167.

extinct pig.[941] This is rather interesting since this tooth had been presented as evidence in the 1925 "monkey trial" as "evidence" for the evolutionary model.[942] When the tooth of an extinct pig is mistaken for the tooth of the missing link between apes and men, it shows how subjective modern science has become. Though high school and college textbooks show drawings of the missing links from apes to men, the fact is that this art merely depicts the vivid imagination of scientists. No undisputed missing link between apes and men has been discovered.

Archaeopteryx was once thought to be a transitional form between reptiles and birds.[943] It had features resembling that of a reptile (teeth, lizard-like tail, and claws). But, archaeopteryx also had wings and feathers similar to a bird. Still, the archaeopteryx was fully developed. It did not have half-wings or the like. Archaeopteryx has now been classified as a bird. This is due to the fact that every characteristic of archaeopteryx can be found in some genuine bird, though some of its features are not found in reptiles.[944] It should also be noted that the supposed evolution of reptiles into birds is highly improbable. The lungs of a reptile have millions of tiny air sacs, while the lungs of birds have tubes. In order for a transitional form to exist between a reptile and a bird it would have to breathe without having fully-developed lungs.[945]

---

[941]Morris, *Science and the Bible*, 58.

[942]Ibid.

[943]Huse, 110.

[944]Morris, *Science and the Bible*, 267-268. See also Huse, 110-112.

[945]Huse, 112.

An extinct, small three-toed animal called Eohippus was once thought to be the ancestor of the modern, large, one-toed horse.[946] It is now doubtful that Eohippus should have ever been classified in the horse family. Eohippus is probably an extinct type of hyrax.[947]

Evolutions believe that invertebrates (animals without backbones) have evolved into vertebrates (animals with backbones). However, no transitional form between the two has ever been found.[948]

This lack of transitional forms is very problematic for the evolution model. It has been over 130 years since Darwin wrote *The Origin of Species*. Still, no missing links have been found. Due to this absence of evidence for evolution, modern evolutionists like Stephen Jay Gould have proposed a new model called "Punctuated Equilibrium."[949] Whereas evolution means "gradual change," Punctuated Equilibrium teaches that the changes occurred so suddenly that transitional forms did not survive long enough to be fossilized. It appears that Punctuated Equilibrium is an attempt to explain away the absence of evidence for evolution—but it fails as well.

Since there is no evidence of missing links in the fossil record, evolution should be rejected. The lack of transitional forms in the fossil record is evidence against evolution and in favor of the creation model, which teaches that there are no missing links.[950]

---

[946]Morris, *Science and the Bible*, 54-55.

[947]Ibid.

[948]Huse, 44.

[949]Geisler and Anderson, 150-153.

[950]Ibid.

MUTATIONS

Evolutionists need a mechanism that explains how evolution has supposedly occurred. Many evolutionists believe that mutation is this mechanism.[951] However, mutations merely scramble the already existing genetic code. No new genetic information is added.[952] Yet, for evolution to have occurred, a mechanism is needed through which new genes are produced. Therefore, mutations fail to explain evolution. Evolutionists claim that they believe the present interprets the past. However, there is no mechanism in the present that spontaneously produces new genetic information. Until such a mechanism is found, evolution can only be accepted by "blind faith."

HEISENBERG'S PRINCIPLE OF INDETERMINACY

Heisenberg's principle of indeterminacy is a theory in quantum physics. Quantum physics deals with the atom and the motion of subatomic particles.[953] The principle of indeterminacy states that it is impossible to determine both the position in space of a subatomic particle and that particle's motion at the same time.[954] Therefore, subatomic particle

---

[951]Morris, *Science and the Bible*, 46-47.

[952]Ibid.

[953]*The World Book Encyclopedia* (Chicago: World Book, Inc., 1985), vol. 16, 4.

[954]Roy E. Peacock, *A Brief History of Eternity* (Wheaton: Crossway Books, 1990), 56-59.

movement is currently unpredictable for man. This simply means that scientists aren't yet able to accurately predict where a specific particle will be at a given moment. Some scientists have wrongly concluded from this that things can occur on the subatomic level without a cause. If this were true, the scientists reason, then it would be possible that the universe just popped into existence without a cause. However, if this were the case, it would not favor either evolution or creation. If things can come into existence without a cause, then the entire basis for modern science crumbles. All experiments would be a waste of time, for any given phenomena could have come into existence without a cause. Therefore, there would be no need to study the elements of the universe any longer. Modern science would die.

Albert Einstein believed that Heisenberg's principle did not prove that things can occur without a cause. Einstein held that the causes actually do exist, though man may not be able to find them.[955] Man is limited in knowledge, and there may be some causes he is unable to find.[956] Heisenberg's principle, therefore, cannot come to the aid of evolution; the universe (since it had a beginning) needs a cause. It should also be noted that even if quantum events occurred without a cause, it would still not mean that something has been produced from absolutely nothing. After all, some things has to exist for a quantum event to occur (i.e., a sub atomic particle, space).

---

[955]Ibid., 59.

[956]Moreland, *Scaling the Secular City*, (Grand Rapids: Baker Book House, 1987), 38-39.

CONCLUSION

In conclusion, evolution is not a proven fact. It is assumed to be true by many scientists, but they have offered no convincing proofs. There is no evidence for the evolution model. This can be seen in the many unproven assumptions held by evolutionists.

First, there is no evidence for spontaneous generation. The belief that life evolved from non-life contradicts both the cell theory and the law of biogenesis. The Miller-Urey experiments have failed to produce life in the lab (if they were successful, it would be evidence for the creation model and intelligent design, not the evolution model).

Second, there is no evidence for the evolutionary assumption that the universe is eternal. If an evolutionist believes the universe is eternal (most evolutionists deny this), the evolutionist must accept this by faith. All the available scientific evidence shows the universe had a beginning. Most Evolutionists assume that the universe burst into existence from nothing, totally without a cause, but this assumption goes against reason and all the available scientific evidence.

Third, there is no evidence that intelligence could come from non-intelligence. Intelligence shows evidence of design; it could not have been produced by chance.

Fourth, no evidence has been found proving that multi-celled animals came from single-celled animals. (Even the human embryo does not evolve into a human; it has its full human genetic code at conception.[957])

Fifth, there is no evidence for the evolution of animals with backbones from animals without backbones.[958] Though

---

[957]Huse, 120.

[958]Ibid., 44.

there should be multitudes of transitional forms between the two groups, none have been found.

Sixth, there is no evidence for the common ancestry of fish, reptiles, birds, and mammals.[959] Common anatomy could point to a common Designer; it does not necessarily point to common ancestry.

All these major steps that evolution is supposed to have taken are assumed to have occurred; yet, they have not been proven to have occurred. Therefore, evolution itself is an unproven assumption. Those who dogmatically proclaim it as truth spend more time explaining away the scientific evidence against their view than they do providing evidence for their view. Any scientific model which lacks plausibility should be abandoned. Such is the case with evolution.

Evolution needs God, but God does not need evolution. If evolution is true, then God is needed to bring the universe into existence from nothing, to bring life from non-life, and complex life forms from simple life forms. In each case, a miraculous superseding of natural laws is needed. However, if God exists, He doesn't need evolution. He could have either started the long evolutionary process or He could have created the universe in six literal days. God could have used evolution, but if He did, He covered His tracks. He left no evidence. Since God is not the author of deception, it is reasonable to conclude that evolution is a myth, devoid of any scientific evidence and not worthy to be considered true.

---

[959]Ibid.

Chapter 24

Paranormal Apologetics

A recent method of defending the Christian faith can be called *Paranormal Apologetics*. This approach attempts to give a Christian explanation for many of the paranormal experiences people are having today. These paranormal experiences include: UFO sightings, alien abductions, haunted houses, near death experiences, out of body experiences, and bigfoot sightings.

It is easy for Christian scholars to dismiss these reports as products of someone's wild imagination. But, if this is the approach that Christian apologists take, many opportunities to reach unsaved people in our society will be forfeited. As our culture turns its back on God, a door has been opened to the world of the occult. People are having real experiences and they are looking for real explanations. The Bible has the explanations they seek; but, if Christian apologists do not provide the scriptural explanations for these paranormal experiences, then these people will likely be deceived by neo-pagan, New Age thought.

In this chapter, a few examples of apologists who have answered the call to explain paranormal data will be discussed. Though there are many apologists now researching some of the many paranormal issues, the apologists mentioned below will suffice as a summary of paranormal apologetics.

Cris Putnam

Cris Putnam is one of the few Christian apologists who recognizes the need for defenders of the faith to update their apologetic arguments to deal with a changing culture. Putnam argues that Christian apologists need a "supernatural worldview."[960] Though not all apologists would agree with Putnam's conclusions, he should be applauded for tackling some of the most controversial issues of our day: near-death-experiences, out of body experiences, clairvoyance, telepathy, precognition, remote viewing, haunted houses, apparitions of deceased humans, and spiritism.[961]

Too often the Christian apologist sounds just like an atheist, denouncing every supernatural claim as fraudulent or a mistaken interpretation of a natural event. But, the biblical worldview is a supernatural world view. Supernatural events have occurred and can still occur in this world. These events could be caused by God and His angels or by Satan and his demons. In fact, Putnam is open to the possibility that God may allow deceased humans (saved and unsaved) to visit the land of the living (the Bible speaks of Samuel the prophet, Moses, and Elijah coming back).[962] In fact, contrary to the

---

[960]Cris Putnam, *The Supernatural Worldview: Examining Paranormal, PSI, and the Apocalyptic* (Crane, MI: Defender, 2014), 1-2, 29-31.

[961]Ibid., 149-347.

[962]Ibid., 340-347.

view of many other Christians, Putnam is open to the possibility that demons are not fallen angels, but the ghosts of dead men.[963] He is not dogmatic that all demons are ghosts of deceased humans, but he does believe that some ghosts are.[964]

Putnam is even open to the possibility that extra-sensory perception might be a natural ability latent in most humans.[965] Though paranormal knowledge could come from God or Satan, Putnam believes it is also possible that it comes from latent natural abilities of man. Though Putnam sees in near-death-experiences outstanding evidence for life after death, he also believes many people who have these experiences are being demonically deceived into believing that all people go to heaven.[966] Though many apologists might disagree with some of Putnam's conclusions, they should follow his example by bringing their apologetic expertise into the domain of the paranormal. Many Americans are looking for answers to paranormal questions—the Bible provides those answers.

Christian UFO Researchers

In recent years, many Christian thinkers have addressed the UFO phenomenon. As far back as 1981, Christian philosopher Norman Geisler had the courage to intelligently answer questions, during a cross-examination in the *McLean v. Arkansas Board of Education* trial, about

---

[963]Ibid., 279-284, 347.

[964]Ibid.

[965]Ibid., 193-254.

[966]Ibid., 186-187.

UFO's and aliens. Geisler expressed his biblically-based opinion that the UFO and alien phenomenon were demonic deception. Geisler stated that he interviewed numerous people who had experienced UFO phenomena.[967]

In 1992, Christian researcher William Alnor authored a book entitled *UFOs in the New Age: Extraterrestrial Messages and the Truth of Scripture*.[968] The book was endorsed by Tal Brooke, a leading expert on the occult and the president of the *Spiritual Counterfeits Project*. In this book, Alnor shows that not all UFO sightings and alien abduction reports are fraudulent. But, Alnor argues that these visitors are not from other planets. When all the data is taken seriously, only a supernatural explanation will suffice. Alnor concludes that these "alien" visitors are actually demons promoting a neo-pagan, New Age message.[969] In fact, numerous New Age cults have built their views upon alien encounters.[970]

In 2004, Gary Bates authored *Alien Intrusion: UFOs and the Evolution Connection*. In this book, Bates noted that although ninety to ninety-five percent of UFO sightings have natural explanations, the remaining sightings cannot be so easily dismissed.[971] Bates notes that research shows that the "alien" visitors are non-physical entities who are able to

---

[967]Norman L. Geisler, *Creation and the Courts* (Wheaton: Crossway Books, 2007), 91-92, 350, 369-370.

[968]William M. Alnor, *UFOs in the New Age: Extraterrestrial Messages and the Truth of Scripture* (Grand rapids: Baker Book House, 1992).

[969]Ibid., 134-164.

[970]Ibid., 80, 177, 192-198.

[971]Gary Bates, *Alien Invasion: UFOs and the Evolution Connection* (Green Forest, AR: Master Books, 2004), 149-150.

physically manifest themselves to human.[972] The message they often proclaim contradicts Christianity, and these "space brothers" often depart when the name of Jesus is invoked by the abductee.[973] These "alien" entities fit the general description of what the Bible calls demons or unclean spirits.

In 2002, Hugh Ross, Kenneth Samples, and Mark Clark authored a work dealing with the UFO phenomenon.[974] This book showed that it is scientifically impossible for beings from other planets to have travelled all the way to earth.[975] Also, UFOs have been known to violate the laws of physics. Examples of this include: 1) UFOs making ninety-degree turns or sudden stops at speeds approaching fifteen thousand miles per hour, 2) UFO spacecraft randomly changing size, shape, or color, and 3) UFOs suddenly disappearing and reappearing at will.[976] The evidence indicates that these "space brothers" are spiritual deceptive beings, what the Bible refers to as "demons."

Christian UFO researchers Guy Malone and Joe Jordan have both reported that there have been numerous cases in which the aliens have departed as soon as the name of Jesus is invoked by the abductee.[977] In fact, aliens attack

---

[972]Ibid., 248-249.

[973]Ibid., 256-264, 280, 287-288, 291-294.

[974]Hugh Ross, Kenneth Samples, and Mark Clark, *Lights in the Sky and Little Green Men: A Rational Christian Look at UFOs and Extraterrestrials* (Colorado Springs: NavPress, 2002).

[975]Ibid., 55-64.

[976]Ibid., 70.

Christianity and often deny that Jesus is God and Savior. Why would "aliens" travel ninety billion light years merely to attack one specific religion?[978] Malone and Jordan are convinced that the space brothers are actually demons who attempt to deceive mankind.

Michael S. Heiser earned a Ph.D. in ancient Semitic languages from the University of Wisconson-Madison. He is a leading scholar on Old Testament studies and other ancient Semitic literature. Due to his research, Heiser also sees the "space brothers" as deceiving demons whose goal it is to lead mankind astray. These demonic entities claim that they are our creators and guardians. Heiser sees this as an attempt to convince humans to reject belief in God, and embrace the idea that we come from the space brothers, and we owe them our allegiance.[979] That a scholar of Heiser's stature is willing to do in-depth research concerning the real nature of the controversial UFO phenomena is a healthy sign for the current state of Christian apologetics in America.

Gary Habermas and J. P. Moreland: Near-Death Experiences

Two leading Christian apologists, Gary Habermas and J. P. Moreland, researched the phenomena known as near-death experiences. Habermas and Moreland discussed numerous cases where people gave detailed eyewitness

---

[977]Interviews with Joe Jordan and Guy Malone are discussed in Nick Redfern, *Final Events* (San Antonio: Anomalist Books, 2010), 191-197, 201-207.

[978]Ibid., 203.

[979]Heiser is interviewed in Nick Redfern, *Final Events*, 198-200.

testimony of events while they were clinically dead.[980] In many cases, the patients had no brain waves or heart beat while they continued to witness what was occurring.[981] Their research showed that this was excellent evidence for life after death and the existence of the human soul.[982]

Bigfoot Sightings

Very few Christian apologists have researched Bigfoot sightings. Yet, scholarly work done by non-Christians has shown that these sightings should be taken more seriously.[983] The research of Grover S. Krantz, an anthropologist from Washington State University, is a case in point. He thoroughly studied Bigfoot footprints found in 1970 in northeast Washington State. He noted that the footprints were three to four times larger than a human footprint. He estimated that, due to the depth of the prints, the weight of the entity causing the footprints was approximately 700 pounds. The stride is much longer than a human stride. Krantz also provided evidence that the footprints could not have been hoaxes since the foot itself had moving parts and any sophisticated footprint-making-machine would not have been able to

---

[980]Gary R. Habermas and J. P. Moreland, *Immortality: The Other Side of Death* (Nashville: Thomas Nelson Publishers, 1992), 76-80.

[981]Ibid.

[982]Ibid., 29-42, 81-105.

[983]Michael A. Cremo and Richard Thompson, *The Hidden History of the Human Race* (Badger, CA: Bhaktivedanta Book Publishing, 1996), 215-232. The authors are not Christians. Their research needs to be addressed from a Christian perspective.

385

traverse all the rugged terrain (i.e., hills, valleys, ridges, etc.) necessary to make all the tracks.[984]

Christian apologists need to investigate these sightings and give a biblical response to the data. Bigfoot is not a missing link between apes and men; for, evolution is scientifically and biblically untenable. But, Bigfoot is also probably not some unknown specie of animal life. Christian apologists need to deal with all the available evidence concerning Bigfoot, even evidence that is often ignored by non-Christian Bigfoot investigators. For example, several reports show that Bigfoot can materialize and dematerialize at will. Bigfoot has even been conjured up through the use of a Ouija Board or through other occultic practices.[985] Also of interest is the fact that a horrible smell (often described as burning sulfur) often accompanies Bigfoot sightings, alien abduction cases, and demon possession. It is possible (if not likely) that in all these phenomena demonic activity is prevalent.[986]

Edmond Gruss: The Ouija Board, and Demon Possession

Edmond Gruss, a former Master's College professor, began writing on the dangers of using the Ouija Board as early as 1973.[987] His researched culminated in his work *The Ouija*

---

[984]Ibid., 219.

[985]Nick Redfern, *There's Something in the Woods* (San Antonio: Anomalist Books, 2008), 130-131, 133-135.

[986]Ibid., 131.

[987]Edmund Gruss, *The Ouija Board: A Doorway to the Occult* (Phillipsburg, NJ: P & R Publishing, 1994), vii. On this page, Gruss mentions some of his earlier works on this topic.

Board: A Doorway to the Occult, published in 1994.[988] In this work, Gruss documented numerous twentieth-century cases of demon possession that were linked to dabbling with the Ouija Board. Gruss presents several cases reported by eyewitnesses. He reports cases of strange sounds of tapping coming from inside of walls, the hearing of footsteps when no walking person is visible, the levitation of inanimate objects, welts spelling words on the body of a possessed, and rocks flying through the air from amazingly far distances. (Some of the rocks would disappear upon contact with the ground, while others would remain.)[989]

Gruss notes some of the "characteristic symptoms" of demon possession: unusual strength, seizures filled with anger and rage, periods of trance-like states, self-destructive tendencies, visible conflict within the personality, violent opposition to Christ, speaking in different voices (sometimes, in different languages not previously known by the possessed person), and supernatural knowledge.[990] Gruss emphasizes that all possible psychological causes must be ruled out before the diagnosis of demon possession can be made.[991] Gruss's book acknowledges the power and authority of Jesus Christ as the only effective means of casting out demons.[992]

---

[988]Ibid., entire book.

[989]Ibid., 130-153.

[990]Ibid., 179-181.

[991]Ibid., 134, 182.

[992]Ibid., 192-193. See also Merrill F. Unger, *Demons in the World Today* (Wheaton: Tyndale House Publishers:, 1971), 187-203.

Conclusion

American culture can no longer be classified as "Christian." In fact, it is unlikely that America is still a secular (i.e., non-religious) culture. More likely, America is now neo-pagan. There has been a revival of ancient paganistic beliefs in this country. The pagan gods have returned. Even the hedonism (pleasure seeking world view) of "non-religious" Americans closely resembles ancient Pagan practices.

Hence, Christian apologists must not only be prepared to defend the faith against atheistic attacks; he must also be willing and able to make a defense of Christianity against neo-pagan attacks. As the door to the demonic realm has been opened in America, more and more paranormal (i.e., demonic) activity is taking place. If the Christian apologist does not persuasively explain the paranormal activity that is taking place, then, by default, he will completely lose the battle for this culture to the neo-pagans. In fact, the neo-pagans have made great gains in media, politics, business, and education. The Christian apologist must not spend all his time debate issues of the past; we must also make a strong defense of the faith in the arena of the paranormal.

Chapter 25

The Apologetic Methodology of Walter Martin

During his lifetime, the late Dr. Walter Martin (1928-1989) was the world's leading authority on non-Christian cults. He earned a Master degree from New York University and a Ph.D. in comparative religions from California Coast University. He was the original "Bible Answer Man" and the founder and director of the Christian research Institute. His work *The Kingdom of the Cults* continues to be the standard textbook dealing with a Christian exposition and response to non-Christian cults. Walter Martin's apologetic methodology can be classified as "comparative religious apologetics."

Martin defined a cult as "a group of people gathered about a specific person or person's misinterpretation of the Bible."[993] Martin stated that "the cults contain many major

---

[993] Walter Martin, *The Kingdom of the Cults* (Minneapolis: Bethany House Publishers, 1985), 11.

deviations from historic Christianity"; yet, they still claim to be Christian.[994]

This chapter will summarize Martin's exposition and refutation of several non-Christian cults. Since most cults consider the Bible to be God's Word (though they misinterpret its contents), Martin was able to refute these cults by presenting scriptural passages that contradict their teachings. Martin dealt with numerous cults in his works; those discussed below will suffice to show how Martin did his comparative religious apologetics.

MORMONISM

Mormonism is also known as the Church of Jesus Christ of Latter-Day Saints. Joseph Smith founded this cult in New York State in the 1820's.[995] Smith moved the cult first to Ohio, then to Illinois. After Smith's death in Illinois, he was succeeded by Brigham Young, who moved his followers to Utah in the late 1840's.[996] There the cult grew to what it is today.

Mormonism has several sacred writings. The Bible is considered God's Word, so long as it has been translated correctly.[997] *The Book of Mormon* is supposedly an inspired account of the Hebrews who left the Holy Land for America

---

[994]Ibid.

[995]Gordon B. Hinckley, *Truth Restored* (Salt Lake City: The Church of Jesus Christ of Latter-Day Saints, 1979), 1-30.

[996]Ibid., 102-103.

[997]Walter Martin, *The Maze of Mormonism* (Santa Ana: Vision House, 1978), 45.

around 589BC.[998] Smith claimed *The Book of Mormon* was revealed to him by an angel named Moroni.[999] The historical inaccuracies contained in *the Book of Mormon* are well documented.[1000] Evidence has been presented indicating that a retired pastor named Solomon Spalding was the real author of *The Book of Mormon*.[1001] Though Spalding intended this work to be a novel, Joseph Smith gained access to it after the death of Spalding and proclaimed it to be divine revelation.[1002]

Doctrine and Covenants is another sacred Mormon writing. It contains most of the unique Mormon doctrines (priesthood functions, plurality of gods, eternal progression, principles of polygamy).[1003] *The Pearl of Great Price* contains "the Book of Moses" (which deals with the first six chapters of Genesis), "the Book of Abraham" (Abraham's supposed writings while in Egypt), and the official history of the Mormon church.[1004] Mormons, in addition to their sacred

---

[998]Ibid., 48.

[999]Ibid., 47.

[1000]Gleason L. Archer, Jr., *Survey of Old Testament Introduction* (Chicago: Moody Press, 1974), 509-512.

[1001]Martin, *The Maze of Mormonism*, 59-69.

[1002]Ibid., 59.

[1003]*Doctrines and Covenants* (Salt Lake City: The Church of Jesus Christ of Latter-Day Saints, 1982).

[1004]*Pearl of Great Price* (Salt Lake City: The Church of Jesus Christ of Latter-Day Saints, 1982).

writings, accept the prophecies of their living prophets as authoritative revelation from God.[1005]

Walter Martin clearly demonstrated that Mormon doctrines contradict the Bible in essential areas. Mormon theology denies the Christian doctrine of the Trinity. Though Mormons believe the Father, Son, and Holy Spirit are three separate Persons, they reject the Christian view that they are one God. The Latter-Day Saints teach that the Father, Son, and Holy Spirit are three separate gods.[1006] This is consistent with the Mormon doctrine of the plurality of gods, the teaching that there are an infinite number of gods in existence.[1007] This contradicts the biblical teaching that only one true God exists (Exodus 20:1-6; Deuteronomy 6:4; Isaiah 43:10; 44:6; 45:5-7, 14, 22; 1 Corinthians 8:4-6; 10:19-20; 1 Timothy 2:5). In a strange twist of theology the *Book of Mormon* teaches the doctrine of the Trinity (2 Nephi 31:21; Alma 11:44)! Still, Mormon teaching contradicts both the Bible and their own *Book of Mormon* by denying the doctrine of the Trinity.

Not only do Mormons teach the plurality of gods, they also believe that male Mormons can someday become gods.[1008] This is called the doctrine of eternal progression. Mormon prophets have taught that God was once a man, and that He became a god; likewise, men can also become

---

[1005]Josh McDowell and Don Stewart, *Handbook of Today's Religions* (San Bernardino: Here's Life Publishers, 1983), 68.

[1006]Bruce R. McConkie, *Mormon Doctrine* (Salt Lake City: Bookcraft, 1966), 576-577.

[1007]Ibid., 577.

[1008]Ibid., 238-239, 577.

gods.[1009] Martin points out that the Bible teaches that there is only one true God, and that there never were nor ever will be any other gods. God proclaims, "Before Me there was no God formed, and there will be none after Me" (Isaiah 43:10). In fact, it is not God who said that men could become gods; Satan is the originator of that lie (Genesis 3:5).

Walter Martin showed that the Mormon church proclaims a different Jesus than the Jesus of the Bible. Their Jesus is not God the second Person of the Trinity. The Mormon Jesus is one of many gods. He was not always God. In fact, the Jesus of Mormonism is getting better; He is still progressing in His godhood.[1010] Again, the Latter-Day Saints are refuted by the Bible which teaches that Jesus was God from the beginning. He never became a god (John 1:1, 14), for, "Jesus Christ is the same yesterday and today, yes and forever" (Hebrews 13:8).

Mormons do not accept the Bible as the final Word of God; they add their own "sacred" books. However, the Bible declares itself to be "the faith which was once for all delivered to the saints" (Jude3). Scriptural warnings against adding to God's Word are ignored by Mormons (Proverbs 30:5-6; Revelation 22:18-19). The fullness of God's revelation to man culminated in the incarnation and ministry of Jesus (Hebrews 1:1-3). Those who knew Jesus personally (the apostles) were His authoritative witnesses (John 15:26-27; Ephesians 2:20). Any future "revelation" must be tested by the authoritative witness of the apostles. When this is done, Mormonism fails the test.

[1009]Daniel H. Ludlow, ed. *Latter-day Prophets Speak* (Salt Lake City: Bookcraft, 1948), 71-79.

[1010]McConkie, 129.

Mormonism proclaims a different salvation than that of the Bible. Salvation in Mormonism is attained by exercising faith in Jesus, plus Mormon baptism, good works, and obedience to Mormon ordinances.[1011] This contradicts the Christian doctrine of salvation by God's grace alone through faith in Jesus alone (John 3:16-18; 14:6; Romans 3:10, 23; 6:23; Ephesians 2:8-9). Mormonism teaches that Jesus died so that all men would be resurrected and then judged according to their works.[1012] The Bible, however, teaches that Jesus died so that all who trust in Him for salvation would receive the free gift of eternal life (John 1:29; Ephesians 1:7; 1 Peter 2:24; 3:18; 1 John 1:7). The biblical view of salvation is through the work of Christ; the Mormon view of salvation is through human effort.

Mormons believe that their church alone has the true priesthood.[1013] Scripture declares that all believers are priests of God (1 Peter 2:4-5; Revelation 1:6). All true believers are called priests because they intercede on behalf of others and they offer their bodies as living sacrifices to the Lord (Romans 12:1-2). The Old Testament priesthood with all its symbols and ceremonies was fulfilled in Christ (Colossians 2:16-17; Hebrews 10:1, 10-14). Jesus is the only mediator that mankind needs (1 Timothy 2:5). People do not need the Mormon priesthood to find eternal life; people need Jesus, the true Jesus of the Bible.

The Mormon practice called baptism for the dead is unscriptural.[1014] The Word of God declares that people do not

---

[1011]Ibid., 669-672.

[1012]Ibid., 669.

[1013]Ludlow, 183-189.

get a second chance for salvation after death (Luke 16:19-31; Hebrews 9:27). Therefore, one should not be baptized for another person who has died.

Joseph Smith and Brigham Young practiced polygamy despite the fact that it was forbidden in the Bible.[1015] Jesus said that, "He who created them from the beginning made them male and female . . . and the two shall become one flesh" (Matthew 19:4-5). Paul demanded that an elder or deacon must be "the husband of one wife" (1 Timothy 3:2, 12). Joseph Smith and Brigham Young were not qualified to be elders or deacons in a local church, not to mention founders of a new "Christian" religious movement. Even the *Book of Mormon* admits that the Old Testament saints who practiced polygamy greatly displeased the Lord (Jacob 2:24).

Obviously, Mormonism is a perversion of the Word of God. Mormonism is not the one true faith; it is a non-Christian cult. As Walter Martin has demonstrated, when Mormonism is tested against scripture, it fails miserably.

JEHOVAH'S WITNESSES

Walter Martin also refuted the Jehovah's Witnesses cult. The Jehovah's Witnesses (also known as the Watchtower Bible and Tract Society) trace their roots to Charles Taze Russell. He began to teach Bible studies in the 1870's. Though Russell was raised in a Christian home, he thought that the scriptural teaching of eternal torment was unjust. He also believed that Christ's return would be invisible. He denied Christ's deity and bodily resurrection, as well as salvation by grace. He began to believe that his own interpretation of the

---

[1014]McConkie, 72-73.

[1015]Ibid., 577-579.

Bible was the supreme authority.[1016] He predicted that Armageddon would occur in 1914; this prophecy obviously failed.[1017]

After Russell's death, Joseph Franklin Rutherford succeeded him as president. Rutherford retained the doctrines of Russell, and added the emphasis on "Jehovah" as the only true name for God.[1018] Rutherford's predictions of Armageddon also failed in 1918 and 1925.[1019]

The Jehovah's Witnesses "translated" their own version of the Bible called the *New World Translation* of the Bible. This translation is not supported by any reputable Greek or Hebrew scholar. In John 1:1, all recognized translations refer to Jesus as "God." But, in the Jehovah's Witnesses' translation Jesus is called "a god."[1020] Other passages in the *New World Translation* contain questionable readings that strip Christ of His deity.[1021]

Walter Martin showed that the Jehovah's Witnesses deny Christ's deity. They have become experts in explaining away scriptural passages that attribute deity to Jesus (Isaiah 9:6; Zechariah 14:5; John 1:1; 5:17-18; 8:23-24, 58; 10:30-33;

[1016]Martin, *Kingdom of the Cults*, 38-46.

[1017]George A. Mather and Larry A. Nichols, *Dictionary of Cults, Sects, Religions and the Occult* (Grand Rapids: Zondervan Publishing House, 1993), 158.

[1018]Martin, *Kingdom of the Cults*, 47-48.

[1019]Mather and Nichols, 158.

[1020]*New World Translation of the Holy Scriptures* (Brooklyn: Watchtower Bible and Tract Society of New York, Inc., 1961), 1151.

[1021]Martin, *Kingdom of the Cults*, 71-83.

20:28; Philippians 2:5-7; Colossians 2:9; 2 Peter 1:1; Revelation 1:17-18). However, these passages do in fact teach that Jesus is God. Though Jehovah's Witnesses often sound confident when attacking these verses, their unique interpretations (or translations) of these passages lack scholarship. Downplaying Christ's deity, Jehovah's Witnesses often overemphasize passages which speak of the limitations of Christ's human nature (Matthew 24:36) and His submission to the Father in order to provide salvation for mankind (John 14:28; Philippians 2:5-8). The Watchtower interprets Colossians 1:15 and Revelation 3:14 to mean that Jesus is the first being that God created. However, the former verse actually declares Christ to be the supreme ruler over all creation since He is its Creator (Colossians 1:15-17). Revelation 3:14 declares Christ to be the origin of all creation. In other words, He is the source of all created existence.[1022]

Jehovah's Witnesses also deny the Christian doctrine of the Trinity. Though the Bible teaches that there is only one God (Isaiah 43:10; 44:6), the Word of God declares that the Father is God (Galatians 1:1), the Son is God (Titus 2:13), and the Holy Spirit is God (Acts 5:3-4). The Scriptures also maintain that the Father, Son, and Holy Spirit are three distinct Persons (Matthew 3:16-17; 28:19; John 14:16, 26). Therefore, there is only one God, but this one God exists eternally as three equal Persons. This is the Christian doctrine of the Trinity. However, the Jehovah's Witnesses teach that only the Father is God. They consider Jesus to be a lesser god; He was God's first creation.[1023] Jehovah's Witnesses believe that the

---

[1022]McDowell and Stewart, 47-49.

[1023]*Let God be True* (Brooklyn: Watchtower Bible and Tract Society, Inc., 1946), 34-35, 37, 88, 91.

Holy Spirit is nothing more than God's active, impersonal force.[1024] However, the Bible clearly identifies the Holy Spirit as a Person. He is called "another Helper" (John 14:16), and He bears witness of Christ (John 15:26). He can be lied to (Acts 5:3-4) and grieved (Ephesians 4:30). He also speaks (Acts 8:29; 10:19; 13:2; 21:11). Though the doctrine that God is three Persons, but one Being, goes beyond human understanding, it is not contradictory. The doctrine of the Trinity is biblical. To deny this doctrine is to oppose the clear teaching of Scripture in this area.

The Watchtower Society denies that Jesus rose bodily from the dead. They teach that He was raised as a spirit being.[1025] However, Jesus predicted that He would raise His own body from the dead (John 2:19-21). Jesus also proved He had risen bodily from the dead by showing the apostles His wounds, allowing them to touch His body, and by eating food with them (Luke 24:36-43; John 20:26-27).

Jehovah's Witnesses deny that Christ will visibly and bodily return to earth someday.[1026] They believe that Jesus invisibly returned to Brooklyn, New York in 1914.[1027] This contradicts the biblical teaching that Jesus' return to earth will be bodily and visible (Revelation 1:7; Matthew 24:23-31; Acts 1:9-12). Christ will return to the nation of Israel (Zechariah 14:3-5), not Brooklyn, New York. And, when Jesus returns, every eye will see Him (Revelation 1:7).

[1024]Ibid., 89.

[1025]*Reasoning from the Scriptures* (Brooklyn: Watchtower Bible and Tract Society, Inc., 1989), 334-335.

[1026]*Let God be True*, 185-188.

[1027]Ibid., 189-192, 208-209.

The Watchtower denies salvation by God's grace alone through faith in Jesus alone (John 3:16-18; Romans 3:10, 20-23; Ephesians 2:8-9; 1 Peter 3:18; 2 Corinthians 5:15, 21). They teach that Jesus' death removed the effects of Adam's sin on mankind so that people can now save themselves by living a righteous life until death.[1028]

Jehovah's Witnesses deny the existence of the human soul. They believe that after death man ceases to exist until he is resurrected to be judged. This is called soul-sleep.[1029] However, the Word of God declares that when a believer dies, he or she immediately goes to be with the Lord (Acts 7:59; Philippians 1:21-24; 2 Corinthians 5:8). The Bible also teaches that nonbelievers who die do not ceases to exist, but go immediately into conscious torment (Luke 16:19-31).

The Jehovah's Witnesses also deny the eternal, conscious torment of the wicked. They teach that annihilation is the final state of the lost.[1030] However, the Word of God declares that nonbelievers will be "thrown into the lake of fire" where they will be "tormented day and night forever" (Mark 9:47-48; Revelation 14:9-11; 20:10, 15).

The Watchtower society contradicts the Word of God in many other areas as well. They refuse to salute the United States flag or fight in any war to defend this nation.[1031] This disobeys the biblical commands to submit to the governing authorities and render them the honor they are due (Mark 12:17; Romans 13:1-7). Jehovah's Witnesses condemn the

---

[1028]Ibid., 297-301.

[1029]Ibid., 57-67.

[1030]Ibid., 68-80.

[1031]Ibid., 226-242.

usage of any name for God other than "Jehovah."[1032] Yet, Jesus instructed His disciples to call God "our Father" (Matthew 6:9). The Watchtower organization claims to be God's prophet,[1033] but the Word of God shows their organization to be a false prophet: their prophecies have failed (Deuteronomy 18:20-22), they have produced the "bad fruit" of heresies (Matthew 7:15-23), and they have proclaimed the return of a hidden, invisible Christ—Jesus taught His return to earth would be visible to all (Matthew 24:23-27; Revelation 1:7). Therefore, their claim to be the "witnesses" of Jehovah is false.

CHRISTIAN SCIENCE

Besides the Latter-days Saints and the Jehovah's Witnesses, Walter Martin also refuted several other non-Christian cults. One is the Christian Science cult. The Christian Science cult was founded by Mary Baker Eddy in 1866.[1034] Christian Science teaches that God is an impersonal force and that sin, death, pain, and sickness are illusions.[1035] Christian Scientists also deny the existence of the material realm.[1036] They deny that Jesus is the Christ. Instead, they view Jesus as a mere man who exercised His "Christ consciousness" to a greater extent than any other person. All

---

[1032]Ibid., 21-32.

[1033]Ibid., 189-190.

[1034]Martin, *Kingdom of the Cults*, 133.

[1035]Mary Baker Eddy, *Science and Health with Key to the Scriptures* (Boston: The First Church of Christ, Scientist, 1971), 113, 115, 293, 336, 447, 468, 472, 480, 482, 584, 586, 587.

[1036]Ibid., 468.

people have the "divine idea" or "Christ consciousness" within them and some exercise it better than others.[1037] Salvation in Christian Science is the recognition that sin and death are illusions.[1038] Jesus' death on the cross does not cleanse anyone from sin.[1039]

In response to Christian Scientists, Christians must declare that God is a personal Being who can communicate with and love His creatures (Exodus 3:14; John 3:16). He is not the impersonal force proclaimed by Mary Baker Eddy. The Bible teaches that sin, death, pain, and sickness are real (1 John 1:8-10; Romans 3:23; Hebrews 9:27; Romans 6:23). Scripture relates that the material universe does exist (Genesis 1:1; Colossians 1:15-16). The Bible identifies Jesus as the Christ (1 John 5:1) and as God in the flesh (John 1:1, 14). The Word of God reveals that man can only be saved through Jesus (John 3:16-18; 14:6) and that salvation was provided when Jesus died on the cross for man's sin (1 Peter 2:24; 3:18).

THE UNITY SCHOOL OF CHRISTIANITY

The Unity School of Christianity is an offshoot of Christian Science.[1040] Founded by Charles and Myrtle Fillmore, this cult teaches that man is divine; all have the "Christ-consciousness" within them.[1041] Unity views Jesus as merely a man who exercised His Christ-consciousness more

---

[1037]Ibid., 473, 583.

[1038]Ibid., 588, 590, 593.

[1039]Ibid., 23-25, 45-46.

[1040]Martin, *Kingdom of the Cults*, 279.

[1041]Ibid., 284-286.

than any other man.[1042] Sin, the devil, and eternal punishment do not exist; they are illusions.[1043] Salvation in the Unity cult is through reincarnation, and everyone will eventually be saved.[1044] Unlike Christian Science, the Unity School of Christianity does believe in the existence of the physical world.[1045]

The teachings of the Unity cult can be refuted in much the same fashion as those of Christian Science. However, a scriptural refutation of reincarnation should be added when dealing with Unity. The Bible teaches that it is appointed for man to die once, not many times (Hebrews 9:27). The Word of God makes it clear that Jesus alone was punished for our sins (Hebrews 1:3; 1 Peter 2:24; 3:18); man does not need to be purged for his own sins through reincarnation. Jesus clearly taught that a deceased person cannot return to this world for a second chance (Luke 16:19-31).

THE UNIFICATION CHURCH

Walter Martin exposed and refuted the false teachings of the Unification Church. The Unification Church was founded in 1954 by the Reverend Sun Myung Moon.[1046] Moon taught that mankind fell spiritually when Eve had sexual intercourse with Lucifer, and that mankind fell

---

[1042]Ibid., 284-285.

[1043]Ibid., 286.

[1044]Ibid.

[1045]Ibid., 286-287.

[1046]Ibid., 338-339.

physically when Eve later had sexual intercourse with Adam.[1047] Moon instructed his disciples that Jesus prematurely died, having only provided for man's spiritual salvation.[1048] According to Moon, Jesus failed to provide physical salvation for mankind by raising a family who would inherit His sinless nature. He died before He could procure such a family. Now, it is up to Moon to physically save mankind.[1049] Though he has never openly declared so, Moon strongly implies that He is the Lord of the second advent.[1050] His cult denies the deity of Christ.[1051]

When witnessing to Moon's followers, it should be pointed out that the Bible teaches that the Fall of mankind was due to disobedience of a clear command of God (Genesis 3:1-6). It had nothing to do with sex. The Scriptures teach that Jesus did not fail, and He accomplished salvation completely for mankind (1 Peter 2:24; 3:18; Hebrews 10:14; Matthew 20:28). Even the physical redemption of believers was accomplished by Christ's death, though it won't be realized until Christ's return (1 Corinthians 15:50-57; Revelation 20:1-6). People do not need Moon to save them. Jesus is the only Savior. Moon is also not the Lord of the second advent, for Jesus taught that He Himself would return to earth (John 14:1-3; Acts 1:9-11; Revelation 22:20).

[1047]Walter Martin, *Cults Reference Bible* (Santa Ana: Vision House, 1981), 59.

[1048]Ibid., 59-60.

[1049]Ibid., 60.

[1050]Ibid.

[1051]Ibid., 59.

THE WAY INTERNATIONAL

The Way International was founded by Victor Paul Wierwille.[1052] This cult denies that Jesus is God. According to them, Jesus did not pre-exist His conception in the womb of Mary.[1053] Wierwille taught the doctrines of soul-sleep and annihilation of the wicked.[1054] Since sins are thought to have no detrimental effect on the human spirit once saved, repentance is seldom stressed in the cult.[1055]

When confronting members of this cult, the Christian apologist must defend the deity of Christ (Isaiah 9:6; John 1:1, 14; Titus 2:13; 2 Peter 1:1) and argue for His pre-existence (John 1:1-14; 8:58; 17:5; Colossians 1:15-17). The defender of the Christian faith should refute the concept of soul-sleep (Luke 16:19-31; 2 Corinthians 5:8) and give scriptural support for eternal conscious torment in hell (Revelation 14:9-11; 20:10, 15). Those in the Way International need to be informed that sin does effect the spiritual nature of man. God calls men and women to flee from their sinfulness (John 8:11, 31-36; 1 John 2:1; Romans 3:31; 6:14-18; 1 Corinthians 6:18; Hebrews 10:26-27).

[1052]Ibid., 71.

[1053]Victor Paul Wierwille, *Jesus Christ is not God* (New Knoxville: The American Christian Press, 1975).

[1054]Martin, *Cults Reference Bible*, 78.

[1055]Mather and Nichols, 311.

SCIENTOLOGY

Scientology was founded by L. Ron Hubbard.[1056] Scientology teaches that mankind is descended from a race of uncreated, all-powerful gods called thetans. Thetans surrendered their power in order to come to earth. They gradually evolved from non-life to life, and eventually into humans who had forgotten their own deity. Scientologists counsel others to overcome their problems by remembering their own deity.[1057] This is often done through past-lives-regression therapy.[1058] The deity of Christ, the sinfulness of man, and the eternal flames of hell are all denied by this cult.[1059] When dealing with Scientologists, Christians should show that the belief that man is divine originated with Satan (Genesis 3:1-6). It must be pointed out that all are sinners (Romans 3:10, 23) who need Christ's salvation (John 3:16-18; 14:6). Evidence for Christ's deity and eternal conscious torment should be presented, and reincarnation should be refuted.

THE UNITARIAN UNIVERSALIST ASSOCIATION

The Unitarian Universalist Association is the result of a merger between two heretical groups.[1060] The Unitarian

---

[1056]Ibid., 251.

[1057]Ibid., 252.

[1058]Ibid., 253.

[1059]Martin, *Kingdom of the Cults*, 348-349.

[1060]Ibid., 501.

405

Church denied that Jesus is God and taught that God is only one Person (the Father).[1061] The Universalist Church taught that all people will ultimately be saved.[1062] These two heretical movements merged in 1959.[1063] This cult teaches that all religions lead to God, the Bible contains errors, and the impossibility of miracles.[1064] Since this cult denies inerrancy, the best approach for the apologist to take is to use historical evidences to argue for the deity of Christ and the inspiration and inerrancy of the Bible. An apologist must also be able to provide evidence for the possibility of miracles when dealing with this cult.

THE NEW AGE MOVEMENT

Though Walter Martin died in 1989, he was already aware of the fact that Eastern thought and ancient pagan ideas were becoming popular in America. Martin saw that comparative religious apologists must be able to deal with and refute the false teachings and dangerous practices of what has become known as the New Age Movement. The New Age Movement is growing rapidly in America.[1065] It is probably the biggest threat Christianity faces going into the twenty-first century.[1066] Therefore, Christian apologists must be able to dialogue with new agers and be able to refute their teachings.

[1061]Ibid.

[1062]Mather and Nichols, 295.

[1063]Martin, *Kingdom of the Cults*, 501.

[1064]Mather and Nichols, 286-288.

[1065]Walter Martin, *The New Age Cult* (Minneapolis: Bethany House Publishers, 1989), 7-8.

[1066]Ibid.

The New Age Movement is the immersing of western culture with eastern thought.[1067] It is largely responsible for the current revival of ancient occultism in the United States.[1068] New Agers believe in a coming new age of spiritual enlightenment and peace towards which man is evolving.[1069] New Agers seek a one world government and the destruction of nationalistic barriers between the peoples of the earth.[1070] The New Age Movement is not a conscious conspiracy (on the human level) to take over the world, though its thrust towards a one world government may be demonically inspired.[1071] Rather, it is a network of numerous groups who share similar beliefs and goals.[1072]

History of the New Age Movement. The New Age Movement had its roots in the ancient occultism (secret arts) of Sumeria, India, Egypt, Babylon, and Persia.[1073] However, its move into western culture has been fairly recent. The Theosophical Society is responsible for bringing the New Age Movement to America.[1074] Founded by Helena Blavatsky in

---

[1067]Ibid., 13.

[1068]Ibid., 15.

[1069]Ibid., 33-34.

[1070]Douglas R. Groothuis, *Unmasking the New Age* (Downers Grove: Inter-Varsity Press, 1986), 116-117.

[1071]Elliot Miller, *A Crash Course on the New Age Movement* (Grand rapids: Baker Book House, 1989), 202.

[1072]Ibid., 14-16.

[1073]Martin, *The New Age Cult*, 15.

[1074]Ibid., 15-17.

1875, this cult promoted seances, spiritism and Hindu thought in the United States.[1075] The Theosophical Society had three primary goals. First, it sought to declare the universal brotherhood of all mankind. Second, it desired to teach others the unity of all religions. Third, it encouraged others to tap into the spiritual powers within man.[1076] This led to the current interest of many Americans in the New Age Movement.[1077] The Theosophical Society taught that the world is awaiting many avatars (manifestations of God who reveal spiritual truth to the world).[1078] Blavatsky considered Jesus, Buddha, and Mohammad to be avatars.[1079]

Annie Besant and Alice Bailey were later leaders of the Theosophical Society.[1080] Their books are still popular today within new age circles.[1081] Bailey claimed to have communicated with several spirit guides.[1082] Her books are published through a company called "Lucius Trust," formerly known as the "Lucifer Publishing Company."[1083]

[1075]Ibid., 15.

[1076]Bob Larson, *Larson's Book of Cults* (Wheaton: Tyndale House Publishers, 1982), 327.

[1077]Martin, *The New Age Cult*, 15.

[1078]Ibid.

[1079]Ibid.

[1080]Ibid., 16-17.

[1081]Ibid., 17.

[1082]Ibid., 16.

[1083]Ibid., 129.

American culture had been dominated by the Christian world view from about 1620 to 1860.[1084] After Charles Darwin published his *Origin of Species*, American culture began to take on more of a secular mindset (1860-1960). Though most Americans rejected philosophical atheism (the belief that no God exists), they accepted practical atheism. In other words, they lived like no God existed. They rejected the traditional morality taught in the Bible. Moral relativism became popular. Still, Americans were not satisfied with materialistic pleasures; they longed for spiritual experiences. Even so, they did not want an authoritative God who would forbid some of their practices. This left many Americans open to eastern influences. This may also partly explain the "hippie culture" and the widespread experimentation with hallucinogenic drugs. The 1960's were famous for large-scale rebellion against materialism and authority. With many Americans starving for a religious experience, this country abandoned its secular outlook and opened the door to the occult. It was in this context that the New Age Movement became popular in America.[1085]

Common New Age Beliefs. The New Age Movement is antithetical to Christianity. The New Age Movement accepts a pantheistic world view, the belief that God is the universe.[1086] God is thought by New Agers to be an impersonal force.[1087] Obviously, this contradicts Christianity, for the Bible teaches that God is not identical to the universe; rather, God created the universe (Genesis 1:1; John 1:1-3;

[1084]Geisler and Anderson, *Origin Science*, 82-83.

[1085]Groothuis, *Unmasking the New Age*, 37-56.

[1086]Ibid., 18-21.

[1087]Ibid., 20.

Colossians 1:15-17). God is therefore separate from the universe. The God of the Bible is not impersonal. He is a personal God who loves the people He has created and has communicated to them in His Word (John 3:16; 2 Timothy 3:16-17; 2 Peter 1:20-21).

New Agers teach that all humans are God since they are part of the universe (which they equate with God).[1088] On the other hand, the Bible states that man is not God (1 Samuel 15:29; Ezekiel 28:1-2, 9-10; Matthew 19:25-26). In fact, the lie that humans are or can be god was originated by Satan (Genesis 3:1-7; Isaiah 14:12-14). Since New Agers believe they are God, they see no need to be saved.[1089] The Bible, however, teaches the need for all people to be saved (Romans 3:10; 23; 6:23; John 3:16-18; 14:6). New Agers refuse to acknowledge the reality of sin.[1090] However, the Bible teaches that sin is real. All are sinners; all need the Savior, the Lord Jesus (Romans 3:10, 23; 1 Peter 2:24; 3:18; 1 John 1:8-10).

New Agers accept the doctrine of reincarnation.[1091] Reincarnation teaches that the individual soul passes through the cycle of death and rebirth. The soul reanimates a different body (whether animal or human) after death until all negative karma is done away with. Then the individual soul is absorbed into the world soul.[1092] This is in direct opposition to biblical teaching. The Bible proclaims that "it is appointed for man to

---

[1088]Ibid., 21-22.

[1089]Martin, *The New Age Cult*, 29-30.

[1090]Ibid.

[1091]Ibid., 32-33.

[1092]Norman L. Geisler and J. Yutaka Amano, *The Reincarnation Sensation* (Wheaton: Tyndale House Publishers, 1986), 28-30.

die once . . ." (Hebrews 9:27). Jesus' story of Lazarus the beggar and the rich man illustrates that man does not get another chance beyond this life (Luke 16:19-31). Rather than reincarnation purging a soul from sin, Jesus alone paid for the sins of mankind (John 1:29; Hebrews 1:1-3; 1 Peter 2:24; 3:18).

Many New Agers believe the external world is merely an illusion; it does not exist.[1093] Still, they live as if it does exist: they clothe and feed themselves. They do not jump off of high buildings. A belief system that cannot be consistently lived should be seriously reconsidered.

New Agers are often moral relativists. They deny there is right and wrong.[1094] Obviously, the Bible disagrees for the scriptures teach absolute moral laws that are above all mankind (Exodus 20:1-17; Micah 6:8; Isaiah 5:20; 1 John 1:8-10). New Agers do not live consistently with their belief in moral relativism. They do live as though some things are wrong. They protest the production of nuclear weapons.[1095] They march to save the whales, seals, and other endangered species.[1096] They are determined to save the earth from global warming.[1097] Though most New Agers deny the existence of universal moral values, they clearly judge certain things as being "wrong." If New Agers were consistent with their moral

---

[1093]David K. Clark and Norman L. Geisler, *Apologetics in the New Age* (Grand Rapids: Baker Book House, 1990), 151-155.

[1094]Ibid., 71.

[1095]Martin, *The New Age Cult*, 65.

[1096]Ibid.

[1097]Miller, 107-111.

relativistic leanings, then they could not even judge the barbarous actions of Adolph Hitler.

New Agers commonly teach that there is no absolute truth.[1098] However, this is a self-refuting belief. If the belief that there is no absolute truth is true, then *it* would be an absolute truth (universally true). Therefore, it is self-refuting, and it must be false. Hence, some things must be universally true.

New Agers seek the establishment of a one-world government.[1099] They believe that man himself will bring a new age of peace to the earth.[1100] However, God wants the world divided into separate nations until Jesus returns to rule (Genesis 11:1-9). A man-made, one-world government may eventually lead to the global dictatorship headed by the antichrist (Revelation 13:3-7). The Bible teaches that there will be wars until the end, and that mankind will not be able to establish peace on earth by himself (Daniel 9:26; Matthew 24:6-7). Jesus taught that in the last days the love of man would grow cold (Matthew 24:12). Only Jesus, the true Prince of Peace, will be able to bring lasting peace to the planet (Isaiah 9:6-7; Revelation 11:15; 19:11-16). A one-world human government will only expedite man's self-destruction.

New Agers believe mankind is evolving and getting better. But, history agrees with the biblical depiction of man as eroding morally. In fact, this century has been the bloodiest century in human history. New Age optimism about the future

---

[1098]Douglas Groothuis, *Confronting the New Age* (Downers Grove: Inter-Varsity Press, 1988), 72-76.

[1099]Miller, 111-127.

[1100]Ibid.

is clearly unwarranted. Man is not getting better; he is getting worse.

New Agers often say that all religions lead to God.[1101] Again, this contradicts the teaching of Scripture. Jesus taught that salvation comes only through faith in Him (John 3:16-18; 14:6; Acts 4:12). Jesus taught that those who reject Him do not have a saving relationship with God the Father (Luke 10:16). Thus, the Bible denies that all faiths lead to God.

New Agers deny that Jesus is uniquely God.[1102] They deny that salvation comes only through Jesus and that man is lost without Him.[1103] Obviously, the New Age Movement is not compatible with biblical Christianity.

Common New Age Practices. Two common New Age practices are channeling and eastern meditation.[1104] Channeling is the practice whereby a person voluntarily allows himself to be possessed by a spiritual entity who then speaks through the possessed person. The spirit entity is thought to be the spirit of a deceased human.[1105] The Bible forbids people to attempt to communicate with the dead (Deuteronomy 18:9-12; Isaiah 8:19). The Word of God also indicates that the dead cannot communicate with the living (Luke 16:19-31). Therefore, the spirit entities that possess and speak through people are probably demons; they are not spirits of dead humans. The Bible commands men and women to test

---

[1101]Groothuis, *Unmasking the New Age*, 27-29.

[1102]Douglas Groothuis, *Revealing the New Age Jesus* (Downers Grove: Inter-Varsity Press, 1990), 17-21.

[1103]Ibid.

[1104]Miller, 36, 141.

[1105]Ibid., 141-142.

the spirits (1 John 4:1-3). The apostle Paul predicts that in the last days men will fall prey to doctrines taught by demons (1 Timothy 4:1). The content of channeled messages contradicts the gospel message of salvation only through faith in Jesus.[1106] Paul stated that any human or angel who brings a message that contradicts the gospel is accursed (Galatians 1:8-9).

New Agers commonly practice eastern meditation.[1107] Eastern meditation encourages a person to empty his mind of all rational thought. This is believed to create an environment in which a mystical union with the impersonal god can take place.[1108] Eastern meditation differs essentially from biblical meditation. In biblical meditation, the person's mind is emptied of sinful desires. Still, the mind is focused on principles from God's Word (Psalm 1:1-2; Joshua 1:8). Therefore, in biblical meditation, the mind is never left completely empty. On the other hand, eastern meditation is content-less. One surrenders control of one's mind by the cessation of rational thought. Once a person loses control of his mind, demonic control may take place. Mantras are repeated during new age meditation.[1109] A mantra is a one syllable word that, when repeated over and over, is designed to remove all content from the mind. This practice is in direct disobedience to the teaching of Christ. Jesus prohibited His followers from engaging in the vain repetition which was common among pagan worshippers (Matthew 6:7). The mantras have been shown to have been derived from the

---

[1106]Ibid., 169-174.

[1107]Groothuis, *Confronting the New Age*, 23-24.

[1108]Ibid.

[1109]Miller, 94.

names of Hindu deities (false gods).[1110] Therefore, Eastern meditation invites demon possession through the communion with false gods (1 Corinthians 10:19-21), as well as through the surrendering of the mind.

The New Age Movement is not Christian. It competes with Christianity for the hearts of men and women. Therefore, defenders of the Christian Faith should follow the example of Walter Martin—we must be prepared to refute the doctrines of the New Age Movement.

CONCLUSION

The late Dr. Walter Martin was one of the greatest defenders of the faith in the twentieth century. In his day, he was the foremost expert on exposing and refuting non-Christian cults. His comparative religious apologetic methodology should not be ignored. There will always be pseudo-Christian religions that need to be confronted by Christian apologists.

Walter Martin saw the dangers that non-Christian cults presented to the church. He closed his book *The Kingdom of the Cults* by proposing five major projects for the church to embrace in order to battle the kingdom of the cults.[1111] First, Martin argued for the need for careful research on the background and theology of each cult. The results of this research must be placed into the hands of pastors, missionaries, and lay people. Martin founded his Christian Research Institute in 1960 for this purpose.

Second, Martin suggested the use of computers to gather and disseminate information on the cults. We now see

---

[1110]Ibid.

[1111]Martin, *Kingdom of the Cults*, 400-408.

that this is a reality with literally thousands of apologetic and counter-cult websites on the internet.

Third, Martin called for the publishing of specialized literature (books, pamphlets, etc.) dealing with counter-cult research. This literature must be distributed to lay people as well as clergy.

Fourth, Martin called for a reevaluation of biblical education. He believed that Bible institutes, colleges, and seminaries needed courses and programs in apologetics and counter-cult research. He understood that church leaders needed to be trained in apologetics to the cults. He believed that a course in comparative religions or non-Christian cults should be a requirement for graduation at Bible colleges and seminaries.

And fifth, Martin suggested the sponsoring and promoting of counter-cult conferences. This would expose the church throughout America to counter-cult apologetics and ministries. Today, these conferences take place on a regular basis throughout America. Though the evangelical church has come a long way in comparative religious apologetics since 1960, there is still a long way to go. Only time will tell if the church successfully fulfills the dream of Dr. Walter Martin, the original "Bible Answer Man."

Chapter 26

Cultural Apologetics

Cultural apologists argue that when a nation or culture is built upon the Christian world view it thrives; whereas societies founded on other world views will tend to deteriorate. The work of three Christian cultural apologists has already been discussed in this book. Josh McDowell's work on *The New Tolerance*, C. S. Lewis' book entitled *The Abolition of Man*, and Francis Schaeffer's *A Christian Manifesto* were detailed earlier in this work.[1112] In this chapter, we will build upon their work by discussing different world views and their impact of societies.

Though we have all heard the liberal rallying cry of "separation of church and state," the fact of the matter is this: human government cannot exist in a spiritual vacuum. Human government must be based upon certain presuppositions about

---

[1112]See Josh McDowell and Bob Hostetler, *The New Tolerance* (Wheaton: Tyndale House Publishers, 1998), C. S. Lewis, *The Abolition of Man* (New York: Collier Books, 1947), Francis Schaeffer, *A Christian Manifesto* (Westchester: Crossway Books, 1981), and Francis Schaeffer, *The Complete Works of Francis A. Schaeffer*, vol. I and V (Westchester: Crossway Books, 1982).

man and the universe in which he lives. In short, political and economic theories must be based upon a religious foundation. Thomas Jefferson, the author of *the Declaration of Independence*, recognized this when he penned the words, "all men are created equal." Even the atheists who signed the first *Humanist Manifesto* acknowledged man's reliance upon religious ideas by stating that, "nothing human is alien to the religious."[1113] Human beings are incurably religious, and their governments must have a religious foundation as well.

THE JUDEO-CHRISTIAN WORLD VIEW

The United States government was founded upon the Judeo-Christian world view (i.e., the Bible).[1114] Our founding fathers believed that all men were created equal and in God's image, and that all men have God-given rights that could not be taken away. God instituted human government to protect these unalienable rights.

According to our founding fathers, the need for human government is twofold. First, because man was created in

---

[1113]Paul Kurtz, ed. *Humanist Manifesto I & II* (Buffalo: Prometheus Books, 1972), 9.

[1114]It is true that not all of our founding fathers were Christians. Some were deists; they denied the miraculous elements of Christianity. Still, the founding fathers who were deists were *pro-Christian deists*. They were politically conservative and held to the biblical view of government and morality. On the other hand, *anti-Christian deists* could be found among the leaders of the bloody French Revolution. Anti-Christian deists are politically liberal—they believe that big government has all the answers to man's problems, and that man, through his reason, can save this planet. Anti-Christian deists reject the biblical view of limited government as well as the biblical view of morality. Modern deists usually fall into the anti-Christian deist camp. They often have more in common with secular humanists (i.e., atheists) than with adherents of the Judeo-Christian world view.

God's image, human life is sacred and therefore worth protecting. Second, because man is in a fallen and sinful state, human life needs to be protected, for some humans infringe upon the God-given rights of other humans. Thus, the need for human government is based upon the biblical doctrines of Creation and the Fall.

Our founding fathers took seriously the sinfulness of mankind. They recognized that since human governments are ruled by sinful humans, government power must be limited. No man or group of men should be allowed to have their sinful lust for power go unchecked. Our nation's founders heeded Lord Acton's advice: "power corrupts, and absolute power corrupts absolutely." Therefore, *the Declaration of Independence* and the *United States Constitution* limited the power of government officials in several ways. First, God and His laws were recognized as existing above human government and its officials. Government officials are not above the law; they are answerable to God. Second, global government was rejected. A global government limited in power is an oxymoron. Third, a system of checks and balances and separation of powers (federal and state governments & the three branches of the federal government) were established to prevent the unleashing of a unified assault against the American people and their freedoms. Fourth, the people's rights to worship as they saw fit, elect many of their government officials, peacefully protest the government's actions, and bear arms were protected.

The Constitution does not force Americans to become Jews or Christians, but, because it is based upon the Judeo-Christian world view, it protects a person's freedom to worship according to the dictates of his or her conscience. The form of government America has and the freedoms we enjoy are due to the Judeo-Christian world view. Our founding fathers acknowledged the biblical view of government and

419

morality in their political and economic thought. Political liberals may not like this fact, but it is a historical fact nonetheless. Although political liberals wish to change the religious presuppositions of our government, the alternatives are not very promising. And we must never forget that governments must have a religious base. We will now look at some of the alternatives to the Judeo-Christian basis for human government.

ATHEISM/SECULAR HUMANISM

In *Humanist Manifestos I and II*, atheist leaders proposed to save this planet by working towards a one-world socialistic government based upon the foundation of the atheistic world view.[1115] However, in this century we have witnessed the horrors produced by governments based upon atheism. The totalitarian regimes of the Soviet Union and Red China together have systematically slaughtered more than 80 million of their own people in this century alone.[1116] Atheism, by denying belief in God's existence, is a world view that has no basis for the sanctity of human life. Man is merely molecules in motion, having no intrinsic worth. Since atheists also reject a historical Fall of mankind, man's lust for power is left unchecked. A survival of the fittest mentality is allowed to run rampant among government leaders. While claiming to have the best interests of the populace in mind, government officials are answerable to no one as they seek to increase their power.

[1115]Kurtz, 8, 10, 21.

[1116]R. J. Rummel, *Death by Government* (New Brunswick: Transaction Publishers, 1994), 8.

420

Consistent atheism not only entails a rejection of traditional values, but also a complete denial of any absolute moral laws. Therefore, there is no such thing as right and wrong; the end (the goals of those in power) justifies the means (even if millions are slaughtered). Atheism fails to supply the moral foundation necessary for good government: man-made laws no longer reflect God's moral absolutes. Instead, man-made laws will be arbitray and will protect those in power, and not the multitudes these leaders are supposed to serve. Therefore, if the Judeo-Christian world view is rejected, we must look elsewhere for an alternative religious base for human government.

ISLAM

In the militant Islamic world view of Iran, the government leader (the ayatollah) is viewed as the infallible spokesman for God.[1117] This is the Shi'ite branch of Islam. It perverts the Judeo-Christian world view by allowing a sinful man to stand in the place of God. The results can be the same as that of the atheistic world view since the atheist denial of God's existence causes its government leaders to attempt to replace God as the highest authority. The power of the government leader is not held in check. Whenever a human leader (other than the Lord Jesus who is fully God and fully man) stands in the place of God and claims to speak infallibly for God, oppression will almost surely follow. This was seen during the Carter administration when Ayatollah Khomeni took innocent Americans hostage for 444 days. The militant wing of Shi'ite Islam is known as Hezbollah.

[1117]Timothy Demy and Gary P. Stewart, *In the Name of God* (Eugene: Harvest House Publishers, 2002), 58-59.

The violent side of Islam is not only found in the Shi'ite Islam of Iran, but also in the Sunni Islam of other Muslim countries. Most Muslims in the world are Sunni Muslims. Within the Sunni branch of Islam, two movements deserve our attention. The Wahhabi movement originated in Saudi Arabia in the eighteenth century, and the Deobandi movement began in India in the nineteenth century and is currently popular in Pakistan.[1118] Both branches of Sunni Islam are reform movements within the Muslim world. These groups literally interpret the Koran (the Muslim holy book written by Muhammad) and the Hadith (early and authoritative Muslim traditions). Therefore, they take seriously Muhammad's commands to slay the idolaters or infidels (Surah 9:5; 5:34-35, etc.). They often use force and violence to purify the Islamic faith. This entails terrorist attacks on liberal or modern Muslims as well as acts of unprovoked violence against the non-Muslim world. The Al-Qaida terrorist network, the Taliban, and Osama Bin Laden have links with both Deobandi and Wahhabi Islam. The terrorist attacks against America on September 11, 2001 were the work of Bin Laden and his followers. The current Islamic terrorist organization called ISIS appears to be even bloodier than Al-Qaida.

Though some would argue that violent Muslims, whether of the Shi'ite or Sunni type, are perverting the peaceful and tolerant religion of Islam, the facts tell a different story. Though most Muslims are probably peace-loving people, the Koran and the Hadith call for the slaying of non-Muslims wherever they are found. Muhammad meant Jihad (a holy war fought in the name of Allah, the Muslim God) to be taken literally; he himself conquered non-Muslims with the

---

[1118]Ibid., 59-62, 80-82.

sword. In fact, whereas the first three centuries of Christianity saw thousands of defenseless Christians persecuted, the first three hundred years of Islam were characterized by Islamic military conquests of non-Muslim lands. Professing Christians who kill innocents in Jesus' name pervert the teachings of Christ; Muslims who commit terrorist acts in the name of Allah are following Muhammad's example and obeying the teachings of Muhammad as found in the Koran as well as the Hadith. A "back to the Bible" movement usually leads to religious freedom, while a "back to the Koran" movement will always lead to bloodshed and violence. It is no coincidence that every government heavily influenced by the Islamic faith offers no religious freedom to non-Muslims. In Middle-Eastern Muslim countries, non-Muslims can be executed for trying to convert a Muslim, and in the Sudan more than 2 million professing Christians have been killed by Muslims since the 1950's.

POLYTHEISM

Many tribal peoples in Africa and South America hold to the belief in many gods, called polytheism. The animism (the belief that all nature is animated with spirits) of American Indians was very similar to polytheism. History has shown that polytheism and animism leave their adherents in occultism, superstition, poverty, and anarchy. Human sacrifice is often practiced (i.e., Incas, Aztecs, Mayas). Polytheism offers no unified code of ethics to unite its people, since the gods are often opposed to one another. Ancient dictators were more than willing to bring in their own unifying principle (usually the enforced worship of the emperor or ruler as the superior god) while using polytheism to aid them in suppressing the rights of their people. In short, polytheism often produces a society that lacks a unified direction, thus making that society easy prey for potential dictators. The finite gods of polytheism are not able to sustain a society.

OTHER-WORLDLY PANTHEISM

Pantheism is the belief that God is the universe, and that, since man is part of the universe, man is God. In India, the society and government are based upon this world view due to India's most popular religion—Hinduism. But this type of Hindu pantheism in India is an *other-worldly* pantheism— the emphasis is not on this life, but on future reincarnations. This lessens the incentive of Hindus to alleviate the suffering of others, for the suffering person is working off negative karma. To alleviate his suffering would be to force him to return to this world, in a different body, and to suffer again to work off the negative karma. Thus, helping alleviate a person's sufferings is viewed as a hindrance to that person's spiritual progress. This is why many of the health care workers in India are Christian.

The caste system in India is another consequence of other-worldly pantheism. It is almost impossible for a person to leave the caste (or class) into which they are born, since the person is thought to be in that caste due to the karma he has brought from a former life. Usually, it is assumed that a future incarnation is the only way for a person to move out of their caste. Due to the other-worldly pantheism of India, suffering people are often neglected since they are thought to be working off negative karma.

It should be noted that any reform movements in India attempting to change the caste system are actually contrary to the doctrines of Hindu Pantheism. On the other hand, reform movements in America, such as the abolition of slavery, were actually bringing American life more in conformity to the Judeo-Christian world view.

THIS-WORLDLY PANTHEISM

In contrast to the other-worldly pantheism of India is the *this-worldly* pantheism of Nazi Germany.[1119] In early twentieth century Germany the leadership of the German Church had all but apostacized. In earlier decades, German theologians and philosophers had attacked the authenticity and reliability of the Bible, causing many professing Christians in Germany to lose their confidence in the traditional Christian world view. The German Volk religion filled the void left by the church's apostacy. It became the dominating religious perspective of Germany's leadership. The German Volk religion was a pantheistic ideology which held that the Aryan race is divine and that the German leader (Hitler) was the fullest manifestation of the divine. Non-aryan races were viewed as "sub-human." These races were seen as a threat to human progress, for it was feared that they could pollute the pure genetic make-up of the Aryan (master) race. The emphasis of the pantheism of the German Volk religion was on this life and the supposed future spiritual evolution of the Aryan race. The undesirable "sub-human" races had to be weeded out in order to usher in a "new age" of spiritual enlightenment.[1120]

Thus, the holocaust, which took the lives of more than 6 million innocent Jews, was motivated by the this-worldly pantheism of Adolph Hitler and the Third Reich. The present-day version of this-worldly pantheism is the New Age

---

[1119]Richard Terrell, *Resurrecting the Third Reich* (Lafayette: Huntington House Publishers, 1994), 49-61, 145-168.

[1120] Ibid., 50.

Movement. Both the New Age Movement and the German Volk religion were greatly influenced by the occultic beliefs of Theosophy, a cult founded by the Russian mystic Helena Blavatsky.[1121] The New Age Movement, if it continues to grow in popularity, may produce another holocaust; however, this holocaust may cover the entire earth. New Age leader and author Barbara Marx Hubbard believes that not everyone is ready for the coming New Age of peace and spiritual enlightenment. In fact, she believes that traditional Christians, Jews, and Muslims are holding back the spiritual evolution of mankind because they refuse to acknowledge that man is God. Therefore, reasons Hubbard, one-fourth of mankind needs to be exterminated in order to usher in the New Age.[1122]

Pantheism (in both its this-worldly and other-worldly forms) teaches that God is an impersonal force, not the personal God of the Bible. Being an impersonal force, the God of pantheism is beyond the moral categories of right and wrong. Therefore, ultimately, there are no moral absolutes; what is right for one person is not necessarily right for another person, and visa versa. Usually this moral relativistic view translates into a toleration of willful, immoral behavior (i.e., homosexuality, abortion, euthanasia, sexual immorality,

---

[1121] Ibid., 49, 151-153.

[1122] Tal Brooke, *One World* (Berkeley: End Run Publishing, 2000), 197. Hubbard is an insider with the United Nations and the United Religions Organization. She is not alone in her thinking. Her idea that a large portion of the world's population needs to be exterminated is shared by Cornell Professor David Pimentel. In 1994, he argued before the American Association for the Advancement of Science that the total population of the world should not exceed 2 billion people. Since the world's current population is about 6 billion, Pimentel apparently would like to see 4 billion people "disappear." Pimentel's wild idea was treated with respect by the *Los Angeles Times*. See William Norman Grigg, *Freedom on the Altar* (Appleton: American Opinion Publishers, 1995), 109.

pornography, etc.), as well as an inconsistent lack of toleration of traditional values and beliefs (i.e., the Judeo-Christian world view). Unfortunately, that which a this-worldly pantheistic world view cannot tolerate it usually exterminates. For although the concept that man is God appears to be a high view of man, it is actually devalues human life since it entails the weeding out of undesirables who hold back human progress. (For the New Age Movement the undesirables include traditional Christians and Jews, as well as patriotic Americans who hold to traditional values.)

WHAT ABOUT THE INQUISITION AND THE CRUSADES?

Christianity is often blamed for the terrors of the Inquisition and the bloodshed of the Crusades. In reference to the Inquisition, several things need to be clarified. First, the Inquisition was primarily a killing & torturing of those who opposed the Bishop of Rome. In other words, it should not be viewed as an indictment on traditional, protestant Christianity (i.e., Bible-based Christianity). When the church and the Roman Empire merged, it was the empire that corrupted the church, not the other way around. Second, much of the inquisition dealt with torturing and killing Jews merely because they were Jews and they would not convert to "Christianity." But, true Christians cannot hate Jews. Jesus was Jewish. The apostles were Jewish. The Bible (Old and New Testaments) is Jewish. True Christians pray for Israel and love the Jewish nation since it is God's chosen nation. Jesus said "not everyone who says to Me 'Lord, Lord' shall enter the Kingdom of Heaven, but he who does the will of My Father in heaven" (Matthew 7:21). Third, Bible-believing Christians defend Jesus, not the actions of a fallible church. We do not believe the church is infallible, nor do we believe that the Bishop of Rome (i.e., the Pope) is infallible when he speaks for the entire church in areas of faith or practice. Protestants acknowledge that professing Christians have committed horrors in the name of Christ, but we believe that their actions prove them to be outside the true faith, for "faith without works is dead" (James 2:26). Fourth, during the Inquisition many true Christians were tortured and killed because they refused to submit to the Bishop of Rome. Often, the Inquisition was characterized by professing Christians killing true Bible-believing Christians as well as Jews.

The Crusades involved the waging of war in behalf of the Church of Rome. The early crusades were fought in defense of the Eastern Church as she was being attacked by Muslim invaders. Still, later Crusades morally deteriorated to the point where there is simply no way to justify them. Again, we must remember that these actions were ordered by the Roman Catholic Church. Protestants argue against the church hierarchy having that kind of authority; Protestants reject the notion of papal infallibility. Like the Inquisition, the Crusades show that not all professing believers are genuine Christians.

In a book entitled *Christianity on Trial*, authors Vincent Carroll and David Shiflett sum up the issue well:

> Whatever Christianity's role in the conflicts of the last two millennia, its hands were clean during the bloodiest century on record—the one just past. The body count from the two great barbarisms of the twentieth century, communism and Nazism, is extraordinary enough on its own. Communism's toll ran to perhaps 100 million . . . Adolph Hitler's death machine was equally efficient, but ran a much shorter course . . . Communism was and is proudly atheistic, while Nazism . . . embraced a form of neopaganism. Both were hostile to the organized religions in their midst, and neither genuflected before any power other

than man himself. Yet these movements exterminated their victims with an efficiency that clearly exceeded the most grisly achievement of states produced by Christian zealotry. In that sense, they were worthy heirs to the French Revolution, which erected altars to the Goddess of Reason before the backdrop of a guillotine.[1123]

CONCLUSION

Government cannot be separated from religion. Every government must have a doctrine of man and his place in the universe, and it is here that government and religion overlap. If a government rejects the faith of our founding fathers (the Judeo-Christian world view), then it will accept an alternative world view. But the consequences of that alternative world view will infringe on man's freedom and eventually result in great loss of life, for the dethronement of God is not without consequences. Contemporary man's flight from God will inevitably lead him down the dark, bloody road to tyranny.

[1123] Vincent Carroll and David Shiflett, *Christianity on Trial* (San Francisco: Encounter Books, 2002), 109.

Chapter 27

Narrative Apologetics

Narrative apologists defends the faith by telling stories. Often, people who are not willing to dialogue concerning religious issues enjoy listening to stories. Because of this, several Christian apologists have chosen to use fiction to proclaim and defend the Christian faith. John Bunyan, Fyodor Dostoyevsky, J. R. R. Tolkien, and C. S. Lewis were all willing to use their story-telling ability to defend Christian truth. In fact, Jesus may have been the first narrative apologist. He often used parables to teach and defend His views.

Jesus' Parables

In their recent work *The Apologetics of Jesus: A Caring Approach to Dealing with Doubters*, Norman Geisler and Patrick Zukeran discuss how Jesus defended the faith. Geisler and Zukeran classify one of Jesus' methods of defending the faith as parabolic apologetics since Jesus used parables to explain and defend His teachings.[1124] Parables are

---

[1124]Norman L. Geisler and Patrick Zukeran, *The Apologetics of Jesus: A Caring Approach to Dealing with*

43

true to life stories that teach spiritual truth. Hence, parabolic apologetics is synonymous with what this work calls narrative apologetics.

An example of how Jesus used narratives to defend His teachings and practices is found in Luke chapter fifteen. The Pharisees condemned Jesus for welcoming and eating with "sinners" (Luke 15:1-3). Jesus defended His actions by telling three parables: the Parable of the Lost Sheep (Luke 15:4-7), the Parable of the Lost Coin (Luke 15:8-10), and the Parable of the Prodigal Son (Luke 15:11-32). Jesus' main point is that the godly person will rejoice when sinners repent and turn to God—Jesus was right to associate with unsaved people in an attempt to reconcile them with God.

John Bunyan

John Bunyan used allegory to teach the Christian journey (salvation, sanctification, and glorification) in his novel *Pilgrim's Progress*. This is one of the most widely read book of modern times—it has influenced millions of lives. How many of these readers' hearts were oepned to God's truth because *Pilgrim's Progress* was written as a novel.[1125] Many people who would not read a theological or philosophical work can be reached through the writing of narratives.

Fyodor Dostoyevsky

Fyodor Dostoyevski (1821-8181) was a brilliant Russian writer of the nineteenth-century. In his novel entitled *The Brothers Karamazou*, Dostoyevski tried to deal with the

---

Doubters (Grand Rapids: baker Book House, 2009), 79-88, 187-189.

[1125]Ibid., 188.

problem of evil: how could an all-good, all-powerful God allow the evil and human suffering that takes place in the world? After giving accounts of horrible human suffering, Dostoyevski gave a twofold answer to the problem of evil. First, when an innocent person suffers God is able to build their character—we often spiritually grow the most due to our times of suffering. Second, if a person chooses to deny God's existence he has forfieted the foundation from which any action can be condemned as evil.[1126] Without God, there is no such thing as good. And, if there is no such thing as good, then nothing is evil. And, if there is no such thing as evil, then all things are permissible.[1127] But, man cannot consistently live with the idea that all things are permissible—he must acknowledge that some things are evil and detestable. Man cannot live consistentkly with a world view that denies the existence of God.[1128]

Many people who would never read philosophical or theological works might be reached through novels. Dostoyevski is an example of a Christian who dealt with the difficult issues of life in his writings and steered people in the direction of God.

J. R. R. Tolken

J. R. R. Tolken entertained readers with his works entitled *The* Hobbit, The *Lord of the Rings*, and *The Silmaillion*. Tolken's imagination created places such as the

---

[1126]William Lane Craig, *Reasonable Faith: Christian Truth and Apologetics* (Wheaton: Crossway Books, 1994), 55.

[1127]Ibid., 61.

[1128]Ibid., 66.

"Shire" and "Middle Earth." In *The Lord of the Rings*, the evil Dark Lord Sauron held all the rings of power, except one. If he could find this missing ring his power and dominion would be complete. But, the last ring had fallen into the hands of a hobbit named Bilbo Baggins.

The hobbit Bilbo Baggins passed the ring onto his cousin Frodo. It was now Frodo's mission to save his homeland, the Shire, by traveling across Middle-earth and disposing of the ring in the Cracks of Doom. He could not allow the ring to fall into the hands of the Dark Lord. Nor, could he allow the ring to corrupt himself. The power of the ring would tempt Frodo to use the ring for his own gain. But, Frodo resisted the temptations and endured the trials. Joining him on his dangerous journey were three other hobbits, Gandalf the Wizard, Gimli the Dwarf, an elf named Legelos, Boromir of Gondor, and an exiled king named Aragorn.[1129]

Through his novels, Tolken taught eternal truths. One such truth was the the extreme difficulty of suffering for doing the right thing (i.e., Frodo bearing the burden of the ring to deliver his people). Self-sacrifice on behalf of others is a Christ-like attribute that true heros manifest. Tolken also taught that a hero is often the last person one would expect to be a hero. For even a hobbit can deliver Middle earth from the clutches of the Dark Lord.

C. S. Lewis

C. S. Lewis not only rationally defended the faith, but he also used narratives to defend the truths of Christianity. In his *Chronicles of Narnia*, Aslan the lion (a type of Christ) dies

---

[1129]J. R. R. Tolken, *The Lord of the Rings* (Boston: Houghton Mifflin Company, 1994).

to deliver Narnia from the clutches of the evil white witch (a type of Satan). In Lewis' *Screwtape Letters*, a more experienced demon instructs a "rookie" demon in how to tempt humans and lead them astray. Millions of people who might not have read religious literature enjoyed Lewis' fictional works. Lewis managed to witness to his readers, not just through their reason, but also through their imaginations.

Other Novels Teaching a Christian Message

Several other novels that teach a Christian message could be mentioned. *Les Miserables* teaches the conflict between law and grace. Law demands justice, but has no place for forgiveness. But, grace, while understanding justice, provides forgiveness and redemption. Grace does what the law cannot do: grace delivers and transforms.

The Count of Monte Cristo teaches the extreme difficulties connected with forgiveness, especially when one is betrayed, falsely accused, and wrongly punished. This novel also shows the extremes God will go to as He seeks to save a lost soul.

Films that Promote a Christian Message

A narrative does not have to be found written in a book. It can also be told in the form of a film or a play. Three fairly recent movies that promote a Christian message (or at least a message consistent with Christianity) are *Signs*, *The Passion*, and *I am Legend*.

Signs appears to be a movie about extraterrestrials invading planet earth. But, a deeper meaning behind the action proclaims the failure of modern science to adequately explain all of reality, and the failure of modernist rational thought to explain away miracles. This movie opens the door for traditional religion to join the discussion concerning what reality means.

Mel Gibson's *The Passion of Christ* gives the viewers a realistic portrait of the sufferings and anguish of the Lord Jesus on the night He was betrayed and the day He was crucified. The movie closes with the triumph of Jesus' bodily resurrection. Though the script in is Hebrew and Latin, the subtitles give enough of the biblical text for the Gospel to be proclaimed. May people throughout the world, who would probably not have read the Gospels, were exposed to the truths of the Gospel through this film.

The movie *I am Legend* is more than just an apocalyptic film. This movie has numerous allusions to Christianity. It is a story that shows the dilemma of modern science: it can find cures to diseases, but it can also turn humans into monsters and bring about the destruction of the human race. Salvation is not to be found in science. Faith in God is essential if man is to have hope of deliverance. The butterfly as a symbol of regeneration is a prominent theme in the movie, as is salvation be found in the blood of the hero (who turns out to be somewhat of a type of Christ).

Conclusion

In a what Francis Schaeffer called a post-Christian era, it is not always possible to get people excited about hearing the Gospel preached or Christianity rationally defended. But, if the apologist can use narrative to capture the imagination of his audience, he may be able to proclaim and defend the faith without rational argumentation. Storytelling can be an effective way to defend the Gospel in these postmodern times.

Chapter 28

Combinational Apologetics

Some apologists use more than one approach or method when defending the Christian faith. This is called combinational apologetics. Combinational apologetics should not be mistaken for cumulative case apologetics. Cumulative case apologetics gathers several different *arguments* together to build a case for Christianity. On the other hand, combinational apologetics combines different apologetic *methods*. A few examples of combinational apologetics will suffice.

Norman Geisler

Norman Geisler is primarily a classical apologist. He starts his defense by using philosophical arguments to build his case for God's existence, and then he argues for the truth of Christianity from historical evidences. However, Geisler is also willing to use scientific evidences for God.[1130] Geisler uses big bang cosmology, entropy, and the complexity of life

---

[1130]See chapter five of this work.

to make his scientific case for God. Hence, he combines more than one apologetic methodology in his defense of the faith (i.e., classical and scientific).

Josh McDowell

Josh McDowell is an evidentialist—he utilizes historical evidences to defend Christianity. Still, McDowell also shares his testimony in defense of Christianity. He also engages in both comparative religious apologetics and cultural apologetics. Therefore, McDowell combines at least four different apologetic methodologies in his defense of the faith (i.e., evidentialism, testimonial apologetics, comparative religious apologetics, and cultural apologetics).[1131]

Francis Schaeffer

Francis Schaeffer was a verificational apologist. He treated Christianity like a hypothesis or an explanation. He allowed the Christian hypothesis to be tested. But, Schaeffer was willing to use more than his verificational method. For, he also engaged in cultural apologetics. He argued that Western civilization's rejection of Christianity will ultimately lead to the downfall of the West.[1132]

Blaise Pascal

Blaise Pascal is a psychological apologist. Rather than trying to use reason to argue for the truth of Christianity, Pascal appeals to the heart of man. He pulls the strings of

---

[1131]See chapter eleven of this work.

[1132]See chapter seventeen of this work.

man's emotions and will; he does not treat man as if he was a mere thinking machine. Pascal knew that often man's emotions, desires, and will override his reason. But, Pascal does not stop at psychological apologetics. Once he convinces his readers that they ought to desire God and seek Him with all their hearts, he then uses historical evidences and the evidences of fulfilled prophecies to make his case for the truth of Christianity.[1133]

C. S. Lewis

C. S. Lewis was a verificational apologist. He argued that Christianity alone adequately explains reality. But, Lewis was also willing to use cultural apologetics (his work entitled *The Abolition of Man*), as well as narrative apologetics (i.e., *The Chronicles of Narnia* and *Screwtape Letters*) to defend the faith.[1134]

Conclusion

David Clark, John Warwick Montgomery, William Lane Craig, Edward Carnell, and J. P. Moreland can also be added to the list of combinational apologists.[1135] While combinational apologists should be classified by their primary methodology, it should still be noted that they do not limit themselves to one single apologetic method.

[1133]See chapter twenty of this work.

[1134]See chapters eight and twenty-seven of this work.

[1135]See chapters twenty-one, twelve, six, eighteen, and seven of this work.

Chapter 29

Suggestions for Classifying Apologetic Methodologies

This book has examined of a variety of Christian apologists and their different approaches to defending the faith. It is now time to list these different apologetic methodologies that have been or are being utilized by these defenders of the faith. This chapter will try to refrain from omitting the several apologetic approaches that have been ignored in previous works on apologetic methodologies. This work has identified at least sixteen different ways to defend the faith.

Seventeen Distinct Apologetic Methodologies

1) *Classical Apologetics* is often called the two-step approach to defending the faith. The first step consists of using the traditional arguments for God's existence (i.e., cosmological, teleological, moral, and sometimes the ontological). The second step deals with presenting historical evidences for Christianity. Classical apologists do not change this order—they first argue for God's existence and then move

on to historical evidences for Christianity. Most of the great apologists throughout church history have been classical apologists (i.e., Augustine, Anselm, Aquinas, Bonaventure, Descartes, Paley, etc.). Some of the leading classical apologists of the last seventy years have been: C. S. Lewis, Stuart Hackett, Norman Geisler, William Lane Craig, and J. P. Moreland.

2) *Evidentialism* or *Historical Apologetics* is the method of defending the faith that focuses primarily on historical evidences for the truth of Christianity. Some evidentialists will also argue for God's existence; but, they do not believe God's existence has to be defended first. Unlike classical apologists, evidentialists believe the defender of the faith can start his case for Christianity with historical evidences. John Warwick Montgomery, Josh McDowell, and Gary Habermas are three well-known evidentialists.

3) *Cumulative Case Apologetics* is very similar to the classical and evidential approaches. However, what makes the cumulative case method unique is this: the cumulative case apologist is willing to use numerous arguments for God and Christianity without considering any one argument to be the primary one. The arguments are added together to increase the probability of the case for Christinianity. Paul Feinberg is probably the most famous cumulative case apologist.

4) *Transcendental Presuppositionalism* is the apologetics methodology of Cornelius Van Til and his greatest disciple Greg Bahnsen. Van Til believed that it is almost idolatrous to start one's apologetic with anything but the Triune God who has revealed Himself in Scripture. Hence, Van Til presupposed the existence of the Triune God and then argued that, wihtout this presupposition, reality is not intelligible. Just for man to think presupposes the existence of the God of the Bible. This is Van Til's transcendental argument. He argues that the existence of the true God is the

pre-condition for all thought, morality, and meaning. In short, Van Til argues from God, not to God. Van Til believed that his transcendental argument is the only argument that could be used for Christianity without the apologist compromising his faith. Van Til, and his pupil Greg Bahnsen, were also willing to show that non-Christian belief systems are contradictory.

5) *Dogmatic Presuppositionalism* was the apologetic methodology of Gordon Clark early in his long career. Clark was very rationalistic in his thought—he believed that only that which could be rationally deduced qualified as knowledge. All other ways to find truth fail (i.e., empiricism, subjectivism, irrationalism, pragmatism, etc.). However, even though he exalted man's use of reason, Clark knew that a person could not reason to all his beliefs, for a belief system must start somewhere. Clark argued that man must dogmatically presuppose his first principles and then deduce all other knowledge from this starting point. Clark chose to presuppose the existence of the Triune God who has revealed himself in Scripture, plus the law of non-contradiction. Clark added the law of non-contradiction to his starting point because he believed that, as the source of all logic, God is logic. From this dogmatic starting point, Clark would deduce his system of thought. Clark believed that reality confirmed his Christian presuppositions to be true. He also believed that reality proved all other presuppositions to be false. Clark believed that using anything but his Christian presuppositions led to skepticism. Hence, we must either presuppose Clark's starting point or ultimately face skepticism.

6) *Scripturalism* was the apologetic methodology that Gordon Clark used later in his career as an apologist. Clark's dogmatic presupposition gradually changed over the years, until Clark held the view that truth can only be found in the Bible and whatever can be deuced from the Bible. Late in his

life Clark reached the conclusion that no truth could be found through sense perception, and that all truth is propositional. Only in the Scripture could man find truth. This radical approach to defending the faith and unique view of truth has few adherents today.

7) *Verificationalism* was the method used by Francis Schaeffer. Schaeffer was a student of Cornelius Van Til. He used Van Til's term "presupposition;" but, for Schaeffer, his Christian presuppositions could be tested. Hence, Schaeffer's presuppositions functioned more like a hypothesis, a proposed explanation that could be tested. Therefore, Schaeffer was willing to verify his Christian hypothesis, something Van Til would never do. Schaeffer believed that only the Christian world view adequately made sense of the world in which man lives. Only the Christian explanation works.

8) *God as a Properly Basic Belief* or *Reformed Epistemology* was created by Christian philosopher Alvin Plantinga. Plantinga rejected strong foundationalism (the view that our beliefs should be based upon basic beliefs that were self-evidently true). Instead, he pointed out that many of man's long-held beliefs were considered basic, yet are not self-evident. Man believes in the existence of a real world outside his mind and the existence of other minds without any good evidence for these beliefs. These believes are considered to be properly basic. Plantinga reasons that if man is justified in believing these things without evidence, then the Christian is justified in believing in God without evidence. Plantinga is not opposed to Christians providing others with evidence for Christianity; he merely notes that the Christian is justified in believing in God without any evidence for God.

9) *Combinationalism* is the apologetic methodology that combines several different apologetic methodologies in order to defend the faith. What makes combinationalism a distinct methodology from the cumulative case approach is

this: the cumulative case approach uses several arguments for Christianity; whereas, the combinational approach utilizes several different apologetic methodologies to defend the faith. The leading combinationalist of the twentieth-century was Edward J. Carnell. He used the verificational approach, historical apologetics (i.e., evidentialism), testimonial apologetics (i.e., evidence from transformed lives), and psychological apologetics. Though many leading apologists use more than one methodology, each apologist usually has onr primary method. In Carnell's case, it seemed that his primary approach was the combination of several methodologies. Hence, he is a combinationalist.

10) *Comparative Religious Apologetics* compares and contrasts Christianity with other religions. It attempts to accurately show what other religions teach, and then tries to refute those beliefs. Walter Martin, Winfried Corduan, and Ron Rhodes should be classified as comparative religious apologists. However, apologists who primarily use other methods do at times engage in comparative religious apologetics as well (i.e., Josh McDowell, Norman Geisler, etc.).

11) *Scientific Apologetics* utilizes scientific evidence to argue for the existence of a personal God. Scientific apologists also often argue against evolution (though some scientific apologists are theistic-evolutionists). Some scientific apologists are young-earth creationists (i.e., Henry Morris, Duane Gish, John Morris, Jonathan Sarfati, Russell Humphries, Steve Austine, Paul Nelson, and Kurt Wise); whereas, other scientific apologists are old-earth creationists (i.e., Hugh Ross, Norman Geisler, J. Kerby Anderson, William Dembski, Philip Johnson, etc.). Francis Collins is an example of a scientific apologist who is a theistic-evolutionist.

12) *Testimonial Apologetics* uses the evidence of changed lives to defend the faith. Several apologists (i.e.,

Michael Brown, Barry Leventhal, Josh McDowell, etc.) have used the evidence of their transformed lives to argue for the truth of Christianity.

13) *Psychological Apologetics* turns to the psychological make-up of man to argue for the truth of Christianity. Blaise Pascal was probably the greatest psychological apologist. Edward J. Carnell and Soren Kierkegaard also engaged in some form of psychological apologetics.

14) *Dialogical Apologetics* was formulated by David Clark. Clark's approach to defending the faith is person-centered—it attempts to find what arguments would work best with the particular non-believer being addressed. Dialogical apologetics uses several arguments (i.e., cumulative case), is very ecclectic in its approach (i.e., combinationalism), and argues for Christianity as the best explanantion of reality (i.e., verificationalism). Clark is not an ultra-rationalist; but, he is willing to use reason in a less dogmatic fashion (i.e., soft rationalism). It is possible to classify David Clark's dialogical apologetics as a unique form of combinationalism. But, at least in this work, dialogical apologetics has been given its own category.

15) *Cultural Apologetics* attempts to defend the Christian faith by showing its positive effects on culture, as well as the dangers of removing Christianity from a culture. C. S. Lewis, Francis Schaeffer, Josh McDowell, Vincent Carroll, and David Shiflett are examples of those who have engaged in cultural apologetics.

16) *Narrative Apologetics* attempts to defend Christianity through fiction—the telling of stories. Rather than appealing to the non-believer's reason, the narrative apologist targets his readers' imagination. Jesus Himself engaged in narrative apologetics by telling parables to His

audiences. John Bunyan, Fyodor Dostoyevski, J. R. R. Tolken, and C. S. Lewis were all narrative apologists.

17) A new and very needed method of defending the Christian faith is *Paranormal Apologetics*. This form of apologetics deals with the many paranormal events and experiences that are being reported in America today. These paranormal experiences incude: UFO's and alien abductions cases, haunted houses, demon possession cases, and bigfoot sightings. If Christian apologists do not take these paranormal reports seriously, they will miss the opportunity to reach many people for Christ. The paranormal apologist must carefully investigate paranormal reports and then offer a solidly biblical explanation of the data. Some paranormal apologists include Tal Brooke, Gary Bates, Cris Putnam, and Michael Heiser.

Seven Major Categories of Apologetic Approaches

Breaking down Christian apologetics into seventeen distinct methodologies may at first seem to complicate matters. Many students of apologetic would rather limit the number of methodologies. However, the problem with this reduction of the number of methodologies is that several methodologies are ignored. Also, key apologists often do not fit into any category when the options are limited. It is suggested that each of the seventeen distinct methodologies mentioned above be recognized in order to do justice to the various ways the faith can be defended.

Still, these seventeen apologetic methodologies can be grouped together into seven major apologetic approaches. At first, this would seem to produce the same oversimplification that has been created by previous attempts to classify apologetic methodologies. However, this is not the case, so long as each of the seven major approaches contains enough sub-categories to include all seventeen methodologies. The seven major apologetic apologetic approaches are: 1) traditional apologetics, 2) presuppositional apologetics, 3) verificationalism, 4) basic belief apologetics, 5) comparative religious apologetics, 6) narrative apologetics, and 7) paranormal apologetics.

1) *Traditional Apologetics* is characterized by arguing *to* God. This major category would include: classical apologetics, evidentialism, cumulative case, combinationalism, scientific, testimonial, psychological, dialogical, and cultural apologetics. This approach argues from something else to the God of the Bible.

2) *Presuppositional Apologetics* is characterized by arguing *from* God, not to God. Too often, works on apologetic methodologies treat presuppositionalism as if all presuppositionalists use the same approach. Though it is true to call both Cornelius Van Til and Gordon Clark presuppositionalists, the differences between the approaches of these two presuppositional apologists must not be overlooked. Hence, Van Til's transcendental presuppositionalism and Clark's dogmatic presuppositionalism, and Clark's later scripturalism, should not be confused. Still, all three methodologies can be subsumed under the major category called presuppositionalism.

3) *Verificationalism,* like presuppositionalism, presupposes the truth of Christianity and argues from God, not to God. Still, the verificationalist allows his presuppositions to be tested or verified. Hence, verificationalism is actually distinct from presuppositionalism; it is actually hypothesis-testing.

4) *Basic Belief Apologetics* considers God a basic belief. This is the unique approach of Alvin Plantinga. He believes that a believer is justified in believing in God even if the believer has no evidence for that belief. Basic belief apologetics is a mild form of fideism, in that (unlike fideism)

it does allow its adherents to present evidence for their faith if they choose. Basic belief apologetics should not be called "reformed epistemology" since this is misleading. It implies that all reformed scholars use this apologetic, when that is not the case. Reformed apologists use many different methods to defend the faith.

5) *Comparative Religious Apologetics* deals with refuting other belief systems. This major apologetic approach should not be ignored. If one does not include this approach as a distinct classification, then one implies that some of the great defenders of the faith of the last two generations are not apologists at all—and this is absurd. Walter Martin, Ron Rhodes, and Winfired Corduan are just three of the many comparative apologists who have had, or are having, significant ministries defending the faith.

6) *Narrative Apologetics* is defending the faith through story-telling. Jesus was the first to use this approach by teaching and defending spiritual truths through the telling of parables (i.e., true to life stories that teach spiritual truths). Later narrative apologists include John Bunyan, Fyodor Dostoyevsky, J. R. R. Tolken, and C. S. Lewis.

7) *Paranormal Apologetics* defends the faith by attempting to investigate reports of paranormal activity (i.e., UFO sightings, alien abductions, haunted houses, cases of demon possession, etc.). The paranormal apologist tries to offer a Christian explanation for the data in these paranormal reports.

One Final Suggestion: Apologist-Centered Classification

One final suggestion for classifying apologetic methodologies is this: since it is often very difficult to fit an apologist into one methodology, it may be advantageous to handle each apologist in a distinct manner.[1136] Norman Geisler is a case in point. His primary method of defending the faith is the classical approach—he argues first for God, and then uses historical evidences to defend the truth of Christianity. Still, Geisler is also willing to utilize scientific evidences for God, cultural apologetics, and comparative religious apologetics.

In this apologist-centered classification, the most precise description of the way each particular apologist defends the faith can be identified. Unfortunately, there could be as many apologetic methodologies as there are apologists. Therefore, if the seventeen different apologetic methodologies are recognized, and the seven major classifications noted, then each apologist can be accurately assessed by comparing his unique arguments with the methodologies and classifications listed above. Obviously, this work is not the final word on the classifying of apologetic methodologies. Still, it is hoped that this work will help Christians to more accurately identify the true nature of the several different methods of defending the faith being used today.

[1136]This apologist-centered approach to classifying apologetic methodologies can be seen in three scholarly works on apologetic methodologies: 1) Bernard Ramm, *Varieties of Christian Apologetics* (Grand Rapids: Baker Book House, 1976); 2) Gordon R. Lewis, *Testing Christianity's Truth Claims* (Lanham: University Press of America, 1990); 3) Brian K. Morley, *Mapping Apologetics: Comparing Contemporary Approaches* (Downers Grove: Intervarsity Press, 2015).

Appendix

FIDEISM: THE ENEMY OF APOLOGETICS

Fideism is the belief that religious faith cannot be defended through the use of philosophical, historical, or scientific evidences. Religious faith is viewed as a leap of faith into the non-rational realm. One makes an ultimate commitment apart from any evidence. Objective truths are not considered as important as a person's subjective beliefs. Religious truth is viewed as personal, not propositional.[1137]

Obviously, fideism is the antithesis of apologetics. Apologetics is the defense of the Christian faith; fideism claims that the Christian faith cannot be defended. It can only be believed. For this reason, fideism is the enemy of apologetics. They cannot both be true. In this chapter, the views of several men whose ideas are associated with fideism will be discussed. This chapter will close with a critique of the fideist position.

TERTULLIAN

Though Tertullian, a second century Christian thinker, was a great defender of the faith, he has often been mistaken for a fideist. Tertullian stated, "I believe because it is

---

[1137]Norman L. Geisler, *Christian Apologetics* (Grand Rapids: baker Book House, 1976), 58-59.

absurd."[1138] However, Christian philosophers Norman Geisler and Paul Feinberg point out that Tertullian was not saying that he held to the idea that contradictions are true or that faith is irrational. Rather, he merely meant that he accepted the gospel as true even though the world considered it foolishness.[1139] In other words, Tertullian was merely echoing the teachings of the apostle Paul (1 Corinthians 1:18-31).

Tertullian also stated, "What indeed has Athens to do with Jerusalem?"[1140] Obviously, he was contrasting Greek philosophy and Christian theology. Still, he was probably not opposed to all philosophy, since he often used reason to defend the faith. Tertullian was simply opposed to all anti-Christian philosophy. He refused to judge the gospel by human reason. Rather, he judged the reason of men by God's revelation in the Bible. Still, this did not make him a fideist. He believed that the truth of Christianity had been proven by the blood shed by Christian martyrs.[1141] And, he offered other arguments for the truth of Christianity. In other words, he accepted the evidence of eyewitness testimonies as establishing the truth of the Christian revelation. That being proven, he then judged the philosophies of men by God's wisdom.

Hence, Tertullian was not a fideist. Still, he is often quoted out of context to promote fideism. For that reason, he has been discussed here.

[1138]Ibid., 47.

[1139]Norman L. Geisler and Paul D. Feinberg, *Introduction to Philosophy* (Grand rapids: baker Book House, 1980), 262.

[1140]Geisler, *Apologetics*, 47.

[1141]Dowley, ed., *The History of Christianity*, 112.

452

BLAISE PASCAL

Blaise Pascal (1623-1662) was not a complete fideist. He argued for the truth of the Christian faith, something a fideist would not do. However, it is the way that Pascal defended the faith that moved him closer to fideism. This was due to the fact that he criticized rationalism to the point that he questioned the reliability of man's reasoning processes, or at least fallen man's ability to use his reason in an unbiased way. In Pascal's thinking, man must submit his reason to his will.[1142] To a certain degree, the mind must bow to the heart.

Still, Pascal did not consider Christianity to be against reason. He merely emphasized the point that God cannot be found through human reason alone.[1143] It was here that Pascal developed his famous "wager argument" for God's existence. Pascal believed there were strong rational arguments for or against God's existence. Hence, reason cannot decide. One must choose with one's will whether or not to believe that God exists. The mind must give way to the will. Plus, reasoned Pascal, man does not use his reason in an unbiased manner. Before looking at the evidence for God, man is already biased for God or against God. Each person must decide to choose or not to choose God. Pascal pleads with his readers to choose God. If his readers choose God and He does not really exist, they will have lost nothing. But, if his readers choose God and He does exist, they gain eternal life. On the other hand, if his readers wager their lives against God and win, they win nothing, but if they lose, they lose everything.[1144] Hence, the

---

[1142]Geisler, *Apologetics*, 48.

[1143]Ibid.

wise man will be biased towards God and wager his life on God. There is the possibility of eternal gain and no possibility of loss by wagering one's life on God. However, if one wagers one's life against God, there is the possibility of infinite loss and no possibility of gain. Based on what is at stake, the wise man will hope that God exists—he will be biased towards God. He will be willing to wager his life that God exists.

Though many have found this argument convincing, it is not really an argument for God's existence. Instead, it is an argument that, if a person is wise, that person will be biased towards God, not against God. Some have overemphasized Pascal's view of human reason. They failed to see that Pascal was not anti-rational. He merely stressed that human reason is finite and fallen. It can be mistaken. And, reason is often used by fallen man to defend his biases, rather than to find truth in an unbiased manner. Still, this misinterpretation of Pascal has opened the door to fideism. For Pascal declared that man must test truth with his heart, not merely with his mind.[1145] Man is not a mere rational machine—he also has passions and emotion, and these often get the best of man's reason. Future believers went far beyond what Pascal proposed. Subjective beliefs were beginning to surpass objective truth in importance in the history of philosophical thought.

GOTTHOLD EPHRAIM LESSING

Gotthold Ephraim Lessing (1729-1781) was a critic of the Bible who denied biblical inerrancy. He taught that religious beliefs could not be proven through reason or historical evidences.[1146] He was a fideist in the truest sense.

[1144]Ibid., 49.

[1145]Ibid., 50.

He held that faith rested on subjective experience rather than on objective evidence. He believed that religions should be judged by their effect on the moral conduct of its followers.[1147] Evidence for or against religious truth claims were irrelevant.

Lessing imagined an "ugly ditch" between faith and historical facts.[1148] This ditch could not be crossed. No one can know for sure if the Jesus of the gospels is in fact the true Jesus of history. Religious beliefs could not be defended by appealing to objective facts. Only practical results could be used to determine the worth of a religious system. Testing religious truths is a subjective, inward task. Any appeal to objective evidence is futile.

SOREN KIERKEGAARD

Soren Kierkegaard (1813-1855), the famous Danish philosopher, is known as the "father of modern existentialism." Kierkegaard believed that there were three stages of life: the aesthetic, the ethical, and the religious.[1149] Each stage is separated by a feeling of despair. Also, each stage can only be crossed by a leap of faith.[1150]

A person lives in the aesthetic stage when he exists for his own pleasure. In this stage, the person is *self-centered.*

[1146]Frederick Copleston, *A History of Philosophy* (New York: Doubleday, 1960), book 2, vol. 6, 126-131.

[1147]Ibid.

[1148]Millard J. Erickson, *The Word Became Flesh* (Grand Rapids: Baker Book House, 1991), 115.

[1149]William S. Sahakian, *History of Philosophy* (New York: Harper Collins Publishers, 1968), 343.

[1150]Geisler, *Apologetics*, 50.

Through a leap of faith, a person can enter into the ethical stage. Here, duty comes first. This person is *law-centered*. But when the overwhelming feeling of despair and futility comes, the person can, through another leap of faith, arrive at the religious stage. In this stage, the person is *God-centered*.[1151]

Kierkegaard believed religious truth is personal and subjective, not propositional and objective. He felt that subjective truth is of greater importance than objective truth. To leap into the religious stage, one must leave the realm of reason. Kierkegaard is not saying that religious faith is irrational. He merely means that it is non-rational. Reason does not apply. It is an act of the will that is necessary. A leap of blind faith (apart from reason) is needed to accept religious truth.

For Kierkegaard, God's existence cannot be proven.[1152] Religious faith comes from the heart, not the mind. An act of the will is needed, not an act of the intellect. Since religious truth is subjective and personal, there is no test for truth which can be applied.[1153]

KARL BARTH

Karl Barth (1886-1968) rebelled against liberal theology and started neo-orthodoxy. He rejected the liberal view that man was basically good.[1154] Barth, though accepting

---

[1151]Ibid.

[1152]Ibid., 52-53.

[1153]Ibid., 53.

a critical view of the Bible, recognized that man is limited and sinful. He taught that God is "wholly other" than man. He considered the Bible a human book which contains errors. However, it becomes revelation from God to the individual in the moment of crisis. This crisis is the crisis of faith. It is that moment when a person recognizes God's condemnation of all human effort and that deliverance comes only through God. At this moment, the Holy Spirit uses the Bible as His instrument to bring about a personal encounter between the individual and God. During this encounter, no communication of information takes place. In Barth's eyes, revelation is personal encounter with God, not the making known of information.[1155]

Barth taught that sin blinds man from finding the truth. Only the Holy Spirit can open man's spiritual eyes so that he can see God. The divine-human encounter is purely a subjective experience.[1156] In this encounter, man encounters God. However, man does not encounter any objective truths about Him.[1157]

In Barth's thought, man is incapable of receiving any revelation from God through nature.[1158] Man's spiritual blindness can only be removed by a contact sovereignly initiated by the Holy Spirit.[1159] Obviously, Barth is opposed to apologetics. There is no need to defend the divine-human

---

[1154]Cairns, 445.

[1155]Ibid.

[1156]Ibid.

[1157]Geisler, *Apologetics*, 53-56.

[1158]Ibid, 55.

[1159]Ibid.

encounter since it cannot even be expressed. There is also no need to defend the Bible since it is a human book with errors. Therefore, for Barth and all other fideists, Christianity is to be accepted by faith. It should not be defended.

CONCLUSION

In chapter one of this work, apologetics was shown to be biblically based. First, it was concluded that the Bible commands believers to do apologetics (1 Peter 3:15; Colossians 4:5-6; Titus 1:7-9; Jude 3). Second, the Scriptures speak of God revealing Himself in nature (Psalm 19:1; 94:9; Romans 1:18-22; 2:14-15). Third, God's Word speaks of historical evidences for the Christian faith (1 Corinthians 15:3-8). And, fourth, the early church defended the faith. Examples were given: Peter, John, Luke, Paul, and Apollos. In short, by showing that apologetics is biblically based, fideism has been proven unscriptural.

Still, there is a lesson one can learn from fideists. Though Thomas Aquinas was one of the greatest defenders of the faith, his thought was often misinterpreted as equating faith with intellectual assent to doctrines that could not be proven by reason.[1160] This misinterpretation of Aquinas placed faith into the head with reason, rather than in the heart. The biblical concept of faith as a personal trust in Christ for salvation was lost. In reality, Aquinas taught that there was a clear distinction between "faith that" (intellectual assent) and "faith in" (personal trust in Christ). Still, even though misunderstanding of Aquinas' thought prevailed, the fideists must be credited for reemphasizing the aspect of personal

---

[1160]William Lane Craig, *Apologetics an Introduction* (Chicago: Moody Press, 1984), 9-10.

commitment and trust. However, in the process, they have de-emphasized reason. Though a personal relationship with Jesus must be stressed, before one can believe *in* the Jesus of the Bible, one must believe the facts *about* Him. Revelation without content is no revelation at all.

If one's apologetics is to be biblical, one must learn this lesson from the fideists. The defense of the faith can lead a person to give intellectual assent to the facts of the gospel. Still, the person must *choose,* by an act of his or her *will,* to personally appropriate the truths of the gospel. Mere head knowledge will save no one. A decision of the heart is needed. Though belief in the claims of Christ is necessary for salvation, one must still personally trust in Christ to be saved. One must never turn the gospel into a mere creed by removing the personal, experiential aspects of Christianity. Even so, the fideist has faltered on the other extreme by removing the intellectual content from the gospel. When this has been done, there is no gospel left at all. Gospel means *good news.* There can be no gospel if there is no *news.*

The Christian faith contains both objective and subjective elements. It contains propositional truth (true doctrines) and personal relationship (a personal relationship with God through Jesus Christ). Effective defenders of the faith will proclaim both. To neglect one at the expense of the other is to move away from historical Christianity.

ABOUT THE AUTHOR

Phil Fernandes is the senior pastor of Trinity Bible Fellowship and the founder and president of the Institute of Biblical Defense, an apologetics ministry which trains Christians in the defense of the faith. He also teaches theology, philosophy, and apologetics for Crosspont High School and Shepherds Bible College. All four ministries are located in Bremerton, Washington. Fernandes also publicly lectures throughout the country on apologetic issues.

Dr. Fernandes has earned a Ph.D. in philosophy of religion from Greenwich University, a Doctor of Theological Studies from Columbia Evangelical Seminary, and a Master of Arts in Religion from Liberty University. He has also earned a Master of Theology and a Bachelor of Theology from Columbia Evangelical Seminary. Fernandes is currently completing a Doctor of Ministry in Apologetics degree from Southern Evangelical Seminary. He has studied apologetics under leading apologists Gary Habermas, Norman Geisler, and Richard Howe.

He has lectured and debated in defense of Christianity on university campuses (such as Princeton, Washington State University, University of North Carolina—Chapel Hill, State University of New York, etc.) and in public schools. Dr. Fernandes has debated some of America's leading atheist voices (i.e., Michael Martin, Jeff Lowder, Dan Barker, Reggie Findley, Doug Krueger, and Robert Price). Fernandes is a member of the following professional societies: the Evangelical Theological Society, the Evangelical Philosophical Society, the International Society of Christian Apologetics, and the Society of Christian Philosophers.

Dr. Fernandes is the author of numerous books including: *The God Who Sits Enthroned: Evidence for God's Existence* (1997), *No Other Gods: A Defense of Biblical Christianity* (1998), *God, Government, and the Road to Tyranny: A Christian View of Government and Morality* (2003), *Contend Earnestly for the Faith: A Survey of Christian Apologetics* (2008), *Evidence for Faith: Essays in Christian Apologetics* (2009), *The Atheist Delusion: A Christian Response to Christopher Hitchens and Richard Dawkins* (2009), and *Hijacking the Historical Jesus: Answering Recent Attacks on the Jesus of the Bible* (2012). Fernandes also contributed to the work entitled *Vital Issues in the Inerrancy Debate* (edited by David Farnell).

Dr. Fernandes resides in Bremerton, Washington with his lovely wife Cathy. They have two grown daughters and three grandsons.

More than 1,400 audio lectures, sermons, and debates by Dr. Fernandes can be downloaded from the internet website: instituteofbiblicaldefense.com by clicking on the sermonaudio button. Dr. Fernandes' sermons, lectures, and debates have been downloaded several million times throughout the world.

The Institute of Biblical Defense can be reached through the address, e-mail address, and phone number listed below:

The Institute of Biblical Defense
P. O. Box 3264
Bremerton, WA. 98310

(360) 698-7382

phil@biblicaldefense.org

CPSIA information can be obtained
at www.ICGtesting.com
Printed in the USA
FFHW012327181019
55659859-61498FF